Legal Aspects of Medical I

CHURCHILL LIVINGSTONE MEDICAL TEXTS

Epidemiology in Medical Practice
Second edition
D.J.P. Barker and G. Rose

Pain: its Nature, Analysis and Treatment
Michael R. Bond

Geriatric Medicine for Students
Second edition
J.C. Brocklehurst and T. Hanley

Essentials of Dermatology
J.L. Burton

Essential Ophthalmology
Hector Bryson Chawla

Elements of Medical Genetics
Fifth edition
Alan E.H. Emery

Notes on Psychiatry
Fifth edition
I.M. Ingram, G.C. Timbury and R.M. Mowbray

Physiology: a Clinical Approach
Third edition
G.R. Kelman

Tumours: Basic Principles and Clinical Aspects
Christopher Louis

Nutrition and its Disorders
Third edition
Donald S. McLaren

The Essentials of Neuroanatomy
Third edition
G.A.G. Mitchell and D. Mayor

Urology and Renal Medicine
Third edition
J.B. Newsam and J.J.B. Petrie

Clinical Bacteriology
P.W. Ross

Sexually Transmitted Diseases
Third edition
C.B.S. Schofield

Notes on Medical Bacteriology
J.D. Sleigh and Morag C. Timbury

In Introduction to General Pathology
Second edition
W.G. Spector

Child Psychiatry for Students
Second edition
Frederick H. Stone and Cyrille Koupernik

Introduction to Clinical Endocrinology
Second edition
John A. Thomson

Notes on Medical Virology
Sixth edition
Morag C. Timbury

Clinical Pharmacology
Third edition
P. Turner and A. Richens

Immunology: an Outline for Students of Medicine and Biology
Fourth edition
D.M. Weir

Clinical Thinking and Practice: Diagnosis and Decision in Patient Care
H.J. Wright and D.B. MacAdam

LIVINGSTONE MEDICAL TEXTS

An Introduction to Clinical Rheumatology
William Carson Dick

A Concise Textbook of Gastroenterology
M.J.S. Langman

Introduction to Clinical Examination
Second edition
Edited by John Macleod

An Introduction to Primary Medical Care
David Morrell

Psychological Medicine for Students
John Pollitt

Respiratory Medicine
Malcolm Schonell

Cardiology for Students
Max Zoob

Legal Aspects of Medical Practice

Bernard Knight
MD (Wales), FRC Path, DMJ
of Gray's Inn, Barrister-at-Law.
Professor of Forensic Pathology,
Welsh National School of Medicine,
University of Wales, Cardiff.
Honorary Consultant Pathologist,
South Glamorgan Health Authority (Teaching).
Home Office Pathologist

THIRD EDITION

CHURCHILL LIVINGSTONE
EDINBURGH LONDON MELBOURNE AND NEW YORK 1982

CHURCHILL LIVINGSTONE
Medical Division of Longman Group Limited

Distributed in the United States of America by Churchill Livingstone Inc., 19 West 44th Street, New York, N.Y. 10036, and by associated companies, branches and representatives throughout the world.

First edition 1972
Second edition 1976
Third edition 1982

ISBN 0 443 02558 4

British Library Cataloguing in Publication Data
Knight, Bernard
Legal aspects of medical practice. – 3rd ed.
– (Churchill Livingstone medical text)
1. Medical laws and legislation – Great Britain
I. Title
344.104'41 KD2945

Library of Congress Catalog Card Number 81–67494

Printed in Singapore by
The Print House (Pte) Ltd.

Preface to the Third Edition

The relentless changes in legislation have necessitated considerable revision in this edition, especially in relation to coroner's procedure and the constitution and functions of the General Medical Council. These chapters have been completely rewritten, along with that on Transplantation, where an official Code of Practice has consolidated procedures.

Once again, much attention has been paid to the systems of certification and disposal of the dead in Scotland, the Irish Republic and in Northern Ireland, where thankfully the teaching of legal medicine is relatively alive and well!

I am very grateful to Professor J.K. Mason of Edinburgh, Professor W.A. Harland of Glasgow, Dr J.F. Harbison of Dublin and Professor T.K. Marshall of Belfast for their detailed advice on procedures in these Celtic counties, but hasten to take any responsibility for any errors in transcribing their comments into print.

I would also like to thank Mr John Salaman, MA, FRCS, my colleague in Cardiff and currently President of the British Transplantation Society, for advice on the transplantation issues.

Two of Her Majesty's coroners, Mr Glyn Evans and Dr John Burton respectively, President and Honorary Secretary of the Coroner's Society, kindly gave much information concerning the recent changes in coroner's procedure.

I sincerely hope that both medical students and practitioners will continue to find that this small book provides an accessible and readable source of up-to-date information on an aspect of medicine which so commonly arises in everyday practice.

Cardiff, 1982 B.K.

Preface to the First Edition

During recent years – a period in which legal actions involving doctors have greatly increased – the various medical defence societies have expressed concern over the falling standard of medico-legal awareness amongst newly qualified doctors.

This is due partly to the decline in the teaching of forensic medicine in our medical schools – in England and Wales, all established chairs disappeared by 1970 and the subject has been dropped from qualifying examinations in all but one university.

Though the pressures of an increasingly crowded curriculum have contributed to this recession in forensic medicine, some of the fault comes from within the discipline itself. For too long, the medical schools have been teaching forensic *pathology*, at the expense of forensic *medicine*. The former is a specialised postgraduate subject, not required by the majority of doctors apart from certain minimum needs in the examinations of injured patients and dead bodies. Far more necessary is a sound knowledge of medical ethics, of the ever-thickening jungle of legislation and administrative regulations as they impinge upon medicine, and an appreciation of the disciplinary and legal consequences of irregularities in medical behaviour.

To these ends, the present book is directed. There are many excellent textbooks of forensic medicine, but the majority are heavily biased towards forensic pathology, attempting to combine both fields. To do this, a book of large size and compendious content is required, much of which would be of little use to the senior student, junior doctor and the general practitioner. It is to these that the present book is directed, the emphasis of practicality always being kept in mind. Many of the larger books give insufficient space to recent legislation, to modern procedures such as transplantation and to the legal aspects of consent, medical reports and medical ethics generally.

Certain aspects of forensic medicine have become superspecialised, so much so that the average forensic pathologist himself has abandoned claims to a comprehensive detailed knowledge. Pre-eminent amongst these are toxicology and forensic serology, only the general outlines of which are considered in this book.

As medicine progresses and becomes ever wider in its scope, it is patently obvious that the student cannot be expected to absorb all that is new, together with established practice. In the field of legal medicine, it seems time to abandon any pretence at forcing the minutiae of criminal pathology upon students at the expense of teaching them the practical medico-legal aspects of their future work. It is hoped that this book will at least begin to provide the type of teaching that will be of most use, anything further being readily obtainable from more comprehensive texts.

Cardiff, 1971 B.K.

Contents

1

The ethics of medical practice

Medical ethics may be described as a code of behaviour accepted voluntarily within the profession, as opposed to Statutes and regulations imposed by official legislation. In many areas, these are synonymous: for example, originally ethical matters constituting 'infamous conduct' have for over a century been guarded by an official body, the (General) Medical Council.

Numerous aspects of medical practice still fall outside official legislation, but are none the less relevant to a doctor's behaviour and conscience, the limits being set by the approbation or disapproval of his colleagues. Much of medical ethics consists of good manners and civilised behaviour in the general sense, but there are certain matters which are peculiar to the practice of the profession of medicine. In Britain, those aspects of medical behaviour which fall outside formal legislation, are largely left to the conscience of the individual doctor, but the British Medical Association, through its Ethical Committee, has a particular interest in codifying, publicising and enforcing these ethical considerations upon its members. Its powers of enforcement are limited to censure and expulsion of members of the BMA and it naturally has no authority over non-members, apart from setting an example, maintaining a standard and drawing attention to new problems. Since 1979, the newly-constituted General Medical Council also has a 'Standards Committee', with a responsibility to draw up guidelines for the profession on matters of professional conduct and medical ethics. The British Medical Association consolidated its views on current ethical considerations in a booklet published in 1980, entitled *The Handbook of Medical Ethics*.

CODES OF MEDICAL ETHICS

The oldest code of medical ethics is the one well known to medical and lay persons alike, the Hippocratic Oath. Though now some 25 centuries old, its basic tenets remain as valid as ever, but the archaic language and formulation, however historically attractive, have become anachronistic, leading to its restatement in the Declaration of Geneva. Formerly, the Hippocratic Oath was pledged by new doctors at graduation ceremonies, though this is now rare. Even so, the newly-admitted practitioner still accepts its spirit and intentions. A translation of the Hippocratic Oath is given at the end of this chapter.

Following the gross transgression of medical ethics during the Second World War, the World Medical Association (founded largely at the instigation of the British Medical Association) restated the Hippocratic Oath in a modern style, this being known as the *Declaration of Geneva*. Upon this, an International Code of Medical Ethics was based.

DECLARATION OF GENEVA

At the time of being admitted as a Member of the Medical Profession I solemnly pledge myself to consecrate my life to the service of humanity.
I will give to my teachers the respect and gratitude which is their due;
I will practise my profession with conscience and dignity;
The health of my patient will be my first consideration;
I will respect the secrets which are confided in me;
I will maintain by all the means in my power the honour and the noble traditions of the medical profession;
My colleagues will be my brothers;
I will not permit considerations of religion, nationality, race, party politics or social standing to intervene between my duty and my patient;
I will maintain the utmost respect for human life from the time of conception; even under threat, I will not use my medical knowledge contrary to the laws of humanity.
I make these promises solemnly, freely and upon my honour.

The English text of the *International Code of Medical Ethics* is as follows:

DUTIES OF DOCTORS IN GENERAL

A DOCTOR MUST always maintain the highest standards of professional conduct.
A DOCTOR MUST practise his profession uninfluenced by

motives of profit.

THE FOLLOWING PRACTICES are deemed unethical:

1. Any self-advertisement except such as is expressly authorized by the national code of medical ethics.
2. Collaborate in any form of medical service in which the doctor does not have professional independence.
3. Receiving any money in connection with services rendered to a patient other than a proper professional fee, even with the knowledge of the patient.

ANY ACT OR ADVICE which could weaken physical or mental resistance of a human being may be used only in his interest.

A DOCTOR IS ADVISED to use great caution in divulging discoveries or new techniques or treatment.

A DOCTOR SHOULD certify or testify only to that which he has personally verified.

DUTIES OF DOCTORS TO THE SICK

A DOCTOR MUST always bear in mind the obligation of preserving human life.

A DOCTOR OWES to his patient complete loyalty and all the resources of his science. Whenever an examination or treatment is beyond his capacity he should summon another doctor who has the necessary ability.

A DOCTOR SHALL preserve absolute secrecy on all he knows about his patient because of the confidence entrusted in him.

A DOCTOR MUST give emergency care as a humanitarian duty unless he is assured that others are willing and able to give such care.

DUTIES OF DOCTORS TO EACH OTHER

A DOCTOR OUGHT to behave to his colleagues as he would have them behave to him.

A DOCTOR MUST NOT entice patients from his colleagues.

A DOCTOR MUST observe the principles of 'The Declaration of Geneva' approved by the World Medical Association.

These modern codes are already under pressure from the progress of events, as current attitudes to termination of pregnancy and even euthanasia may require constant revision of such codes.

With the memory of illegal experiments upon humans during the Second World War and with the great increase in clinical trials of new drugs and other novel methods of treatment, the World Medical Association drew up in 1964, a Code of Conduct for doctors intending to embark upon any experimental scheme of treatment. This code is known as the *Declaration of Helsinki* and its provisions should be studied whenever clinical trials are proposed.

In Britain, each Area Health Authority has an ethical committee, whose function it is to screen all research projects involving clinical trials, to ensure that no breach of ethics will occur.

General ethical considerations

Ethical behaviour is necessary right across the whole spectrum of medical practice, the overriding consideration being the welfare of the patient. It is easy to expand into prolix, pontifical generalisations about ethics, but the purposes of this book would be better served by discussing a representative series of specific matters, so that the principles described might be seen to apply to the whole range of medical activities. It must be emphasised that ethical behaviour is a self-imposed duty upon each doctor, and that no pride can be taken in behaviour calculated to avoid official censure, but which still remains professionally repugnant or undesirable. The disapproval of one's colleagues should be at least as great a deterrent as the authority of courts of law, the General Medical Council or National Health Service Tribunals.

Ethical responsibilities to patients

Though reinforced by the presence of the General Medical Council, the terms of service of the National Health Service and the ever-present threat of civil action for negligence, the conduct of a doctor towards his patient is very largely determined by his own feelings of professional responsibility and awareness of ethical considerations. The well-being of the patient transcends any thought of financial advantage, convenience or professional advancement.

The patient is entitled to information about his illness, within limits determined by the doctor who alone can tell what measure of information should be disclosed. Conversely, a doctor's strict duty to his patient is not to disclose such information to any other person, except those properly entitled to receive it. Naturally, the parents or guardians of small children are entitled to full disclosure, but as the age of a young person approaches 16, the position alters. Especially in regard to matters concerning pregnancy, the consent of a young person between 16 and 18 should be obtained before disclosure is made to the parents. Where a sensible, well-orientated young person even of 14 years is concerned, the doctor must judge for himself whether the patient's reluctance for disclosure to the parents should be honoured.

PROFESSIONAL SECRECY

Part of the Hippocratic Oath affirms 'Whatever in connection with my professional practice or not in connection with it, I see or hear, in the life of men, which ought not to be spoken of abroad, I will not divulge, as reckoning that all such should be kept secret'. Even if a medical graduate does not formally affirm this Oath at qualification, he accepts its spirits and intentions as his ideal standard of professional behaviour. Thus both on ethical grounds and also because unwise breach of confidence may place him at the receiving end of a civil action (the classic leading case is Kitson *v.* Playfair, where a doctor's unwise revelations to his family about his sister-in-law's pregnancy cost him £12 000!) every practitioner should be cautious of statements made outside the professional milieu.

The respect of such confidences obtained in the doctor-patient relationship forms something of a conflict between law and ethics.

Professional confidences may be broken only under one of the following conditions:

(a) *Consent of the patient to disclosure of relevant information*
Where disclosure is to be anything but informal, such as to relatives, it is wise to obtain written consent or at least, witnessing of oral consent.

(b) *As a statutory duty laid down by law*
Examples are the notification of infectious diseases, certification of birth, death, etc., various industrial diseases and other situations mostly related to Public Health Acts. A recent and controversial addition is the enforcement by the courts of the obligation by a doctor to reveal the identity of a patient treated after a road accident, under certain provisions of the Road Traffic Act. Similarly, the 1967 Abortion Act and the 1971 Misuse of Drugs Act are examples of statute law obliging doctors to notify certain facts about their patients to the authorities.

In *Northern Ireland*, Section 5 (1) of the Criminal Law Act (N.I.) 1967, puts an obligation on every citizen to report to the police whenever he believes a grave offence has been committed and he has information which would help to bring the perpetrator to justice. This does not mean of course that doctors need make enquiries about the circumstances in which wounds have been inflicted but when wounds speak for themselves, such as a stab wound or bullet wound, the police should be informed. Some doctors might still be reticent about initiating such a report, understandably because patients must feel free to have treatment without becoming entangled with the law. Nevertheless, if the police learn that a serious crime has been committed and they make enquiries, the doctor must co-operate and answer their questions.

A further exception, in the same vein, was introduced by the Prevention of Terrorism (Temporary Provisions) Act 1976. Section II puts a duty on every citizen to notify a police constable or a member of H.M. Forces whenever he believes he has information which might assist a) in preventing an act of terrorism or b) in securing the apprehension, prosecution or conviction of a person involved in an act of terrorism, i.e. violence for political ends.

(c) *By order of a Court of Law*

When requested to divulge information by a judge, magistrate or coroner, the doctor may demur, but continued refusal is at the risk of fine or imprisonment for contempt of court. Where the doctor honestly believes that disclosure would be a breach of confidence, he may request the court to respect his silence, or if this is refused, he may request that he gives the information in writing so that it is not made public. If these requests are not met, he has no choice but to divulge or risk imprisonment. All matters voiced in court are absolutely privileged, and carry no risk of a subsequent action for defamation or breach of confidence.

(d) *In the interests of the community*

The most difficult situation of all for the doctor is where his ethical inclination towards silence battles with his conscience concerning the welfare of the community. Such instances arise when his patient holds some position in society where illness may prove a public hazard. Instances in the past have been swimming-bath attendants with infective venereal disease, food handlers with chronic infections and public service vehicle-driver with severe cardio-vascular disease. In the most glaring examples, the doctor's duty is rarely in doubt. He should first employ all his persuasion to obtain the patient's consent to his notifying the proper authority, or refer the patient to an appropriate consultant to give added weight to his opinion. If this fails, then he should inform the patient that the gravity of the situation as it concerns the public good, is such that he must forfeit his claim to professional confidence. Where such obvious grounds exist the doctor may be confident that no subsequent civil action will lie against him. In cases of less obvious urgency, there is always a conflict in the doctor's mind. No set rules can be given, each practitioner having to work out his own course of action, though the defence societies can be of the utmost assistance in this matter.

Privileged communications

Inseparable from the matters discussed above, is the liability for subsequent civil action upon confidences or defamatory statements divulged by the doctor. Indemnity from civil action is given by law in two degress:

Absolute Privilege is that which applies to any statements made in a Court of Law (or Parliament) and extends to statements made to solicitors or barristers in the course of preparation for a Court hearing. Nothing said in these circumstances can be used as grounds for an action for libel or slander.

Qualified Privilege. Outside a Court of Law, certain breaches of confidence or defamatory statements by a doctor may be protected if certain conditions are observed. The statement must not be malicious and must be made in good faith to a party having a duty to receive it. For example, official notification of disease, certificates of death etc., are privileged, but only when transmitted to the Medical Officer of Health or Registrar entitled to receive them. Similarly, informing the Superintendent of Baths or the manager of a bus company about dangerous disease in their employees is privileged, as long as the information is strictly confined to the person having an interest in receiving it.

The dangers of wandering beyond these very tight lanes of communication are often not appreciated, and though there is naturally a gap between theoretical perfection and everyday practice, a doctor must be wary of even casual confidences within his own family, as such information has inadvertently been made public in the past, to the considerable mental distress and financial loss of the doctor.

In some countries, it is a statutory obligation to report to the police or other authorities, any case of gunshot wounds or other evidence of possible criminal wounding seen by a doctor in the course of his practice. No such obligation exists in Britain (except in Northern Ireland) and it is left to the individual conscience of the doctor. In general, unless the patient gives consent, he should make no effort to notify the police unless:

1. There is the possibility of repetition of grave illness or even death, such as might occur from the persistent activities of a professional abortionist, using septic methods.
2. Where evidence of attempted poisoning exists: here, further medical proof should be obtained, as well as persuasion to obtain the patient's consent to disclosure. It has been suggested that any approach to the authorities in such a case should be via a private interview with a senior police officer or Chief Constable.
3. A more common circumstance is in connection with injuries to children which are suspected of being inflicted by the parents. This is discussed more fully under the section on the 'battered child' but the matter of professional confidence is very relevant to this issue. In the past, the whole syndrome was unrecognised largely because of the reluctance of doctors to believe that parental abuse existed or because of their reluctance to dilvulge their suspicions, so that proper investigation could be made. The decision to break professional confidence in these circumstances can be most difficult, but is vital if further injury and even the death of a child is to be averted. The opinion of another practitioner or paediatrician should be obtained and where a decision is made, the assistance of the specialised officers in child welfare sought, rather than any approach to the police. The Inspectors of the NSPCC and Children's Officers act with extreme circumspection and tact.

Abortion is a topic which presents its own special problems regarding disclosure. It can be said immediately that where abortion has been performed or attempted by the woman herself, it is no part of any doctor's business to inform the authorities, though technically this is a crime under the Offences Against the Person Act. No one, least of all the police, wishes to know about such cases. Where the signs and circumstances indicate that a professional abortionist has been at work, then the consent of the woman must be obtained before approaching the authorities. Where serious ill health or danger to life has come about, perhaps as a result of sepsis from unskilled abortionists, then the patient should be urged to allow disclosure, being assured that the victims of such operations never suffer prosecution. If no consent is obtained, the matter should end there. Though a famous direction to the contrary was made by Mr. Justice Avery in 1914, the Royal College of Physicians took legal advice at that time, and issued a directive that it was no part of a doctor's duty to divulge information about criminal abortions without the patient's consent. Again this is a case where ethical responsibilities must be weighed against the amount of harm present or potentially present in a community. Naturally, if death occurs, then the Coroner must be informed with full disclosure of the circumstances.

Disclosure of medical records

The importance of accurate medical records is mentioned elsewhere, but at this point it is appropriate to discuss the circumstances in which practice or hospital records may be divulged to another person. With the advent of the National Health Service and increase in litigation, there has been a general loosening-up of the exchange of written confidential information, much of it in an unwise fashion. As a general rule, medical records should not be released to a lay person without good cause. Whenever possible, records should be transmitted only to another doctor. In hospital, the notes of any patient belong to the hospital authority and not to the doctor in charge. This does not apply to private patients.

Where any legal action concerning negligence of medical or nursing staff is concerned or even suspected, records should not be allowed into the hands of solicitors without prior consultation with the legal representatives of the hospital management committee. Records should not be given to employers, insurance companies or their representatives without the consent of the patient (or his immediate relatives, if he is deceased or mentally incapacitated). The records should not be allowed into the possession of the patient if the medical attendant thinks that information therein would be harmful to his own interests. In cases not concerning the reputation of the hospital or doctor, no reasonable request for records should be refused from solicitors or insurance companies dealing with compensation claims etc., providing the patient's consent has been obtained.

Records or information should not be offered spontaneously. There is no obligation to provide the records, the only absolute authority being that of a court order for 'discovery' of such documents, though recent changes in legal procedure have made it easier for lawyers to obtain records, even where a case has not yet been set down for trial. Section 32 of the Administration of Justice

Act 1970 gives the High Court the power to compel any person who is not a party to a legal action to deliver up records to the applicant, who might be the plaintiff or the defendent. In actual practice, the court usually stipulates that the records be seen only by a doctor acting for the applicant, but this rule can be avoided and hence solicitors and even the patient may be able to read the records. Section 31 of the same Act gives access to the records of a doctor who himself is being sued by a patient.

Ethical relations with other doctors

The greatest care should be taken when dealing with a patient, not to criticise or denigrate the professional ability of another doctor, even by innocent implication. Differences of opinion over diagnosis and treatment are legitimate, but should be conveyed in a way which will not undermine the patient's confidence in the other doctor. This especially concerns the patients referred to hospital by a general practitioner (where the outspokenness of a young hospital doctor is often inversely proportional to the length of his experience) and less commonly, to specialist consultations in domiciliary practice. Where there is a marked difference of opinion, it should be settled by direct contact between the two doctors, not via the patient. Where such conduct is calculated to lead to attraction of patients from the practice of another, the matter is even more serious, and apart from the ethical aspect, serious consequences might arise if brought to the notice of the General Medical Council.

Where the patient of another doctor attends a second practitioner for diagnosis or treatment, the patient should be advised to return to his own doctor. If he refuses, the best course is to contact the original doctor and settle the matter in a way which arouses no professional controversy. Under the National Health Service, a patient may change doctors either by obtaining the original practitioner's consent or by giving 14 days' notice to the Area Health Authority.

Where a hospital doctor has been treating the patient of a general practitioner, there should be no undue extension of supervision after the patient has been discharged and the patient should be returned to the care of the family doctor within the limits of the individual case and the complexity of the treatment. This emphasises the need for early and full communication between hospital and the general practitioner, so that appropriate treatment may be continued by the latter.

New practices

Apart from express legal restrictions, it is unethical for the partner or assistant of a practitioner to set up in the same area as his previous principal, as the professional introduction which he has gained from his previous employment with the principal gives him an unfair advantage in the attraction of patients. Even though the National Health Service may have a practice vacancy in that area, the previous assistant or partner should observe the ethical convention of removing himself either in space or time from the original practice. It is common for the principal to enter into a protective legal agreement, restricting the local activities of his associates, but even in the absence of this safeguard, the junior should not set himself up in overt opposition. On the other hand, such restrictive covenants in a contract must be reasonable, so that the distance from the principal's practice and the number of years set as a bar must not constitute an inequitable hindrance. The geographical radius in which practice should not be commenced varies greatly according to the district, being naturally much smaller in an urban as opposed to a rural practice. Where a restrictive covenant exists, its contravention may be countered by a claim for damages or an injunction to resist the continuance of the new practice.

Domiciliary consultations

It is part of a practitioner's responsibility to his patients to arrange for a specialist consultation when he thinks it medically necessary or when the patient or his relatives make a reasonable request for such consultations.

Such a consultation is a *consultation*, not a surrender of his handling of the case to another. The patient should ideally be seen by both practitioner and consultant at the same time, the practitioner being fully prepared to provide all possible information and ancillary investigation where relevant. The practitioner's choice of consultant should be determined solely by his opinion about the suitability of the specialist to advise in the given case, and not to any personal association, especially in the matter of a fee. It is in connection with specialist consultations that the old evil of 'dichotomy' mainly arose: this objectionable practice consisted of fee-splitting between practitioner and consultant, whereby the consultant transferred part of his fee to the original practitioner as an encouragement for further consultations. This practice, now fortunately virtually unknown, is not only grossly unethical, but might be a criminal offence, as it constitutes a bribe in contravention of the Prevention of Corruption Act. Whether criminal proceedings arise or not, the practice might lead to disciplinary proceedings before the General Medical Council and erasure from the Register.

Industrial medical officers

Where the patient of a general practitioner works in a place where the employer possesses a medical officer, careful regard must be given to the relationship of the two doctors. Though the industrial medical officer's function is confined to medical matters relating to employment, it is impossible to draw a sharp division between various aspects of the worker's health. The BMA have drawn up ethical rules for industrial medical officers, and some of the most important points are:

1. Apart from emergency treatment, the industrial medical officer should not undertake treatment which is normally the responsibility of the worker's general practitioner, except in co-operation with the latter.
2. When the industrial medical officer discovers medical facts which in the worker's interest, should be made known to his family doctor, he should always communicate them.
3. Where such facts emerge, the works doctor should urge the employee to attend his general practitioner, rather than attempt treatment himself.
4. Except in emergency, the industrial medical officer should not refer a worker direct to hospital except after consultation with the general practitioner.
5. It is generally not the function of the industrial medical officer to examine employees in connection with absence from work: if this does become necessary, he should only do this in consultation with the family doctor.
6. The industrial medical officer should not, without the consent of the parties concerned, express an opinion as to liability in accidents or concerning industrial diseases, except when so required by a competent court or tribunal.

School medical officers

The same delicate relationship as with industrial medical officers may exist with doctors employed by the local authority to examine schoolchildren.

The examination of schoolchildren is a statutory requirement, except when consent is expressly withheld by parents.

When a school doctor discovers some medical condition in a child which requires treatment, he should not refer the child to a specialist or hospital without first communicating with the family doctor, who has the option of assuming responsibility for such further medical care. As with industrial medical officers, no reply within a week from such a written notification is held to indicate that the family doctor is willing for the second practitioner to assume responsibility for the condition which he discovered. If such a course is taken, the school medical officer should keep the family doctor informed and supply copies of any specialist reports obtained concerning the child.

Acceptance of patients

A doctor has no legal obligation to accept any patient for medical care, unless directed to him under the terms of service of the National Health Service. A *private* practitioner certainly has no obligation to accept anyone whom he does not wish to treat. However, once accepted, his responsibility is absolute until such time as the relationship is ended by either:

1. The voluntary withdrawal of the patient himself from treatment.
2. A doctor having a patient removed from his National Health Service list by requiring the Family Practitioner Committee to do so. This takes effect either: (i) On the date of acceptance of the patient by another doctor or assignment to another doctor by the FPC, or (ii) on the eighth day after the FPC has been requested to remove the patient, unless on that date, the doctor was treating the patient at intervals of less than seven days. In the latter eventuality, the responsibility of the doctor ceases on the eighth day after he notifies the Committee that the course of treatment is finished.
3. Naturally, the death or distant removal or either party.

The general practitioner in the National Health Service is required under his terms of service to render *emergency* treatment to any patient, whether on his list or not. Though this is a statutory requirement, it is also an ethical responsibility of every doctor, whether in the National Health Service or not.

On ethical grounds, a patient should *not* be accepted under the following conditions, except with the express consent of the present medical attendant of the applicant:

Any patient or member of a patient's household, whom the second doctor has previously attended either as a consulting practitioner, or as a deputy for a colleague.

Any patient or member of a patient's household, whom he has attended within the previous two years as an assistant or locum.

Any patient who at the time of the application is in the active clinical care of a colleague, unless he is personally satisfied that the colleague concerned has been notified by the patient that his services are no longer required.

Any patient who applies because of temporary unavailability of his regular medical attendant. Here, the second practitioner should provide treatment for the time being only, and notify the regular medical attendant as soon as it is practicable, returning the patient to his care.

Surgery and consulting premises

Under the terms of the National Health Service, a practitioner is required to provide proper, adequate and clean premises for the examination and treatment of patients. Practitioners are liable, as are other owners or occupants of premises, for injuries sustained by patients attending these premises. Though some such accidents are impossible to guard against completely, obvious defects in structure, flooring, lighting etc., should be eliminated, and adequate insurance obtained against such third party risks.

The direction of the public to the premises by means of notices and exterior plates, is not governed by any set rules, but general ehtical principles and common sense will govern the appearances of the approach to the surgery. A plate of conventional size may carry the practitioner's name, degrees and surgery hours. Though the BMA ethical committee disapprove of specialist descriptions apart from 'Physician and Surgeon', the practice of announcing the particular branch of medicine in which the occupant specialises is quite common. The objection to such description is that it might encourage direct approach of a patient to a consultant without the desirable intervention of the general practitioner.

Consulting rooms should not be under the same roof as other premises which might be held to attract potential patients. Examples are dentists', chemists' and opticians' premises and hotels. In connection with the latter, it is an invidious and unethical practice to encourage or permit hotels, clubs, etc., to refer itinerant guests to any given practitioner. The deposit of a visiting card in hotel, club or business premises is an example of advertising or canvassing, any aspect of which may lead to disciplinary procedures by the General Medical Council. Care must be taken to avoid innocent contravention of this rule, and for instance, no notice should be placed in the local press or any public place announcing removal of surgery premises or a change of surgery hours. If such notification is necessary, it should be done by circularisation of all patients by personal letter.

With the exception of abortion, sterilization and contraception, the ethics of general medical practice in the Republic of Ireland do not differ greatly from the United Kingdom. The first two of the above three exceptions are dealt with in the relevant sections elsewhere in this book. The most recent statutory change affecting Health Services in Ireland is the introduction of Family Planning under the Health (Family Planning) Act 1979. Prior to this Act, the importation, manufacture, distribution and sale of any form of contraceptive, either instrumental or pharmaceutical, was forbidden. The new Act enables Health Boards to provide family planning clinics and attempts to bring existing voluntary family planning clinics under State control. The dispensing of contraceptives is confined to qualified pharmaceutical chemists, so that family planning clinics must employ such a chemist if they wish to continue in operation. The Act requires all contraceptives including condoms to be available on medical prescription only, and to be for *bona fide* family planning, i.e. for legally or common law married couples only. The Act only became operative in November 1980 and its operation is proving difficult, due to non-cooperation by both the medical profession and pharmaceutical chemists. The Act specifically forbids the importation of any device such an intra-uterine device which prevents conception by any potentially abortifacient means.

THE HIPPOCRATIC OATH

'I swear by Apollo the physician, and Aesculapius and Health, and All-heal, and all the gods and goddesses, that, according to my ability and judgement I will keep this Oath and this stipulation – to reckon him who taught me this Art equally dear to me as my parents, to share my substance with him, and relieve his necessities if required; to look upon his offspring in the same footing as my own brothers, and to teach them this art, if they shall wish to learn it, without fee or stipulation; and that by precept, lecture and every other mode of instruction, I will impart a knowledge of the Art to my own sons, and those of my teachers, and to disciples bound by a stipulation and oath according to the law of medicine, but to none others. I will follow the system of regimen which, according to my ability and judgment, I consider for the benefit of my patients, and abstain from whatever is deleterious and mischievous. I will give no deadly medicine to anyone if asked, nor suggest any such counsel: and in like manner I will not give to a woman a pessary to produce abortion. With purity and holiness I will pass my life and practise my Art. I will not cut persons labouring under the stone, but will leave this to be done by men who are practitioners of this work. Into whatever houses I enter, I will go into them for the benefit of the sick, and will abstain from every voluntary act of mischief and corruption; and, further, from the seduction of females or males, of freemen or slaves. Whatever, in connection with my professional practice, or not in connection with it, I see or hear, in the life of men, which ought not to be spoken of abroad, I will not divulge, as reckoning that all such should be kept secret. While I continue to keep this Oath unviolated, may it be granted to me to enjoy life and the practice of the Art, respected by all men, in all times. But should I trespass and violate this Oath, may the reverse be my lot.'

2

The General Medical Council

Until the mid-nineteenth century, there was nothing to enable the public to distinguish properly trained doctors from 'quacks'. In 1841, nearly 5000 of the 15 000 persons then practising medicine in England held no qualifications. Of those qualified, many of the qualifications were local and a doctor practicing in one city was not allowed to practice elsewhere. This unsatisfactory state of affairs led to 17 Medical Bills being presented in Parliament, but they were all defeated until the Medical Act of 1858. This established a 'General Council' whose prime object was to assist the community to identify reputable medical practitioners. It was directly responsible to the Privy Council.

A series of further Acts has ensued, the most recent being that of 1978, which made radical changes in the composition of the Council, (called 'General Medical Council' after the 1950 Act). The Council receives no grants from public funds and derives its income from retention fees paid by doctors together with other types of registration fees.

PRESENT COMPOSITION OF THE GMC

Due to considerable disquiet in the early 1970s about the composition of the GMC, the Merrison Report of 1975 recommended sweeping changes, including the election of a majority of members directly by the medical profession. This report led to the Medical Act of 1978, from which stems the present composition and functions of the newly-formed GMC.

As from September 1979, the Council consists of 93 members made up as follows:

50 members elected by postal vote from the registered medical practitioners of the United Kingdom. The Republic of Ireland is no longer represented, now having a Medical Council of its own. England has 39 members, Scotland 6 members, Wales 3 members and Northern Ireland 2 members.

21 members appointed by universities with medical faculties.
13 members appointed by Royal Colleges, Faculties and the Society of Apothecaries.
7 lay members and 2 medical members nominated by the Privy Council.

The Council itself elects a President from amongst its members, the present President being Sir Robert Wright. All members must retire on reaching the age of 70 years.

The GMC is administered by a Registrar who has a number of Assistant Registrars and a large permanent staff, who reside at 44, Hallam Street, London WIN 6AE, the Registration Division being nearby in Gosfield Street.

FUNCTIONS OF THE GENERAL MEDICAL COUNCIL

The medical register

All the Council's functions derive basically from the establishment and maintenance of the Medical Register which is the definitive list of doctors licensed to practice as 'registered medical practitioners' in Britain. In this country, there is no necessity for any person to be either medically educated, qualified or registered with the GMC, in order to practice medicine. This is unlike the sister profession of veterinary surgeons, who have a legal monopoly to treat animals.

Inclusion in the Register is legal proof of a doctor's professional status and confers upon him various legal benefits and responsibilities. Unless included in the Register he may not hold appointments within the National Health Service or Public Services, he may not prescribe dangerous drugs nor treat certain classes of serious disease. Neither may he issue statutory certificates such as birth, death and cremation certificates. He is also subject to the code of ethics and behaviour as established by his professional colleagues acting through the Council.

A doctor remains on the Register until death (which is notified to the GMC by the Registrar of Births and Deaths) unless:

1. He fails to reply to the Registrar's enquiries. This is the most common cause of removal from the Register, due to the GMC losing track of the doctor's address. In recent years, this has assumed greater importance, as there is now an annual fee payable for the retention of the doctor's name on the Register. Failure to pay the fee results in erasure from the Register, though reinstatement is automatic upon paying the arrears, together with an administration charge.

2. A practitioner may request removal from the Register, usually when he ceases to engage in medical practice.
3. Removal (including suspension) may be directed on disciplinary grounds (see below).

Until 1970, a doctor was either on or off the Register. By the Medical Act of 1969, an intermediate state of suspended professional animation was instituted, whereby the Disciplinary Committee of the GMC could *suspend* a doctor for a fixed period of time. Suspension may also be partial, in that certain functions such as the power to prescribe dangerous drugs may be forbidden the doctor in appropriate circumstances for a certain period of time (see below).

Medical education

Closely related to the original function of the Council in protecting the public from incompetent practitioners, the supervision of medical education is directed towards ensuring an adequate minimum level of competance of new medical graduates. Though the direction of the curriculum is less strictly controlled than in former years, the GMC still maintains a primary interest in both undergraduate and post-graduate education, this being a major reason for the inclusion of appointed members from all the medical schools and Royal Colleges. The Council has the power to inspect qualifying examinations and the Medical Act of 1950 gave the additional power of visiting medical schools. They also issue a periodical booklet entitled 'Recommendations on Basic Medical Education', which though advisory rather than mandatory, is normally followed by teaching institutions in designing their curricula. Close monitoring of the examinations and the pass rates is carried out by the Education Committee of the GMC. An increasing role in postgraduate education is foreseen, under the provisions of the 1978 Medical Act. This is related to the probability of Specialist Registration of all doctors, in line with the practice in the European Community.

The Medical Act of 1950 also introduced the compulsory preregistration house-officer year and also laid down a minimum time for the medical course.

The Council also has the discretion to recognise any additional higher qualifications and a number of these are now included in the official description of doctors in the Medical Register.

Registration

The heaviest work-load of the Council is the registration of doctors, especially those from overseas. Radical changes in the procedure have occurred in the last few years and now registration consists only of the following categories, as 'temporary registration' has been phased out.

1. Doctors qualifying in the United Kingdom obtain *provisional registration* on graduation and *full registration* after satisfactorily completing a pre-registration year. Nationals of any country within the European Economic Community holding registrable qualifications granted in a Member State are eligible either for full registration or for registration as a visiting EEC practitioner, or for limited registration.

2. *Limited registration* was introduced in 1979 to supercede the former system of temporary registration. In order to be eligible for limited registration a doctor must hold a qualification accepted by the Council for the purpose. Qualifications granted in 84 countries have been accepted for this purpose. Unless the doctor has previously held temporary registration, he must also pass a test of knowledge of English and of professional knowledge and competence (the PLAB test) conducted by the Professional and Linguistic Assessments Board. The PLAB test is financed by the Council, the Board consisting of members appointed by the non-university licensing bodies and certain other colleges, together with experts in linguistics.

Limited registration may be granted by the Council for specified appointments or for a range of practice, only in respect of supervised employment. It cannot be granted to any individual for a period exceeding an aggregate of five years. Thus limited registration is registration for either a particular appointment or a particular type of appointment and if the appointment lapses and the doctor wishes to work elsewhere, he must re-apply for an appropriate extension.

Doctors with limited registration may apply for transfer to full registration which may be granted if the Council thinks fit, having regard to the knowledge and skill shown and experience acquired by the doctor.

3. Visiting overseas specialists may be temporarily registered as a fully registered medical practitioner for the purpose of spending time in the United Kingdom for some specialist purpose.

Full registration under reciprocal arrangements still applies to a number of overseas universities, mainly in Australia, New Zealand and South Africa.

Disciplinary functions of the GMC

Though the other functions mentioned above provide by far the largest part of the Council's workload, it is the disciplinary functions which are the most well-known from the point of the view of the lay press.

The first Medical Act in 1858 empowered the Council to erase from the Register any doctor convicted of any felony, misdemeanour, crime or offence or judged after due enquiry by the Council to have been 'guilty of infamous conduct of a professional respect'. This last rather dramatic phrase persisted until the Medical Act of 1969, when it was replaced by the words 'serious professional misconduct'. This power of the GMC is intended to protect the public and not to be a punitive measure against offending practitioners, though the deterrent value is obvious.

The categories of 'serious professional misconduct' are never closed, as with medical negligence, but fairly well-defined groups of offences are the usual cause of erasure or suspension from the Register. The removal of a doctor's name from the Register, either permanently or temporarily, is the greatest professional disaster than can overtake a medical practitioner, as he is then unable to carry on his profession in the usual sense of the word, as he cannot be employed by the NHS or public services and cannot sign most certificates or prescriptions.

The GMC cannot advise or discuss individual cases with practitioners (e.g. a doctor cannot obtain advice in respect of some projected course of action which he fears might be construed as professional misconduct) because the Council has a statutory disciplinary function. It therefore cannot be seen to be acting as both counsel and judge in the same case. However, the GMC issues a 'Blue Booklet' entitled *Professional Conduct and Discipline: Fitness to Practice* which gives detailed guidelines for standards of professional behaviour and outlines what might be construed as breaches of these standards, together with the details of the disciplinary machinery. Since 1980, this booklet also describes the new 'Fitness to Practice' aspects, described later.

As erasure or suspension is the most serious professional disaster which can overtake a doctor, the disciplinary machinery of the GMC should be fully understood by every practitioner.

Disciplinary enquiries may arise from two sources:

1. Accusations of serious professional misconduct may be made to the GMC either from members of the public (including professional colleagues) or from certain public officials whose duty it is to communicate such accusations. This latter class includes various officials concerned with the administration of the National Health Service especially after committees of enquiry etc. at Health Au-

thority level. Where the accusation is made by a member of the public or individual doctor, it must be in the form of a statutory declaration i.e. a legal document sworn before a Commissioner of Oaths.

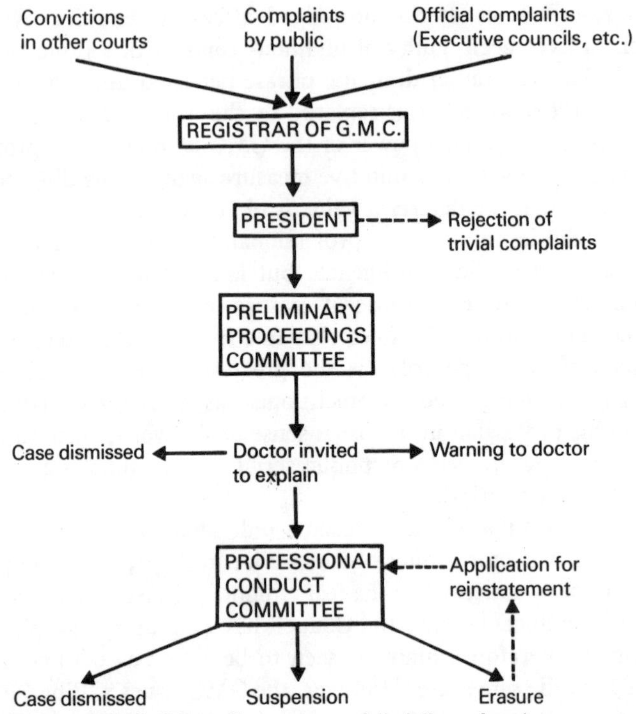

Fig. 1 General Medical Council – sequence of disciplinary functions

2. The police and some law court officials have a statutory duty to report to the GMC all convictions of doctors in the courts. This excludes trivial offences such as parking and minor motoring offences etc. Until 1970, the Divorce Courts were obliged to notify the GMC of any practitioner appearing as co-respondent in a divorce action, but now the GMC only considers such cases if the injured party makes a direct claim to the Council of serious professional misconduct on the part of the doctor.

On receipt of the notification of complaints, they are scrutinized by the Registrar and the Council's Solicitor may be asked to make enquiries to establish the facts. Obviously false, malicious or otherwise unfounded trivialities are rejected at this stage. The Registrar submits the remainder to the President, who decides whether any further action should be taken. He may direct that the doctor be contacted to clarify the circumstances, which may then result in the matter being closed. Where there appears to be some case to answer, the complaints are referred to a special committee, the Preliminary Proceedings Committee, whose function is similar to 'examining magistrates' who decide whether a case be sent for trial. At this stage, the doctor is informed of the allegations made against him and is invited to submit a written explanation (Fig. 1).

The Preliminary Proceedings Committee may decide either (a) to refer the case to the Professional Conduct Committee (b) to send the doctor a warning letter, (c) to take no further action. The second course is most commonly employed, the doctor being warned of the possible consequences of such conduct.

A minority of cases are referred by the Preliminary Proceedings Committee to the Professional Conduct Committee, which is conducted in a formal way, with barristers representing both the Council and usually the subject of the complaint, who is normally represented via his defence society.

Where the complaint arises as a result of a conviction the courts, the Council has no power to query the *fact* of conviction, but only to decide whether it amounts to a serious professional misconduct. At the conclusion of the hearing, the Committee may take one of the following courses:

1. To admonish the doctor and conclude the case.
2. To place the doctor on probation by postponing judgement.
3. To direct the doctor's registration be conditional on his compliance (for a period not exceeding three years) with such requirements as the Committee think fit to impose for the protection of members of the public or in his own interests.
4. To direct that the doctor's registration shall be suspended for a period not exceeding one year.
5. To direct the erasure of the doctor's name from the Register.

Where judgement is postponed, the doctor is given an opportunity to conduct himself correctly during the period of postponment and to obtain references from professional colleagues as to his conduct. When next considered by the Council, the case will normally be concluded if the reports are satisfactory. If not, then the other disciplinary alternatives may proceed.

Conditional registration means that restrictions are imposed upon the doctor in certain specified areas, such that he may not, for example, be allowed to prescribe dangerous drugs or may only work under supervision.

Suspended registration means removal from the Register for a specific period not exceeding 12 months. During that time the doctor cannot practice as a registered medical practitioner. A further period of suspension or even erasure may be ordered during that time.

Where a doctor's name is erased from the Register, he cannot apply for restoration until at least 10 months have elapsed.

Where a doctor has suffered an erasure or suspension, he has a period of 28 days in which to give notice of appeal to the Judicial Committee of the Privy Council. During that period his registration is not affected unless the Professional Conduct Committee had made a separate order that it should be suspended forthwith, they being satisfied that it is necessary to do so for the protection of the members of the public or in the best interests of the doctor.

Fitness to practice

Since 1980, as a result of the changes under the 1978 Medical Act, the Preliminary Proceedings Committee have an alternative course to referring cases to the Professional Conduct Committee. This is the new and somewhat controversial concept of 'fitness to practice' which is supervised by the new Health Committee.

One of the complaints of the Merrison Committee was that where a doctor by reason of physical or mental infirmity was unfit to practice, the only method of removing him from the Register was via the disciplinary machinery, which was inappropriate if the doctor's incapacity was due to sickness. The new machinery brings into being a means whereby a doctor can be prevented from practising if his physical or mental state makes him a risk either to his patients or himself. The procedure does not erase him from the Register, but suspends it or attaches conditions to it. The majority of these cases concern addiction to alcohol or other drugs or to mental illness. It is foreseen that many doctors unfit to practice will be persuaded voluntarily to cease practice, at local level, either by their own medical colleagues or possibly through the 'Three Wise Men' procedure of the Health Authorities. Where such local measures are unsuccessful, then recourse may be made to the Health Committee of the GMC.

Where the Council receives information suggesting that the fitness to practice of the doctor is seriously impaired, it will first be considered by the President or other members of the Council appointed for the purpose. If he is satisfied that a case exists, the doctor will then be informed of this and invited to agree within fourteen days to submit to examination by at least two medical examiners, who will be chosen by the President from panels of examiners nominated by professional bodies. It is then open to the doctor at this stage to nominate his own medical practitioners to examine him and send their own findings to the President.

The results of the medical examination will be communicated to the doctor, who will be asked to state within 28 days whether he is prepared voluntarily to accept the recommendations of the medical examiners as to the management of his case. If he does so, then no further action will be taken. If he refuses to be medically examined or to accept the recommendations, then the President with two other members of the Council may refer the case to the Health Committee, which may also be alerted by the Preliminary Proceedings Committee where complaints come via the disciplinary channel, until it becomes obvious that a health factor is involved.

The Health Committee may suspend the registration of a doctor for a period not exceeding 12 months, or impose conditions on his registration for a period not exceeding three years. These cases will be reviewed by the Health Committee from time to time.

Main categories of serious professional misconduct

Though the potential reasons for erasure or suspension from the Register are limitless, the majority of cases arise from one of the so-called 'Six As'.

Abortion. The illegal termination of pregnancy, if notified as result of a conviction in the criminal court, it almost always an immediate cause for erasure, even on the first occasion. Even following the reform in the law brought about by the Abortion Act of 1967, criminal abortions are still performed by doctors. Lesser degrees of culpability in this connection may arise due to the letter of the Act not being followed, e.g. performing abortions in premises not officially recognised. It is imperative that all terminations of pregnancy be carried out in the prescribed manner, wih more than one doctor assenting to the decision and the procedure being carried out only in a proper institution. This is discussed fully in a later chapter.

Alcohol. Abuse of alcohol is one of the most common causes for warning to doctors by the GMC and if the offence is repeated, erasure or suspension from the Register. The most usual type of offence is drunken driving, though occasionally repeated convictions for other forms of drunkenness have led to erasure, especially when the doctor's ability to carry out his professional duties is impaired.

Commonly, the first offence for drunken driving is dealt with by the Preliminary Proceedings Committee with a warning letter, but further infringements lead to a grave risk of erasure. Occasionally, serious drunken driving offences, such as causing the death of a person by dangerous driving, have led to erasure on the first occasion.

Rarely, drunkenness has led to criminal proceedings for manslaughter, the classic case being R. V. Bateman, where a doctor attended a woman in childbirth when he was intoxicated, caused her death by avulsing part of the uterus and intestines during a forceps delivery. Such extreme cases are very rare, but serious professional misconduct with alcohol as the basic cause is increasingly common. It is an unfortunate fact that the medical profession has the highest rate of alcoholism in the country, a rate that is increasing anually.

Adultery. The professional consequences of a doctor's adultery with a patient have changed significantly in the past few years, mainly due to the advent of a more permissive society. The Merrison Report recommended that such adulterous relationships with a patient should cease to be regarded automatically as serious professional misconduct, unless it was shown that the behaviour was likely to damage the crucial professional relationship between the doctor and patient.

This interpretation is now generally accepted by the disciplinary machinery of the GMC though it is still possible for them to consider any case where a doctor has misused his professional privileges to gain entry to the woman's family.

Actual adultery need not be proved, if it is shown that an improper relationship exists beyond the permitted range of professional contact. Formerly, Clerks of Divorce Courts were obliged to report to the GMC all doctors who had been cited as co-respondents, but this practice ceased in 1970. The GMC only considers such cases if the injured party in a divorce action makes a complaint to them. Where adultery has been accepted by the court, the GMC must accept this as a fact and only consider whether such adultery constituted professional misconduct.

Though disciplinary action is now relatively uncommon in this situation, the possibility still exists. A woman need not necessarily be a patient of the doctor, but if the acquaintance has been formed through his attending another person in the household, this may be deemed to be an abuse of professional privilege. Also, if a doctor ceases to attend the woman professionally before improper association takes place, this need not absolve him from misconduct, as the original association was gained through his professional position. Having said this, it is currently unusual for disciplinary action to be taken in such cases unless a florid breakdown of the doctor-patient relationship within the family has been facilitated by the doctor's professional advantages.

Addiction. Doctors, by virtue of their prescribing powers, have all too often fallen prey to addiction to therapeutic substances such as pethidine, morphine, heroin, barbiturates and amphetamines. Anaesthetists have also been prone to addiction to various substances such as cyclopropane or nitrous oxide. All these substances and many others have led to frequent appearances of doctors before the disciplinary machinery of the GMC and in many cases to subsequent erasure or suspension. This is obviously a situation where suspension of the doctor from practice is necessary both for the protection of patients and for his own well being, so that he may be removed from access to the drug. Not infrequently, conditional suspension with restriction of his powers to prescribe may be proposed by the GMC for a certain period.

Apart from personal addiction, offences against the Misuse of Drugs Act in respect of irregularities in prescriptions, supply and records may form grounds for referral to the GMC.

Advertising. The position of a doctor in regard to self-advertisement or allowing others to proclaim his skill, is one of the most confused aspects of professional misconduct. The very restrictive attitude of the past is no longer applied, due partly to the different structure of medicine and partly to the greatly increased impact of the media in the community.

Since the more static patient lists of the National Health Service, there is far less likelihood of a mass migration of patients from one doctor to another following some publicity. Also, the greatly increased education and awareness of the community in medical matters has demanded far more public exposition of medical topics. Doctors are fully entitled to participate in this information transfer, so long as it does not confer personal professional advantages upon them. Gone are the days of early television, where doctors sat with their backs to the camera so that they would not be recognised!

There has been some complaint in past years that the attitude of the GMC is inconstant to this problem and sometimes allegations are made that the risk of a doctor attracting censure from the GMC is inversely proportional to his eminence in the profession. These complaints are largely ill-founded, but it is difficult to draw general guidelines, as each episode of alleged advertising must be judged on its own merits. It is obviously unethical for any practitioner to perform or condone any form of publicity which draws attention to his professional merits if thereby he stands to gain personally in a financial or professional manner.

In some classes of doctor, this is obviously impossible – the Public Health official or morbid anatomist for instance, could hardly be expected to gain patients or pecuniary advantage from any form of public notice. Yet it is difficult to draw distinctions between doctors and also doctor's circumstances may change – the community physician of today may be a general practitioner tomorrow. It remains a fact that compared to previous years when anonymity was absolute, the appearance of medically-qualified persons on radio, television and in newspaper articles is an everyday occurrence. The public have a right to be kept up to date with medical advances and opinions and especially in small communities, it is patently impossible to conceal identity. It is up to the individual practitioner to decide what is ethical and what is not.

The more obvious forms of advertising are now rare, such as overt publications drawing attention to some professional skill, either in newspapers, public places or upon the doctor's premises. The plate outside a doctor's premises should be unobtrusive and convey no more information than the name, qualifications and surgery hours. It has been held in the past that descriptions of specialties i.e. 'Consultant Gynaecologist' are objectionable, but the practice is so widespread as to be accepted.

More recently, the attention of the GMC has been directed to the use of notices such as 'Slagthorpe Health Centre' displayed outside a group practice. Fears have been expressed that this might suggest that this group practice has some official recognition over and above any other medical practices in Slagthorpe, to the possible professional detriment of other doctors. However, the appending of a geographical name to Health Centres is now so widespread as to be virtually beyond reversal.

Advertising also presents problems in relation to private clinics and specialist services, such as cosmetic surgery and hair transplantation etc. Here the organisation may be directed by lay persons, over whom the GMC has no jurisdiction. Objectional advertisements in newspapers cannot be controlled directly, but doctors who work for the lay directors of such organisations may themselves be censured by the GMC for allowing themselves to be associated with undesirable advertising. Canvassing for patients (i.e. direct invitations to attend) is quite wrong, whether done by work of mouth or written means. It is also not correct for a doctor to advertise a change of surgery hours, for example, in a public notice or newspaper. This should only be done by individual circularisation of existing patients by private note, or a notice displayed in the interior of the surgery premises.

Association. This was a common offence in the last century and an important part of the General Council's work in the early years. It is now very rare for such complaints to come to the GMC's notice. They consist of 'covering' unqualified assistants. This was once particularly common in midwifery work, where unqualified women were employed as midwives on behalf of the doctor. Association does not restrict proper employment of the numerous types of medical auxillary and technician, nor the training of nurses and medical students as long as the doctor retains personal responsibility and exercises effective supervision. Naturally, in any emergency situation, including childbirth, the assistance of an unqualified person would never be held to be 'association'.

Other practices carrying the risk of disciplinary proceedings

An increasing cause for investigation, censure and possibly erasure by the GMC is the abuse or neglectful handling of the many forms of certification required by modern community medicine. Serious inaccuracies in certification, either through oversight or deliberate falsehood, may lead to removal from the Register.

These include the whole range of certification, especially those where some pecuniary benefit is obtained by the doctor or by the patient. Though the pressures of both overwork and persistent, vociferous patients in general practice may lead to careless or unwise certification, this should be guarded against with the utmost care. Sick notes, cremation certificates and certificates entitling patients to various grants are relatively frequent causes for action by the GMC.

Another common cause for the GMC's attention in relation to financial matters is the improper behaviour of a doctor in respect of fees and expenses. Dichotomy or 'fee-splitting' was in former years a much more common offence than at present. This practice referred to the calling-in of a specialist by a practitioner, when the consultation fee would be split between the two doctors. This provided an incentive for practitioners to consult one particular specialist, who might not necessarily be the best person for the patient's benefit. Other dubious activities include commercialisation of a patent medicine: the financial or proprietary interest in a chemist's shop to which patients may be referred for dispensing of prescriptions: prescribing drugs or surgical materials or appliances in which a doctor has a commercial stake i.e. he is a partner or principal shareholder in some drug company etc. This interest has to be direct and substantial and the mere holding of shares in some large pharmaceutical company constitutes no offence. Breaches of professional confidence i.e. medical secrecy, may also lead to disciplinary proceedings.

Failure to attend a patient is, in the isolated instance, a matter of complaint pursued through the machinery of the NHS or via a civil action for negligence. However, if persistent or flagrant neglect of professional duties is alleged, then the GMC may well take notice in respect of professional misconduct. The GMC is not concerned in matters of errors of diagnosis or treatment.

Last, but by no means least, an increasing cause for both NHS enquiries, GMC investigation and even criminal proceedings for fraud, is the deliberate falsification of claims by doctors for remuneration and expenses. An increasing number of allegations are being brought for obtaining money by deception and fraudulent claims in respect of all types of medical fees, extra-duty payments, subsistence allowances and travelling expenses.

Where such incorrect claims are shown to be deliberate and wilful, the doctor runs a grave risk of being found guilty of serious professional conduct by the GMC, in addition to any other retribution that may be brought by Area Health Authorities or the courts.

Republic of Ireland

A medical registration council of Ireland was set up in 1927, five years after the setting up of the State. Representation on the British GMC continued until 1978/1979 when the recommendations of the Merrison Committee brought about the exclusion of representatives from the Irish Republic. This coincided with recommendations from the EEC with the particular reference to registration of medical specialities. As a result, the Medical Practitioners Act 1978, of the Irish Parliament (Dail Eireann) made several changes. It set up a Medical Council which took over the functions of the old Medical Registration Council.

The Council consists of 25 members comprising a person (usually the Dean), nominated by each of the five medical schools, two persons from the Royal College of Surgeons in Ireland, (one representing surgery and the other anaesthetics and radiology), two persons appointed by the Royal College of Physicians of Ireland, (one representing the medical specialities and the other jointly the specialities of Pathology, Obstetrics and Gynaecology), one person appointed by the Minister of Health to represent Psychiatry, one person to represent general medical practice, ten elected medical practitioners representing the specialities, hospital doctors and general practitioners on different panels, and finally, four persons appointed by the Minister of Health, at least three of whom shall not be registered medical practitioners and shall in the opinion of the Minister represent the interests of the general public.

There are two statutory committees of the Council:

1. The Fitness to Practice Committee

This committee comprises only members of the Council, must contain a majority of elected members and must contain at least one of the laymen on the Council. It is the Fitness to Practice Committee which hears the complaints about medical practitioners and may find a doctor guilty of professional misconduct or unfit to engage in the practice of medicine because of physical or mental disability. The committee has the powers of a High Court judge to hear evidence under oath and to require the production of any medical records of that practitioner concerning a patient. If the committee finds the practitioner either guilty or unfit it reports him to the Council which then erases the name of the practitioner from the register or attaches such conditions as it thinks fit to the retention of that practitioner's name on the register. A doctor has the right of appeal to the High Court against his erasure. Unlike the U.K., the Irish Republic has a written constitution, and this form of appeal is necessary because every citizen has a constitutional right to challenge any person or body which seeks to deprive him or her of his or her livelihood. As in Britain the Council may also erase from the register the name of any practitioner convicted, either inside the State or outside it, of an indictable offence. There is however a constitutional appeal against this decision to the High Court.

2. The Educational Training Committee

This has responsibility for the maintenance of standards in education and training, for the setting up of a post-graduate medical and dental board, and in pursuance of EEC directives, for the setting up of a specialist register. This matter of specialist registration has at present not been implemented.

3

Consent

Consent in the context of the practice of medicine concerns the following three situations:

1. Examination of the living patient for the purpose of diagnosis and subsequent treatment.
2. Examination of the living person for medico-legal purposes.
3. Post-mortem examination and removal of tissues.

The last item is dealt with elsewhere, and this section is concerned with the examination and treatment of the living.

The nature of consent

With a few exceptions, consent to examination and treatment is an absolute requisite before a doctor approaches the patient.

The nature of the consent is determined largely by the nature of the intended examination or treatment. Failure to obtain consent may lead to recovery of damages in a civil action for tort (trespass, assault or battery) or even to criminal proceedings for common, aggravated or indecent assault depending on the nature of the examination or treatment. Though awareness of the need for consent is often disregarded by the doctor – mainly because of the rarity of complaints and because of the day-to-day pressures of medical practice – distressing publicity, litigation and damages are occasionally suffered from neglect of relatively simple precautions.

Consent may either be *implied* or *express:*

Implied Consent. This is provided by the demeanour of the patient and is by far the most common variety of consent in both general practice and hospital practice. The fact that a patient presents himself at a surgery or out-patients is held to imply that he is agreeable to medical examination in the general sense. This however, does not imply consent to procedures more complex than inspection, palpation, percussion and auscultation. Even here, the common courtesies of speech normally request access to the body surface. For other examinations, notably rectal and vaginal and the withdrawal of blood for diagnostic purposes, express permission should be obtained. For more complicated diagnostic procedures and for the various forms of endoscopy and radiology, written permission should be obtained, as for surgical operations.

Express Consent. Aything other than the implied consent described above is express consent. This may be either oral or written For the majority of relatively minor examinations or therapeutic procedures, oral consent is employed, but this should be obtained in the presence of a disinterested third party, usually a receptionist, ward sister or nurse and not a person closely associated with the patient, whose later testimony may be biased. Oral consent, where properly witnessed, is of equal validity to written consent, but the latter has the advantage of easy proof and permanent form, which avoids dispute in any subsequent litigation.

Written consent, as stated, is obtained for all major diagnostic procedures and for surgical operations. It is important to note that written consent should refer to *one specific procedure*, and the former practice of obtaining a 'blanket' permission on admission to hospital to cover any subsequent procedures over any length of time, is to be deprecated. Such written permission should normally be obtained on a special form provided by the institution, and witnessed by a third party. It is also essential that the nature and extent of the therapeutic or surgical procedure should be explained to the patient before obtaining permission, though this idea must naturally be modified by the clinical circumstances, as for example in the case of a very apprehensive patient. This concept of 'informed consent' has come very much into prominence in recent years, because of the increased awareness of the public about medical matters, which are so ofen exposed on television and in the press; and also from a general awareness of 'civil rights', which has eroded the former sometimes patronising attitude of doctors. There is now an acute sense of the 'right to know' amongst a large proportion of patients and informed consent is now almost mandatory. However, there has been some reaction against the concept, especially in the United States, as unwise decisions by the patients to reject treatment because of the potential risks may weigh disproportionately against the benefits of life-saving or health-giving treatment. It is also usual to point out that the procedure need not be carried out by any particular doctor, as this aspect has given rise to court proceedings in the past.

Though not directly concerned with consent, it is appropriate to emphasize here that wherever possible, examination of female patients by male doctors should be made in the presence of a nurse or receptionist, or failing that, a female relative. This is imperative in intimate examinations and also very advisable when short anaesthetics are being administered. Though the pressures of general practice make this impossible on many occasions, a number of cases of imagined or malicious allegations of indecent assault make this a potentially serious matter.

From whom consent is obtained

Conscious, mentally sound adults (adults in this context being persons over 16 years of age) normally give consent themselves. Where procedures involving marital relations are involved, such as sterilisation and termination of pregnancy, the wishes of the spouse are usually sought, though are not always legally necessary (see appropriate chapters).

Though the age of majority in law is now 18 years, adolescents become registrable with the National Health Service at 16 years and this is the age at which they can legally give their own consent (Family Law Reform Act, 1969). Below the age of 16 years, consent should be obtained from the parent or guardian except in the case of emergency. Sometimes the permission of the person *in loco parentis*, such as the headmaster of a residential school, is obtained, but as the situation would almost always constitute an emergency, this is not absolutely necessary.

The age of consent in the Republic of Ireland is generally taken to be eighteen years which is also the age of the voting franchise. Legal Authorities however still regard 21 as the minimum age at which an individual may undertake a contract at law.

Where the parent or guardian of a person below the age of 16 years refuses permission for an urgent diagnostic or therapeutic procedure, the doctor's position is governed partly by personal ethics and partly by a somewhat cumbersome mechanism set up by law. This situation usually arises from religious objections, notably Jehovah's Witnesses in respect of blood transfusion. Where transfusion or other procedure is held to be a life-saving matter, the doctor may proceed according to his own conscience and trust that the courts will uphold his view, if it should come to litigation. Alternatively, he may seek the assistance of the Children's Officer of the Local Authority. An emergency court can be convened at the bed-side at any hour of the day or night, and a Magistrate may authorise the removal of the child's custody from the parents to a 'fit person', usually a Children's Officer, who then authorises the medical procedure. This mechanism is rarely used, and the Department of Health have directed that its employment be abandoned. If the doctor acts in good faith in urgent circumstances, he may rest assured that his decision will be upheld against the parents' objections (*see also* page 00).

Adults unable to give consent

Mentally defective persons are in the same position as minors, and permission is obtained from close relatives or the officer in charge of the institution in which they reside, if no relatives are available. Where certified mental patients are compulsorily detained in an institution, consent to medical treatment should be obtained from them if they are able to comprehend the nature of the procedure. If not, the medical officer in charge should sign the appropriate form – the relatives have no legal standing in the matter. Consent for therapeutic procedures upon unconscious persons is also obtained from close relatives: in an acute emergency when no one is available, consent is justifiably dispensed with. In such cases, care should be taken that surgical procedures do not go beyond the minimum required to save life, and wherever possible, amputation of limbs etc., is postponed until such time as personal permission can be obtained.

Consent in any form must be obtained freely after explanation of the need for the performance of the technique, the latter being modified by the doctor's judgement of the patient's mental state. Consent obtained by duress – that is, force, fear or fraud – is invalid and is no consent at all. Similarly, consent obtained for illegal or unethical procedures is invalid – euthanasia and any mutilating operation would then constitute murder, manslaughter or criminal assault, whether any form of consent from the patient had been obtained or not. Formerly, sterilisation of either male or female came under this heading, but modern practice has now made this acceptable under the proper conditions.

EXAMINATION FOR MEDICO-LEGAL PURPOSES

The foregoing sections have applied to the diagnostic examination and treatment of patients for their own welfare. Examinations are frequently carried out, however, at the behest of a third party, sometimes to the potential detriment of the person examined. Again, except in a limited range of exceptions, consent *must* be obtained in every case. No third party (which especially includes police) can authorise examination without consent, which would then still constitute an assault.

Express permission should always be obtained in these cases, as the person has usually not come voluntarily to the doctor and thus implied consent cannot be assumed. A third party should always be present when oral consent is obtained or should witness a written form of consent.

Examination at the request of the police

As stated, the police have no authority to demand medical examination. The usual reasons for such examination are of accused persons in police stations especially in connection with drunkenness, drunken driving and sexual assaults. The *victim* of alleged criminal actions, especially sexual assaults, is another common reason for examinations requested by police officers. These are usually performed by a retained Police Surgeon, but in an emergency or where none is available, any other doctor may be requested to carry out such examinations. The person, accused or otherwise, has the right to be examined by a doctor of his or her own choice, and it is obligatory under Police Orders that such examination by another doctor be conducted in the presence of a police officer or the police surgeon.

Examination of employees at employer's request

No employer has the right to enforce medical examination upon an unwilling employee. Though certain types of employee, especially in the food industries, may be obliged to submit to medical examination, this occurs under various Public Health Acts and not at the behest of the employer. In former years, examination of female servants who were suspected of being pregnant was a common reason for the employer to request a doctor to examine, and numerous actions for assault subsequently arose.

Examination of schoolchildren

It is normal practice for all children in State schools to be examined medically and dentally, but objection by the parents is always upheld, though in strict law it could be enforced (Education Act 1944, Sect. 49.) The usual procedure is for the parents to arrange for their own private practitioner to conduct an alternative examination.

Situations where consent need not be obtained

Though normal courtesy would request permission before every approach by a doctor, some limited circumstances allow examination to continue even if this is refused. Most of these are concerned with the detection of contagious disease:

- Immigrants may be examined by Port and Airport medical staff on entry into Britain.
- A person suffering from a notifiable disease or tuberculosis may be examined after obtaining an order from a magistrate.
- New admissions to H.M. Prisons may be examined to exclude infectious diseases. This does not extend to anything other than routine external medical examination, nor do the other exceptions listed here.
- Probation orders from a court may direct that psychiatric examination be conducted (Section 28, Mental Health Act, 1959).
- Handlers of food and dairymen may also be required to submit to medical examination if a Medical Officer of Health has reason to suspect infection by salmonella or staphylococcus.
- Members of the Armed Forces must submit to examination.

4

Transplantation of organs and tissues

This subject has leapt into prominence in recent years due to technical advances in organ transplantation. This has raised many problems, not only medical and legal, but ethical and even religious. Few topics have aroused such intense interest and divergence of opinion in both the medical press and lay media, especially television. The public reaction to the subject is very labile and sensitive, as witnessed by the dramatic drop in donations immediately following an inaccurate account of the criteria of brain death shown by a BBC 'Panorama' programme in November 1980.

Some forms of tissue transplantation are long established and arouse no passions amongst the majority of the public – though certain religious sects still object. Blood transfusion is the oldest practical form of tissue transplantation, but as in Western countries the donors are living and suffer no ill effects, no antipathy is aroused. Corneal grafting is another technique where because the controversy about the definition of death in the donor is not relevant, only emotive feelings about disfigurement from removal of the eyes complicate the issue.

The first statute law on tissue transplantation was implemented because of corneal transplants, the Corneal Grafting Act of 1952 being a forerunner of the more comprehensive Human Tissue Act of 1961. This Act controls present legal requirements, though its drafting leaves certain matters undecided and new legislation is required to rectify some ambiguities and omissions.

Of vital importance and great practical use is the booklet *The Removal of Cadaveric Organs for Transplantation – A Code of Practice* published by the Department of Health in October 1979. This covers all practical aspects of the subject and includes the text of the Human Tissue Act 1961 and the criteria for diagnosing brain death etc.

HUMAN TISSUE ACT, 1961 (and the Human Tissue Act (Northern Ireland) 1962)

This deals with three topics:

1. Permission for post-mortem examination, other than those for medico-legal purposes.
2. Removal of cadaver tissues for transplantation.
3. The addition of cremation to methods of disposal of bodies used for anatomical dissection.

Post-mortem examination

This matter is not related to transplantation, but as the provisions in the Act are virtually identical, it is best considered here.

Where a post-mortem examination is desired for 'academic' clinical purposes to determine the *extent* of a disease process (in a case not reportable to a coroner or procurator-fiscal), the following procedure must be carried out. Note that such a clinical autopsy cannot be performed to determine the *nature* of a disease process, as if this was unknown to the clinician, then by definition, the case is reportable to the coroner.

The person lawfully in possession of the body may give permission for post-mortem examination if, having made such reasonable enquiries as may be practicable, he is satisfied that:

a. The deceased person had not indicated during life that he objected to a post-mortem and
b. The surviving spouse or any relative does not object to a post-mortem examination.

The interpretation of these regulations will be discussed below in connection with transplantation, but as far as clinical autopsies are concerned, a printed form, devised in accordance with Health Service practice, is offered to the nearest relative, next-of-kin or executor.

This confirms the absence of objection on the part of the relative, who signs it in the presence of a witness. There is also a sub-section (which can be deleted by the relative if so wishes) which indicates a further lack of objection to the removal of limited amounts of tissue for therapeutic purposes. This is not related to transplantation, but usually to the removal of the pituitary gland. These glands are needed by the Medical Research Council for processing of growth hormone, the only effective treatment for certain forms of infant dwarfism. Unfortunately, the present form does not extend this to material for teaching and research, which are covered by the Human Tissue Act itself.

Another defect in this respect is that far more medico-legal autopsies are performed than clinical ones, so there is no opportunity to request permission for pituitaries etc., as no permission from relatives is needed in coroner's or fiscal cases.

Post-mortems must either be carried out by fully-registered medical practitioners or they must supervise any provisionally registered practitioners performing such autopsies.

Legal and ethical considerations in the obtaining of tissues for transplantation

The type of tissue required for transplantation makes a profound difference to the legal and ethical considerations. For example, where blood transfusion is concerned, no problem arises at all except in some religious sects who object to any form of transplantations. With corneal grafting and the now almost defunct use of artery grafts for vascular repairs, the problems are relatively minor, because these tissues may be removed many hours after death, when there is no problem about determining the moment of death.

It is the recent technical advances in *organ* transplantation that have caused such profound changes in the legal and ethical considerations surrounding the donation of tissues. At the time of writing, the most common organ to be transplanted – and the one with the greatest record of success – is the kidney, but the same questions arise in connection with other organs, notably the heart.

Because of a low level of awareness both in the medical profession and amongst the lay public (added to by some adverse publicity and the unclear state of the law surrounding organ donation), the kidney transplant programme in Great Britain has become seriously hindered by a lack of suitable donor material.

Live donors

The use of kidneys from related live donors is attended by a greater success rate than with the use of cadaver tissues. Patients receiving such a live kidney will have a 93 per cent chance of surviving a year, compared with an 82 per cent chance with a cadaver donation. In Britain, the use of live donors has always been very small compared with other countries, mainly due to the fact that relatives are rarely approached with the request. In Europe as a whole, only 4 per cent of kidney transplants are from live donors, though in the United States 35 per cent are obtained in this way.

Where a live donation is proposed, a full explanation of the procedure involved must be given to the donor, the possible consequences and risks being fully explained. If these risks are accepted, a written witnessed consent must be obtained. In order to avoid any rash decision being taken by the donor in the emotion of the moment, he should be advised to discuss the matter with his or her family and where appropriate, religious advisers. Every assistance and information should be offered by the medical attendants concerned. No donation can be accepted which would cause any significant risk to the life of the donor, no matter how willing the donor is to sacrifice the organ.

Tissues from cadaver donors

As the use of live donation of kidneys is very infrequent outside the United States, most must be obtained from cadavers. Almost all come from acute cerebral catastrophies, notably accidental head injuries and subarachnoid haemorrhage. Though in Britain there are some 6000 fatal road accidents per annum, each of which could theoretically donate two kidneys, the actual number of kidney transplants is only of the order of 850. As about 2000 people each year need transplantation, it is obvious that there is a marked failure of the system intended to obtain cadaver material. About 10 per cent of cadaver renal transplants fail to function, leading to an unfortunate situation where the recipient has to undergo two unneccessary operations, one for the transplantation and a second for the removal of the useless graft. This failure to function becomes progressively more likely with a longer 'warm ischaemic time' i.e. the time during which the kidney remains in the dead body after cessation of the heart-beat. On the continent of Europe, kidneys are normally removed before the cessation of the heart-beat, ensuring a much better survival rate and this practice is now being followed in Britain.

The Human Tissue Act (1961) provides almost identical procedures to the rules for post-mortem examinations, with the addition of permission being granted by the donor himself.

Section 1 states that if a person during his lifetime expresses in writing (or orally in the presence of two witnesses) a desire to donate tissue for transplantation, the person lawfully in possession of the body after death, may authorise the removal of those tissues (which may either be specified organs or tissues, or a general donation).

In other words, this is a 'contracting-in' situation. In fact very few people actually indicate such a desire although some may carry Donor Cards. These cards are issued by the Department of Health and can be signed by the potential donor. The card is carried on the person, so that if the circumstances where donation becomes practicable so arise, legal permission is available without delay.

Section 2 of the Act goes on to rule that, where no ante-mortem permission is given, the person lawfully in charge of the body (see below) may authorise the removal of donor tissues *if having made such reasonable enquiry as may be practicable*, he has no reason to believe that:

1. the deceased had ever expressed any objection to donation and
2. that the surviving spouse or any surviving relative has made any such objection.

Some of these terms must be clarified further. Firstly, *reasonable enquiry as may be practicable* has never been defined in the Act. As there is often extreme urgency as far as time is concerned, in order to obtain tissues or organs in as good a condition as possible, it is obvious that such enquiries cannot extend over a considerable time or distance. The Code of Practice mentioned above concurs with the Department of Health's interpretation that 'in most instances it will be sufficient to discuss the matter with any one relative who had been in close contact with the deceased, asking him his own views, the views of the deceased and also if he has any reason to believe that any other relative would be likely to object'.

In a donor's relatives are inaccessible, it would be impracticable to try to ask them. They might for instance, be young children or seriously ill. In these cases, the designated person can give authorisation for removal, though the facts should be recorded in the case notes.

Secondly, the 'person lawfully in possession of the body' is almost invariably the Health Autority responsible for the hospital where the body is lying. This possession continues until the body is claimed by the next-of-kin, executor, coroner etc. The Act empowers delegation of this possession to any officer or person acting on its behalf. Any administrator or doctor of the Health Authority may give oral permission for the removal of tissues once he has satisfied himself that the provisions of Section 2 have been fulfilled.

As the majority of subjects from whom tissues are taken will be the victims of head injuries, these cases will of necessity be reported to the coroner or procurator-fiscal. No organ donation can be performed in such cases without the permission of the coroner or fiscal, as it is possible that medico-legal investigation of the death might be hampered by such prior operative interference. In fact, this is rarely a practical objection as removal of the kidneys is unlikely to interfere with the subsequent examination of the head injuries. However, where heart transplantation is involved, it is possible that a heart condition may have contributed to the fatal accident, an aspect which might require forensic examination. However, any potential donor with a history of heart disease would be unlikely to be used.

The permission of the coroner is usually a prior 'blanket' consent, rather than individual consultation on every occasion. The coroner's pathologist may also be consulted as to the possible relevance of transplantation donation to the subsequent autopsy.

DONATION PROCEDURES

For organ transplantation, which includes kidney, heart, liver, pancreas, lung etc. the organ must either be removed whilst the circulation is still functioning or removed within a very short time of cardiac arrest, to reduce the warm ischaemic time to a minimum. With kidneys, it was the former practice in Britain to switch off mechanical ventilation and wait for the heart to stop before removing the kidneys. However, this method reduced the success rate of transplantation by a significant percentage. Thus all organs are now removed whilst the heart is still beating and the tissues perfused with oxygenated blood. This forms the most controverisal aspect of donation, as the moment of death is then a more arbitrary point in time.

These issues are fully dealt with in the official 'Code of Practice', some salient points being summarised here.

The choice of donor

An organ donor must be:

1. Deeply and irreversibly unconscious.
2. Without spontaneous respiration, thus sustained on artificial ventilation i.e. must be in an Intensive Care Unit.
3. Must be shown to have irreversible brain death (see below).

Persons with systemic infections, tumours other than primary brain neoplasms, renal disease and severe atherosclerosis are unsuitable for organ donation. These criteria do not necessarily apply to corneal donors, but these should not be children (because of corneal thickness) or patients with eye diseases.

The team of doctors providing care for the fatally ill or injured patient must be – and be seen to be – quite distinct from the transplant team. Nothing should be done to the patient for the purposes of donation that would not have been done in furtherance of treatment e.g. no transfer to another hospital merely to facilitate donation. There is no objection (indeed, it is recommended) that when blood samples are taken for diagnostic or therapeutic tests, an extra sample be sent for tissue typing in anticipation of transplantation.

When the treatment team has cause to anticipate a fatal outcome, the transplant team should be alerted. By this stage, the relatives will have been prepared for the impossibility of recovery and after this is confirmed to them by the treatment team, the matter of organ donation is raised by a member of either team, usually a senior and experienced doctor. Sometimes, it might be more appropriate for a ward sister, family doctor or hospital chaplain to raise the subject. In the case of kidney transplants, permission is granted in the great majority of instances, though inexplicably there is more resistance to corneal grafting.

Where a person has left a Donor Card, this constitutes sufficient legal authority for transplantation to be performed, but it is still good practice and obvious courtesy to discuss the procedure with the relatives. Though their objections legally have no weight, it would be exceptional for a transplant team to proceed in the face of serious objection on the part of the relatives.

A lack of objection from relatives to donation is not normally confirmed in writing – there is no printed form comparable to the post-mortem permission form. However, the outcome of discussions with the relatives should be recorded in the notes – the Code of Practice recommends a 'Transplantation Checklist' to record the sequence of procedures.

As mentioned above, the coroner or procurator-fiscal must concur with the removal of organs in cases which will be reported to him, but not in other instances – though these are relatively few in numbers, such as natural deaths from ruptured cerebral aneurysms and cerebral tumours.

The coroner or procurator fiscal cannot give *sole permission* for the donation or organs – they can only refuse it or express a lack of objection.

Determination of death

Formerly, cessation of respiration and circulation were the criteria for determining death. As all potential donors will of necessity be on artificial ventilation and circulation must be present for the donor tissue to be viable, then some other criterion must be sought. This is brain-stem death.

In Britain, there is no legal definition of death, this being left to clinical judgement. For viable donor organs, cardio-respiratory function must continue after brain-stem death has been diagnosed. Once death has been diagnosed, then there is no legal objection to drugs being given where necessary to maintain the condition of the organs.

Where death is to be determined by the diagnosis of brain-stem death, the fact of death should be confirmed by:

1. A consultant in charge of the case or his deputy who should have been registered at least five years and be experienced in such cases.
2. In addition, one other doctor, who should also be suitable experienced and clinically independent of the first doctor.

Neither of these doctors should be a member of the transplant team. Their opinion about brain death should be carefully recorded in the clinical notes and checklist.

It is ethical and legal to carry out any procedures after brain death has been diagnosed, which will improve the chances of a successful 'take' of the transplant, e.g. drugs to maintain renal function, antibiotics, continuing ventilation and oxygenation and cardiac support.

The removal of organs for transplantation may only be carried out by a *fully* registered medical practitioner (who must satisfy himself by personal examination of the body that life is extinct i.e. that brain-stem death or cessation of cardio-respiratory function is confirmed). This is stated specifically in the Human Tissue Act.

Diagnosis of brain death

The Code of Practice includes two papers produced by the Conference of Royal Colleges and Faculties of the United Kingdom (1976 and 1979), giving criteria and comments on the diagnosis of brain death. These are summarised thus:

1. The patient is in deep coma, which must be shown not to be due to depressent drugs, hypothermia or metabolic or endocrine disturbances.
2. The patient must be ventilated artificially, because spontaneous respiration is either inadequate or absent. Neuro-muscular blocking agents and other drugs (i.e. curare-like) must be excluded as a possible cause of such respiratory failure.
3. There should be no doubt that the patient's condition is due

to irremediable structural brain damage. The diagnosis of a disorder which can lead to brain death should have been fully established.

Diagnostic tests for brain-stem death

1. All brain-stem reflexes are absent.
   Fixed pupils, unresponsive to light.
   Absent corneal reflexes.
   Absent vestibulo-ocular reflexes (ice-water in ears).
   No motor responses in cranial nerves.
   No gag reflex to catheter in trachea.
   No respiratory movements when patient disconnected from ventilator (The arterial pCO_2 level should exceed 50 mm/Hg to allow sufficient stimulus for breathing).
2. The tests should be repeated by two doctors to ensure permanent absence of response. The interval is variable between tests, but may be up to 24 hours in equivocal cases.
3. The persistence of spinal reflexes is not relevant in the diagnosis of brain-stem death.
4. The use of electroencephalography is not essential for the diagnosis, neither is central angiography nor measurements of cerebral blood-flow.
5. Testing should be carried out at a body temperature not less than 35°C, as hypothermia may itself mimic brain-stem damage.

Religious objections to transplantation techniques

Certain religious sects, notably Jehovah's Witnesses, are adamant in their refusal to allow any form of tissue transplantation, which in everyday practice usually means blood transfusion. Any member of such a sect over the age of 16 years is quite entitled to take this attitude, and nothing can be done in the face of his persistent refusal, after adequate explanation about his medical condition. The position, however, is different when a child is concerned. Where a parent or guardian of such a religious belief stubbornly refuses to allow blood transfusion or any other medical or surgical procedure which is held to be necessary either to save life or to treat a serious injury or disease, two paths are open to the attending doctor.

Under the provisions of the Children and Young Persons Act of 1933 (Section 67, 2) the custody of a child can be transferred from the parents to the care of a 'fit person' who can then give consent to the necessary medical treatment. For this purpose, the Children's Officer of the local authority can stand *in loco parentis*, and this procedure can be performed quickly by means of a bedside court, on the authority of one attending magistrate. The Department of Health have advised against using this procedure, where it can be avoided, mainly because of the lack of opportunity for appeal on the part of the parents.

The second course is for the doctor to proceed with the required treatment even against the parent's wishes. A joint committee of the BMA and the Magistrate's Association have studied this problem and concluded that a doctor's first consideration is the health of his patient, irrespective of his own position in law. It is certain that if a doctor in good faith and according to the dictates of his own conscience, carried out such treatment in the absence of parental consent, full support would be given him by his defence society and professional bodies. It is extremely unlikely that any action for assault would ever be successful in a court of law.

Republic of Ireland

There is no legislation concerning these matters in the Irish Republic. Neither the British Corneal Grafting or Human Tissues Acts are applicable there. For transplantation a code of practice has been evolved between the Dublin City Coroner and the transplant surgeons in that city, necessitating death to be certified by two doctors not connected with the transplant team, and also the consent of the nearest relative of the donor. While many citizens have signed kidney donor cards, their validity has yet to be challenged in a Court of Law.

5

Medical negligence

Medical negligence was formerly called 'malpractice', though this is not strictly synonymous, as other forms of irregular medical practice may be malpractice, apart from a dispute between doctor and patient over the standard of medical care. The vast majority of instances of medical negligence lie completely within the civil law and instances where negligence has been so gross as to constitute a criminal offence are exceptionally rare.

Medical negligence is no different in law from any other type of negligence, apart from the fact that the courts adopt a more sympathetic and lenient view towards the doctor than other types of defendant – a fact not appreciated by many doctors, who tend to believe that the reverse is true.

Negligence, medical or otherwise, is a civil wrong known as a *tort*, a difficult concept to describe. In addition, a doctor may be held in breach of *contract*, if his professional behaviour falls short of the requirements of the contract between him and the patient.

For negligence of any kind to be proved, it must be shown that:

1. That the defendant (doctor) owed a duty of care to the plaintiff (patient).
2. That the defendant was in breach of that duty.
3. That the plantiff suffered damaged as a result.

Applied to the medical situation, negligence is the breach of the duty owed by a doctor to his patient to exercise reasonable care and/or skill, resulting in some bodily, mental or financial disability.

The doctor must possess a reasonable degree of proficiency and apply that proficiency with a reasonable degree of diligence. Thus an exceptionally brilliant surgeon may be negligent if he falls to apply his brilliance: conversely, an inadequately proficient or inexperienced surgeon may be negligent even if he strains himself to the utmost, if he has held himself out to the patient to be posessed of sufficient competence.

This degree of competence is not a fixed quality, but varies according to the status of the doctor. Though there is a minimum level of competence for all doctors (which is supposed to be guarded by the qualifying examination and supervision of the General Medical Council before a doctor is admitted to the Register) the standard of skill varies through a whole spectrum from new graduate to senior consultant. No doctor is expected to possess all current medical knowledge nor be able to apply all known diagnostic and therapeutic techniques: but a doctor of a particular standing, as regards grade and experience, is expected to have a standard of knowledge and capability commensurate with his status. Thus a house surgeon is not expected to possess the same skills as a consultant surgeon, but at the same time, he is expected to confine his activities (except in emergencies) to a level of medical care which is within his competence. A house surgeon electing to perform a major surgical operation, not in an urgent situation, might be held guilty of negligence if damage ensues, even though he could not be expected to possess the same experience as a senior surgeon, who should have performed the operation. With the present complexity of anaesthesia, this point has special relevance to the giving of anaesthetics by insufficiently experienced doctors and no junior or non-specialist should trespass outside the limits of his own competence, except in an emergency.

Returning to the three elements of negligence, each must be examined more closely.

The duty to exercise skill and care

Such a duty only exists – and therefore negligence can only occur – when a doctor/ patient relationship is established. This relationship may be formed extremely easily, and by no means depends on any formal acceptance of a patient by a doctor, such as inclusion on a practice list. Even in an acute emergency, once a doctor approaches an ill or injured person with the object of assisting him, then a completely valid relationship is set up, notwithstanding the fact that the patient may be unconscious and quite unaware of the doctor's presence. It is somewhat ironic that actions for negligence have been brought by a patient against a doctor who acted as a 'Good Samaritan' following some roadside accident, but the legal position is quite definite. The number of such actions became so frequent in the United States within recent years, that passing physicians became extremely reluctant to render aid in emergencies and some States brought in legislation to prevent actions for negligence arising from casual treatment at the scene of accidents.

A doctor is not negligent if he does not offer his services in an emergency to a person who is not already his patient as no doctor/patient relationship exists (though the ethics might be questionable and a National Health Service general practitioner has a contractual obligation to treat any emergency). The fact that no payment or other reward is offered or expected, makes no difference to the duty of care, the essential ingredient of which is willingness to examine, diagnose and treat the patient.

Where a doctor examines a patient for some purpose other than providing advice and treatment, no relationship is established and thus no duty of care exists. A doctor conducting a medico-legal examination for any purpose (such as insurance, evaluation of disability, drunkenness etc.) is not there in his capacity as a healer, and no duty of care arises. In these circumstances, there *is* a duty not to inflict any damage upon the patient, and thus if for example, a needle is negligently broken off whilst taking blood, the patient has a right of action. If, however, a doctor reports to an employer, insurance company or compensation board that a patient is healthy, when in fact he is not, the patient has no claim for negligence against that doctor for any loss suffered, as no duty to take care existed between the doctor and the patient. A duty exists, however, between the doctor and the authority employing him to make the examination, but any incompetence in this context, would be a breach of contract, not a tort.

Damage suffered by the patient

However negligent the doctor might be, a patient cannot sue him for negligence if no damage has accrued. He must have suffered some loss which can be measured and compensated for in terms of money. Examples of such loss are:

Loss of earnings, whether due to enforced absence from work or prevention or impairment of his ability to carry on his previous occupation, so that he is forced to take employment at a lower level of salary or from loss of expectation of life and the consequent shortening of the earning period.

Expenses incurred as a result of the damage caused by the negligence, which may be hospital or nursing-home expenses, nursing attention, special treatment, special foods etc.

Reduction in expectation of life, apart from the financial aspect.

Reduced enjoyment of life, from any physical or mental consequence of the negligent act. Examples would be loss of faculty of limb or sense, which would reduce mobility or appreciation of his surroundings.

Especially in the case of women, some physical disability or disfigurement which might reduce the chances of marriage or inability to have further children might also be actionable.

Pain and suffering, whether physical or mental, may also be taken into account, as may mental or nervous shock.

Death may be actionable for the benefit of dependent relatives, the main criterion applied to measure such damage being the loss of potential future earning power, any off-setting by life insurance, pension being taken into account. In this regard, it should be pointed out that damages for the death of a child tend to be very low.

Damages awarded for loss of faculty, pain and suffering, loss of expectation of life, etc., are termed *general damages*, and those for expenses, medical and nursing attention etc., are called *special damages*, which can be computed more exactly. General damages depend upon the Judge's assessment of all factors obtained in the particular case, so that the damages awarded may vary very greatly from case to case. There is thus no fixed scale such as '£1000 for loss of a leg', as it is not the leg that is in issue but the circumstances of the man who lost it.

Breach of duty to exercise reasonable skill and care

A well-worn legal maxim in this respect is that 'the categories of negligence are never closed', emphasising that it is impossible to draw up a comprehensive list of all events which could constitute medical negligence, as these naturally increase as medical technology advances.

There is however a hard core of situations which give rise to the majority of actions for negligence. Before considering these individual cases, some general features of negligent behaviour should be mentioned.

A doctor is not liable for errors of judgement either in diagnosis or treatment. So long as he applies a minimum reasonable standard of skill and care, he cannot be held negligent. A doctor can misdiagnose, and mis-treat a patient without being negligent, even if another practitioner of greater skill would have had more success. A doctor does not guarantee to provide the best possible care, but only care consistent with his professional status.

Normally, the risk of providing negligence rests upon the person bringing the action. An exception to this rule that the 'burden of proof rests on the plaintiff', is in cases where the facts are so obvious that the onus is shifted to the doctor to prove that his own negligence did *not* contribute to this state of affairs. This doctrine of *res ipsa loquitur* ('the facts speak for themselves') applies when, for instance, the wrong limb or digit is amputated at operation. The patient plaintiff does not have to prove that the act was negligent, as it obviously could be nothing else. It is for the surgeon to show – if he can – that the negligence was not his doing. The courts are reluctant to apply this doctrine to any but the most flagrant cases as, in general, the plaintiff has to prove negligence. This is especially so in Scottish law.

Departure from accepted medical practice is another hazard. Though doctors are not expected to be aware of every development in medical science, they are expected to keep abreast of general principles and to follow general lines of treatment. There is great latitude in this, but certain ommissions, rather than commissions, lead to allegations of negligence. Probably foremost amongst these is failure to X-ray suspected fractures, especially of the skull. Radiology of bone injuries has become such an accepted part of investigation that even where the doctor might honestly think that no such investigation is required, the frequency of civil actions has virtually forced casualty officers to submit any but the most trivial injuries to radiology. A similar medico-legal climate made the giving of anti-tetanus serum almost mandatory in all instances of deep laceration, though recent misgivings about the dangers and efficiency of ATS have tended to modify this practice.

COMMON CAUSES FOR NEGLIGENCE ACTIONS

Failure to attend

Though often a matter for NHS Committees and Tribunals (and in certain instances, even the GMC), failure of a general practitioner to respond to a request for attendance may form grounds for an action for negligence. They are particularly frequent where children are concerned, especially in relation to acute abdominal emergencies and chest infections.

Amputation of the wrong limb or digit

This is an increasingly common mishap and one that has caused considerable concern to the defence organisations. Carelessness in hospital notes, and failure to check such notes against the patient in the operating theatre are common causes for this highly actionable misadventure. A similar mistake involves operating on the wrong patient altogether, and the whole 'syndrome' has assumed such serious proportions that one defence society has commissioned a film entitled *Make No Mistake*, drawing attention to these dangers.

Retention of objects in operation sites
This is the classic example which most often comes to mind when discussing medical negligence. Swabs, packs, towels or instruments may be left behind in the abdomen after operation. The responsibility remains with the surgeon, and even if the theatre sister has the actual task of maintaining a swab count, the surgeon must satisfy himself that she is correct before closing the abdomen.

Casualty departments
In the medico-legal sense, the casualty department is the most dangerous part of a hospital (Fig. 2). Until recent years, it was commonly the practice for the least experienced doctors to deal with this most hazardous department, but partly due to the frequency of civil actions, senior staff now frequently assume responsibility for such work, though the hazard to junior staff often still remains, especially at night. Fractures, head injuries and lacerations account for much of the danger, as already mentioned, and junior staff employed in casualty departments should not hesitate to request the advice of more senior colleagues where there is the slightest doubt as to the proper course of action.

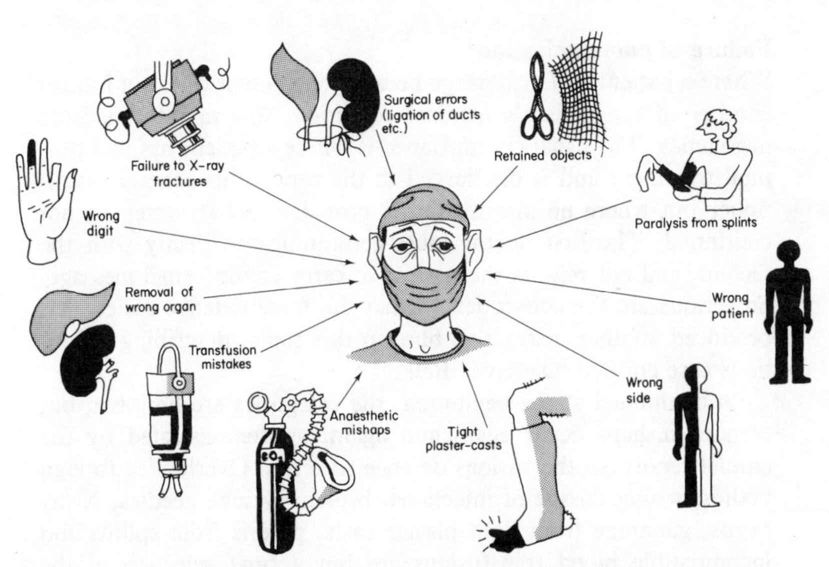

Fig. 2 Common surgical mishaps leading to allegations of negligence

Anaesthesia

Like casualty work, anaesthesia has its own special dangers. Anaesthetists, along with surgeons, present a common target for litigation: the actual administration of the anaesthetic is not usually the cause of complaint, but the many ancillary responsibilities such as transfusion, injections, airways, intravenous catheters, diathermy and hot-water bottle burns may form grounds for allegations for negligence.

Therapeutic hazards

Many forms of treatment hold inherent risks, but these will not provide grounds for negligence, unless the doctor failed to draw the attention of the patient to these potential risks and also failed to take all possible steps to avoid undesirable consequences. Where certain operations carry certain well-recognised risks (e.g. laryngeal paralysis in thyroidectomy) particular care must be taken and if the patient's psychological state allows, the risk should be explained previously. Drugs with well-known potential dangers must also be handle with care. For instance, it would be negligent for a doctor to give penicillin to a penicillin-allergic patient if he was aware of the possible allergy or had not enquired as to its presence. Substances known to cause serious or fatal reactions, such as ATS, should only be administered after either a test dose or an enquiry to ensure that previous injections had been given without mishap.

Failure of communication

Where a patient suffers damage because one doctor does not inform another of the patient's medical condition, this might constitute negligence. The usual circumstance is where a patient has had hospital treatment and is discharged to the care of his general practitioner but where no information is provided and treatment is not continued. The first doctor must communicate directly with the second, and not rely on the patient to carry any informal message. So serious are the consequences that the same defence society has produced another instructive film on this topic, describing a fictitious case entitled 'Ogden *v.* Bell'.

As mentioned at the beginning, the categories are limitless, but certain mishaps occur again and again, as demonstrated by the annual reports of the various defence societies. Overlooked foreign bodies, wrong dosage of injections, broken syringe needles, X-ray burns, gangrene from tight plaster casts, paresis from splints and incompatible blood transfusions are but a brief selection of the cases which daily come to the attention of the defence societies.

Defences against an allegation of negligence

Apart from a denial of the actual occurrence of negligence, even when the fact of damage is proved, a doctor has three possible avenues of defence:

1. Delegation of duties

That any negligence which occurred was not that of the doctor, but of some third party. In the present complex state of medicine, a patient may be dealt with by more than one doctor, as well as non-medical auxiliaries such as radiographers, physiotherapists, technicians of various sorts and of course, the nursing staff. It is sometimes difficult for the plaintiff to know whom to sue, and here the doctrine of *res ipsa loquitur* is of great importance to the plaintiff, as it shifts the onus of refutation back to all those concerned.

The delegation of duties by a doctor and the subsequent responsibility for any mishap has been a matter of dispute over the years, but in hospital practice, has become less controversial since the National Health Service began. Where the fault lies with the non-medical members of the medical team it seems now settled that the hospital authorities assumme full responsibility for these servants. Where a doctor is concerned, there is almost always shared responsibility between the doctor and the hospital management. The proportion of responsibility varies according to the circumstances, and the consultant of a firm tends to bear the brunt of any damages, even when he has delegated his authority to his junior medical staff. As we have said, the common mishap of retained swabs and instruments following abdominal surgery is still the responsibility of the surgeon, even though the theatre sister technically performs the count herself.

When injecting any drug, though the doctor may request the correct substance from an attendant nurse, it is his responsibility to check that he had been provided with the correct substance in the correct strength. Many cases of death and paralysis etc., have occurred from incorrect injections, where the fault has not lain primarily with the doctor, except in that he unwisely accepted the substance without checking the label on the stock bottle which was used to fill the syringe or galley-pot. Spinal anaesthesia provided a considerable proportion of these cases in past years and much of the decline in spinal anaesthesia has been due to the disproportionately large number of mishaps that occurred.

When the actual facts of negligence are not in dispute, much of the function of the court will be to apportion blame and consequent damages on an equitable basis according to the division of responsibility. The Area Health Authority is virtually always joined in these actions as a co-defendant, and for this reason it is now obligatory for all medical staff in hospital service to belong to a medical defence society in order that their legal costs and at least part of the damages may be guaranteed, so that the Hospital Administrators do not risk shouldering the whole claim.

2. Contributory negligence

The second defence available to a doctor is that there was contributory negligence on the part of the patient-plaintiff. Though this will not defeat the claim, it may well appreciably reduce the damages, if it can be shown that subsequent actions of the patient contributed to his own disability. Thus if some negligent act on the part of a doctor results in the initiation of some disability, but the patient either refuses to carry out the recommended treatment for this disability or even actively exacerbates the condition, then there should be reduction of the damages proportionate to the relative contributions of the doctor's original negligence and the subsequent actions of the patient.

3. Consent of the patient

A further defence is that the patient willingly assumed the risk of the injurious event actually taking place, and therefore forfeited any claim to damages by way of recompense. This is the doctrine of *volenti non fit injuria*, a maxim best illustrated by those who willingly take part in amateur sport: if injuries occur, there can be no claim against the other players who cause the injury, as the injured player voluntarily took part in full knowledge of the possibility of damage. The same principle may apply in medical treatmemt, but is much less easy to apply than in the example above. The doctor must have fully explained the risks to the patient, and the patient must have willingly accepted them. Normally, under such circumstances the doctor still has his normal duty of care, and for this maxim to apply, it must usually be shown that the patient insisted upon a course of treatment even where the doctor was reluctant to proceed. More commonly, this defence is good where a patient refuses to complete a suggested course of treatment and discharges himself from hospital. Proof of such discharge against advice must be obtained, in writing if possible, in order to substantiate any later claim against the doctor for negligence.

JOINT LIABILITY FOR NEGLIGENCE

Though in hospital practice, there is a tendency for a consultant to carry the largest portion of the responsibility and subsequent damages, there is no statutory definition of the apportionment of responsibility, and this frequently shared between consultant, junior doctor and hospital management.

In general practice, the normal rules of civil law apply as between partners. By the Partnership Act, 1890, each partner is jointly and individually liable with his co-partners for all acts of negligence committed by the firm. Thus if one partner in general practice commits a negligent act, the patient may sue all partners equally and they may all be liable in damages, even though the other partners may have no part whatsoever in the negligent act. It is common practice when forming a partnership, for there to be a Deed of Indemnity, which provides that if any one partner causes such financial damage to his fellows, he must compensate them for their loss. This indemnity is quite separate from the original action for negligence.

Where a principal in general practice employs an assistant, as opposed to a partner, the usual legal relationship of master and servant apply. The principal is responsible for any negligence of his junior, though the assistant himself may also be jointly liable. Both may be sued by an aggrieved patient, even though the principal has not been professionally concerned. It is up to the patient to choose whether he acts against the assistant or the principal or both. The same applies where the principal employs non-medical servants, such as receptionist or dispenser.

In hospital service, the same relationship does not apply between a consultant and his registrar or houseman, though as stated earlier, there is usually joint liability together with the hospital authority. Here, the legal relationship of the consultant to the assistant does not depend upon the same principle as in general practice, but is based upon the negligence of the consultant in delegating authority to a junior not sufficiently proficient to carry out the delegated duty.

In hospital service, a doctor is not responsible for the negligence of a nurse, who is directly the burden of the hospital management. If however, the nurse's injurious behaviour was a direct result of wrong direction by the doctor, he might find himself jointly liable. Outside hospital, in either a nursing home run by a doctor or in general practice, the relationship of master and servant again holds good, the doctor being liable for the negligence of an employed nurse.

The same principle applies to medical auxillaries, such as radiographers, laboratory technicians, and to medical students, where all these are employed in the hospital service. Unless the wrongful act was a direct result of incorrect instruction by a doctor, the clinician in charge of the patient who sues will not be liable, any action being directed either at the administrators or jointly with them and the non-medical person at fault.

The liability of hospital authorities for negligence of their staff has changed over the years. Originally, it was held that medical and ancillary staff must stand alone in actions of negligence, but a series of decided cases beginning some 40 years ago, introduced first the acceptance that hospitals were responsible or jointly responsible for the negligence of their non-medical staff, and then, especially with the advent of the National Health Service, this concept was extended to cover medical staff.

Though in general, a civil action for negligence may be brought any time up to six years following the negligent act, in the case of personal injuries, which includes any disease or impairment of a person's physical or mental condition, there is a limitation period of three years. Where the effects of the injury etc., are delayed, the three-year period begins to run from the time when such effects first became apparent or should have been apparent with a reasonable degree of observation. This three-year period can be extended in certain circumstances, including deliberate concealment of the disability by the defendants or if the plaintiff was under age or of unsound mind and not in the custody of a parent at the time of the negligent act. Until 1934, negligence sufficient to cause death in a fatal accident prevented any action by the surviving relatives, the potential right to sue being confined to the person himself. Since that year, however, the cause of action for negligence now survives for the benefit of his estate and though there are certain limitations on the type of damages claimable, they may be paid in respect of pain and suffering, loss of expectation of life and for funeral expenses of the deceased. For almost a hundred years before this Act, there was a limited provision for an action to benefit the dependent family of the deceased in fatal accidents, but this was only for the personal maintenance of the dependants and not for the general benefit of the deceased's estate. Damages were assessed solely on the money that the dependants might have enjoyed if the deceased had not been killed.

Medical defence organisations

As it is now obligatory for newly-qualified doctors both to take pre-registration house appointments and thus (as a condition of service) to join a defence organisation, it is no longer so vital to exhort doctors to join such an organisation. It is, however, still worth emphasising that membership should not be allowed to lapse, as even one day without the benefit of their advice, support and indemnity could be professional suicide for a medical practitioner. It is also important to emphasise that when any dispute or allegation of negligence arises, the society must be contacted before any admissions or correspondence are entered into.

Defence organisations in Britain (in alphabetical order)

1. *Medical and Dental Defence Union of Scotland Ltd, 105 St Vincent St., Glasgow G2*
   (tel. 041-221-8381)
2. *Medical Defence Union, 3 Devonshire Place, London WIN 2EA*
   (tel. 01-486-6181)
3. *Medical Protection Society, 50 Hallam St., London WIN 6DE*
   (tel. 01-580-9241)

6

Compensation: industrial injuries and disease

A worker suffering injury in the course of his employment may seek compensation by a civil law suit against his employers or by deriving benefit under the National Insurance (Industrial Injuries) Act, 1946. He may take both courses, but in this case any damages awarded in a civil action may be modified by benefits already derived or to be derived under the statutory provisions. Before this Act was introduced, there was previous legislation (mainly the Workmens Compensation Acts, 1925–1945) which provided for more limited compensation as an alternative to the right to bring a civil action.

In almost all industrial injuries and diseases, medical evidence will be necessary in some form or another, and it is particularly important for a doctor to keep comprehensive records of any injury sustained by a patient during the course of employment. This is particularly important in that there may be a considerable delay between the sustaining of the injury and subsequent legal proceedings. In the case of a civil action, this may extend to a number of years, if time for the development of some disability, plus the waiting time for trial is taken into account. The period of limitation for a civil action involving personal injury is three years from the time either of infliction of the injury or from the time when the effects first became apparent. In the latter case, the claimant must initiate proceedings within 12 months of his discovery of his disability.

National Insurance (Industrial Injuries) Act, 1946

An Industrial Injuries Fund was set up by this Act, to receive compulsory contributions from employer and employee, together with a direct Treasury Grant, for the purpose of compensating victims of industrial injuries and certain prescribed industrial diseases.

As stated above, the Act does not remove the right to initiate a civil action against the employers, but when the court assesses damages, they must make allowance for benefits which have accrued or probably will accrue under the Act, within a five-year period.

For a workman to benefit under the Act, at the time of the injury or disease he must have been in some employment covered by the provisions of the Act: this generally covers any contract of service but excludes self-employment. The injury must have arisen directly by an accident arising out of and in the course of, his employment. If the claimant can show this, then in the absence of evidence to the contrary, the injury or disease is compensatable without further proof of negligence on the part of the employer. Even if the accident happened while the claimant was acting in contravention of any rule or regulation concerning his employment (though it be in direct disregard of the employer's instructions) the claim is still acceptable. It may only be rebutted if the employer can show that the accident arose out of some behaviour that was not concerned with the course of employment. Instances of this would be a workman performing some task for his own benefit on his employer's premises or during his employer's time, or because of irresponsible 'skylarking' or drunkenness. Much debate surrounds the decision of as to whether or not a workman is covered during travel to and from his place of work: if he is in transport provided by the employer, there is usually acceptance of the claim.

Definitions of certain terms used in the Act have been fertile ground for legal argument, and the case-law of industrial injuries litigation is constantly developing. However, 'arising from an accident' is held to mean 'any unlooked for mishap or occurrence' rather than the more strict definition of an accident.

The definitions of 'arising out of and in the course of employment' must also be interpreted in a broad fashion.

Particularly difficult are those cases of sudden death from natural disease, such as coronary occlusion. An increasingly liberal attitude has developed, so that a minimum relation to physical strain during employment is acceptable, even to the point of sometimes granting benefits following collapse whilst travelling to work.

The Act takes virtually no regard of any contributory negligence on the part of the employee, who might deliberately and flagrantly contravene any safety regulation but would still be entitled to compensation if he received injury during the course of his employment.

Where disease is concerned, if he contracts certain diseases listed in the Schedules and this disease is related to the type of employment in which he is engaged, then he becomes compensatable in the same way as a workman suffering an industrial injury. This aspect is capable of further expansion by decisions of the Industrial Injuries Commissioners. Each unscheduled case must be decided upon its individual merits and probability of relation to employment.

TYPES OF INDUSTRIAL INJURY BENEFITS

1. Injury benefit

This is payment during a temporary period of disablement from injury or disease, or for the initial stages of permanent disablement. The maximum period for which this is payable is 156 days from the date of the accident, and is paid at a flat rate with supplementary allowances for dependants. If after the 26th week of this benefit, the injured person still suffers from a 'loss of faculty', he is entitled to disablement benefit.

2. Disablement benefit

This is a pension awarded either for an indefinite term or until medical examination reveals that the disablement has ceased. It is payable during any period in which the claimant suffers from 'loss of faculty', meaning the partial or total loss of the normal use of organs or part of the body, or the destruction or impairment of bodily or mental functions. Assessment is made by taking into account all disabilities including loss of earning power and additional expenses, compared with a person of the same age and sex whose condition is normal. The assessment is stated as a percentage of loss of faculty. For example, loss of a hand plus a foot or severe facial disfigurement or absolute deafness would all qualify for 100 per cent disablement.

Following assessment, a statement is made as to the permanency or otherwise of the disablement, and where a change in condition is likely, either for better or worse, a final assessment may be delayed. Periodic examination by a medical board may alter the percentage, especially in a progressive condition such as serious pneumoconiosis.

The disablement benefit is paid as a weekly pension, except where the assessment is 20 per cent or less, in which case a lump sum is provided (except in the case of pneumoconiosis). There are various supplements to the disablement benefit, such as a special hardship allowances, constant attendance allowance for bedridden patients, dependant allowances and supplements for inability to continue any employment.

3. Industrial death benefits

Where death is caused by, contributed to or accelerated by, an industrial injury or disease, the dependent relatives are entitled to benefits over and above those normally provided by the Social Security Scheme. All such deaths where industrial accidents or diseases may be concerned (especially where a connection is alleged by relatives), must be reported to the coroner, and an inquest held after post-mortem examination. The finding of the coroner is not binding upon the Insurance Officer, though naturally considerable weight is given to his verdict.

PROCEDURE UNDER THE ACT

To claim benefit under the National Insurance (Industrial Injuries) Act, the claimant must:

1. Report the accident immediately to his employers except where the effects of the accident are delayed.
2. Initiate a claim under the Act without delay, officially within 21 days, though extension of this period is allowed where good cause is shown.
3. Claims are made to an Insurance Officer appointed by the Department of Health and Social Security. This must be done in a prescribed form.

The local Insurance Officer may accept or reject the claim himself, or refer it to the Local Appeal Tribunal. If he disallows it, the claimant may also appeal to this Tribunal which again may reject or accept the claim.

The Local Appeal Tribunal consists of representatives of employers and employees. From their decision, if they reject the claim, a final appeal may be made to the Industrial Injuries Commissioner, who must be a barrister of at least ten years' experience. No further appeal is possible, though the right of civil action against the employers always exists.

A Medical Board, consisting of at least two practitioners, examines claimants to assess their disability. Appeals against their opinion are referred to a Medical Appeal Tribunal consisting of two other doctors with a legal chairman.

Apart from this procedure, various legal questions may require decisions. The question of whether a person was in insurable employment must be determined by the Minister. He may refer the matter to the High Court for decision, and an appeal from his own decision also lies to the High Court.

In view of the frequency of claims and the specialised nature of the disease, special provisions and special medical boards exist for dealing with pneumoconiosis. Departments wholly concerned with this work are established in various parts of the country, being termed Pneumoconiosis Medical Panels.

Disablement pensions for members of the Armed Forces do not fall within the Industrial Injuries Act, but arise from the provisions of a Royal Warrant. Somewhat similar methods are used to assess disability, with medical boards consisting of a legal, a medical and a service representative. If the appeal is against percentage assessment, the board consists of two medical and one service representative. As with industrial injuries and diseases, death in a person receiving a 'war pension' must be reported to the coroner.

7

British legal systems and courts of law

The various nations which comprise Great Britain have differing legal systems, with the exception of England and Wales, which are combined.

ENGLAND AND WALES

In England a system of law has evolved from Anglo-Saxon origins, modified by the consequences of the Norman Conquest. Wales originally had a quite separate and advanced code of law, which culminated in the tenth-century codification of Hwyel Dda. Subsequent imposition of English law by both Marcher Lords and the Norman kings and eventually the merging of the countries by Act of Union, 1536, created a uniform legal system in the two countries.

The system is divided into the criminal and civil sections; some courts have an exclusively civil jurisdiction. The inter-relationship of these courts is shown in Figure 3.

Magistrate's courts

These courts deal with by far the greater proportion of criminal offences and a small number of civil matters, mainly family law. Magistrates are voluntary, unpaid 'Justices of the Peace' (J.P.s) who are chosen from amongst the most solid citizens to administer justice in the various boroughs and counties. In larger conurbations, a full-time professional lawyer replaces the magistrates. He is known as a 'Stipendiary Magistrate'.

Magistrates have two separate functions: firstly, they hear and dispose of a large number of petty offences, such as minor motoring offences, minor thefts, assaults and drunkenness charges. Whilst exercising this jurisdiction, they are also known as *Petty Sessions*. Secondly, they act as 'Examining Magistrates' in more serious offences, where they decide if there is a sufficiently strong case for sending the accused to a higher court for trial. More serious offences against property and persons and serious motoring offences etc., come into this category.

They have an intermediate function in cases where the accused may choose whether to be tried and sentenced by the magistrates or to opt for trial by a higher court before a jury. In Petty Sessions, either the J.P.s or the Stipendiary decide the guilt and the sentence: in certain cases, they may refer the case to the Crown Court for sentencing. Where lay magistrates (i.e. J.P.s) are sitting, they must have the benefit of the advice of the Clerk to the Magistrates, a qualified lawyer.

The Magistrate's Court is a frequent place for a doctor to appear in the witness box, especially in relation to minor assaults. Formerly, doctors also appeared in the Magistrate's Court when it was acting as committal proceedings before examining magistrates for more serious offences, such as homicide, serious assaults and sexual offences, but since the Criminal Justice Act, 1967, most committal proceedings are conducted on documentary evidence only and the attendance of witnesses is now rarely required.

Crown Courts

Until the Courts Act, 1972, there were two main levels of higher court above the Magistrate's Court, namely the Quarter Sessions and the Assizes. These have been abolished and replaced by the Crown Courts. Formerly the Quarter Sessions dealt with cases of an intermediate degree of seriousness and the Assizes with the most serious crimes, such as murder. This division is still present within the Crown Court system, which acts on two levels roughly comparable with the former courts. Judges of different grades of seniority sit in the two types of Crown Court but the main difference is that the old circuit system, where perambulating justices pass through Assize towns four times each year, has been abolished and now the Crown Courts sit almost continuously, in order to deal with a far greater volume of judicial proceedings. Such Crown Courts had existed before the Courts Act in London (the Central Criminal Court or 'Old Bailey') and at Liverpool and Manchester. The advantages of these courts led to their introduction throughout the rest of England and Wales.

Most medical evidence is heard at the superior Crown Court, which deals with cases of murder, manslaughter, serious wounding, serious sexual offences and causing death by dangerous driving.

The Crown Courts also have an extensive civil jurisdiction and not infrequently, medical evidence is also heard under these circumstances, especially where death or disablement has occurred

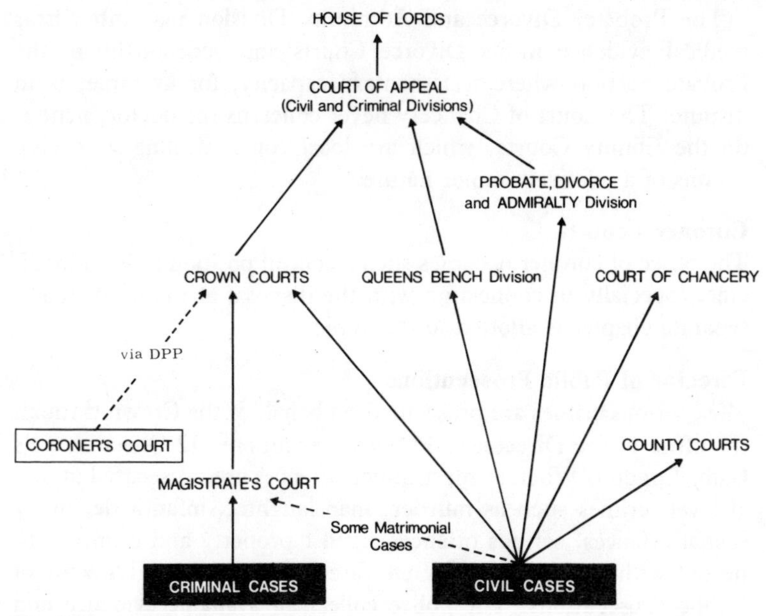

Fig. 3 Inter-relationship of the various courts of law

from motoring or industrial accidents. In London, civil cases are heard at the Royal Courts of Justice in the Strand.

Courts of Appeal

All courts have a channel of appeal to the higher court, though this is not often of much relevance to medical witnesses, as the grounds for appeal are almost always on points of law or appeal against severity of sentence. The various channels of appeal are indicated in Figure 3. Formerly, appeals from the 'Courts of First Instance' went either to the Court of Appeal in Civil Cases or the Court of Criminal Appeal in criminal cases. In recent years, these have been merged into one Court of Appeal, though there are criminal and civil divisions.

Exceptionally, appeals on a point of law of considerable public importance may lie from these Appeal Courts to the House of Lords, which is the ultimate peak of judicial decision.

Other civil courts

Apart from the civil jurisdiction in the Crown Courts and in the Royal Courts of Justice (which are part of the Queen's Bench Division hearing Common Law actions) there are several other divisions of the High Court.

The Probate, Divorce and Admiralty Division may often hear medical evidence in its Divorce Courts and occasionally in the Probate Section where testamentary capacity, for example, is in dispute. The Court of Chancery never concerns the doctor; neither do the County Courts, which are local courts dealing with civil actions of a relatively minor nature.

Coroner's courts

The office of coroner occupies such a central position in legal medicine, especially in connection with the disposal of the dead, that a separate chapter is allotted to this topic.

Director of Public Prosecutions

Most serious crimes are prosecuted on behalf of the Crown through the office of the Director of Public Prosecutions, 12 Queen Anne's Gate, London. Whereas most minor offences are prosecuted at local level, crimes such as murder, manslaughter, infanticide, many sexual offences, serious offences against property and crimes connected with national security etc. are initiated by the Director of Public Prosecutions. The police collect all available evidence and after preparing statements, forward them to the D.P.P., who decides whether or not there is a sufficiently strong case to go forward for trial. Medical evidence is naturally included in the papers submitted to the D.P.P. and not infrequently, the solicitors employed by the Director will seek further amplification from the doctor concerning his evidence.

Medical evidence for the defence

As well as offering evidence for the prosecution in the shape of medical reports, autopsy findings etc., doctors frequently appear in both civil and criminal cases on behalf of the other party, the accused in criminal cases and the defendant in civil actions. Here the doctor almost always appears as an expert witness, frequently appearing to offer an alternative interpretation of the medical facts of the case. In homicide cases, the medical witness for the defence frequently conducts another post-mortem examination or if this is not possible, examines the prosecution evidence on the original autopsy. Though the role of the defence medical witness is naturally to detect any aspects of the medical evidence which are to the favour of the party whose legal representatives have called him, his evidence is still for the benefit of the court and both medical ethics and a sense of justice should prevent him from supressing any evidence which comes to light which is detrimental to the interests of his client.

SCOTTISH LEGAL SYSTEM

The development of Scots law was independent of England until the 1707 Act of Union. Due to strong medieval ties with the continent, the Scottish system owed more to Roman principles than to Anglo-Saxon, though the Napoleonic wars and the consequent dissociation of Scotland and France accelerated closer affinity with English legislative measures. Much statute law emanating from Westminster has brought Scottish law nearer that in the south, though administratively, great differences remain.

As in many European countries, criminal law is administered by a Public Prosecutor. The prime holder of this office is the Lord Advocate, who with the Solicitor-General and Advocates-Depute (collectively known as Crown Counsel), prosecutes on behalf of the Crown before the High Court of Justiciary. These officials preside at Edinburgh but in each Sheriffdom, the Lord Advocate appoints a Procurator Fiscal. The Fiscal prosecutes in the Sheriff Courts and District Courts and in addition to his criminal functions, carries out parallel duties to the English coroner, which will be discussed in the next chapter. The Fiscal prepares the evidence for cases in the High Court and also leads the evidence in Fatal Accidents Enquiries – the latter being extremely important for doctors.

The Lord Advocate's department – the Crown Office – fulfills the functions of the English Lord Chancellor's department, together with a function similar to the English Director of Public Prosecutions. Both the D.P.P.'s office and the Crown Office examine the adequacy of evidence in serious criminal charges and decide whether the case should come to trial, the conduct of the case of the prosecution and the level at which the trial should be held e.g. Sheriff Court or High Court.

In Scotland, there is no equivalent to the preliminary committal proceedings at Magistrate's Court, which reveals evidence to the public and potential jury members. English law has approached Scotland in this respect since the introduction of the Criminal Justice Act 1967, which largely eliminated public committal proceedings.

The nomenclature of the courts in Scotland is quite different from that of England and Wales. The lower criminal court is known as the *District Court* and roughly corresponds to the Magistrates Court in England. Above this is the *Sheriff's Court*, where the Sheriff or a Deputy sits either alone or with a jury. This court covers a wide range of both civil and criminal cases of up to moderately serious nature. The conduct of the prosecution is the responsibility of the Procurator Fiscal in that area. The next court is the *High Court of Justiciary* and approximately corresponds with the English Crown Court. It is held in Edinburgh and on a circuit with sittings in other major towns. Glasgow has by far the greatest number of cases, the circuit being held there monthly. The Lord Justice General and his judges preside over these courts, which have juries of fifteen persons. There is also a *Criminal Appeal Court*, where the accused can take his appeal from the High Court of Justiciary.

The supreme Civil Court of Scotland is the *Court of Session*. The same judges as in the High Court of Justiciary sit in the Session Court under a different title. All manner of civil litigation, including divorce, is heard in these courts. The Court of Session is divided into an *Outer House* for hearing cases of first instance and into an *Inner House* where it hears cases on appeal. The House of Lords in London is the ultimate Court of Appeal in civil cases, but there is no appeal to England on criminal matters.

Other differences in Scottish and English procedure are that the Scottish jury may return a verdict of 'not proven', in addition to 'guilty' or 'not guilty'. However, 'not proven' is equivalent to 'not guilty', as the verdict does not imply guilt. Until recently, the verdict of an English jury had to be unanimous, but this is another instance of English law approaching that of Scotland in that recent legislation has approved the majority verdict, a well-established asset of Scottish legal procedure.

COURTS IN THE REPUBLIC OF IRELAND

The equivalent of the English Magistrate's Court is called the *District Court*, where summary offences are tried without a jury. A District Justice presides and also takes depositions on indictable offences, similar to the committal proceedings of examining magistrates in England. If a *prima facie* case is made out, the District Justice refers the defendant to a higher court for trial by judge and jury.

The next level of court is the *Circuit Criminal Court* which tries lesser indictable offences before a Circuit Court Judge and jury. This sits in principal county towns and in addition to its principal function, also hears appeals from District Courts.

The latter may be held roughly equivalent to the lower level of Crown Court in England: the higher level of Crown Court, which used to be the Assize Court, is represented in Eire by the *Central Criminal Court* in Dublin, which tries major criminal cases including all murder and many manslaughter cases from the whole of the country.

There is a *Court of Criminal Appeal* in Dublin, where three High Court judges sit on appeals from the Criminal Courts. There is also a *Supreme Court* consisting of five judges including the Chief Justice, which is the ultimate court of appeal in criminal matters. In addition there is a *Special Criminal Court*, where a judge of the High Court, a judge of the Circuit Court and a District Justice sit without a jury in certain unusual issues, usually political cases.

There is a parallel system of civil courts which are stratified according to the upper limit of damages or recovery possible. These consist of the *District Court*, the *Circuit Court* (neither of which has a jury), then the *High Court* where a jury is optional. Within the High Court, both common law actions and Chancery and commercial matters are dealt with separately. Again the *Supreme Court* is the ultimate fount of appeal in civil as well as criminal cases.

The *Coroner's Courts*, discussed further in the appropriate chapter, have no powers of committal comparable with the former function of the English coroner in this matter. No verdicts imputing civil or criminal liability by either the deceased or a third party are permissible.

OUTLINE OF COURT PROCEDURE IN ENGLAND AND WALES

Appearance in court is often a bewildering and anxious occasion for any witness, and medical men are no exception to this rule, which explains the frequent reluctance of doctors to become involved in litigation. Even a superficial understanding of the sequence of procedure in court, might assist in removing some of this anxiety.

Using a hypothetical, though common example, let us suppose that a casualty officer has treated a man for extensive superficial injuries alleged to have been caused by an assault. At a later date, two possible legal consequences might arise. The assailant may be arraigned on a criminal charge, or the victim may bring a civil action to recover damages for assault. In the first case, the police will request a statement from the doctor and in the second, the victim's solicitor may request a report. In either event, this emphasizes the need for careful note-taking and medical records. The request for a medical report, especially in the civil case, may come some time after the patient was seen (often many months later) and a busy casualty officer cannot hope to remember details of every case. The actual casualty card or case notes may well form part of the court evidence, and, as further described in another section, the former should be in a logical, clear and complete state.

Considering the criminal sequel, a police officer will call upon the doctor and request a statement as to the time, circumstances, condition and treatment given to the victim. Formerly this statement formed the basis of the oral evidence in the Magistrate's Court when the doctor appeared at either the magistrate's hearing or the committal proceedings. Now that depositions often form the only evidence at committal proceedings, if the charge is a serious one, the next occasion upon which the doctor will be confronted with his own words in a statement may be at the Crown Court. It is therefore highly desirable that the opinions expressed in the report should correspond with what the doctor wishes to say verbally at this later date.

As to actual court procedure, this varies according to the severity of the charge. If the case is dealt with summarily at the Magistrate's Court, the doctor will be notified of the date and time of the proceedings. It is usual for the doctor to be allowed to sit in court if the legal representatives of the defendant raise no objection. When the time to give evidence arrives, he will be sworn in the witness box either by a court usher or by reading the words on a card provided. Normally the oath is sworn upon an English New Testament, but the Old Testament, Koran etc., are available for persons of other religious beliefs. If desired, a witness with no religious beliefs may 'affirm'. Since 1967, witnesses in Wales may both take the oath and give evidence in the Welsh language, as of right.

After being sworn in, the doctor will be led through his written statement by the Prosecutor, who in the Magistrate's Court will either be a solicitor or, in a minor charge, possibly a senior police officer. After this evidence-in-chief has been given and possibly elaborated, the accused person, or more usually his legal representative, rises to cross-examine. In Petty Sessions, this is rarely an arduous experience, and after cross-examination it is the privilege of the prosecuting solicitor or counsel to 're-examine', when he may ask for clarification of previous evidence which may have been challenged by the cross-examiner. No new topics may be raised in re-examination.

When this is completed, the doctor is usually allowed to leave the court, though only after either he or the prosecuting solicitor obtains permission from the bench. This rarely refused, except in complicated cases where recall of the doctor is a possibility.

When attending the Magistrate's Court for committal proceedings (as mentioned, a relatively rare event since the 1967 Act) the same procedure may be seen, though it is uncommon for any cross-examination worthy of the name to take place, this being retained for the subsequent trial at the Crown Courts.

Passing on to these higher courts, the atmosphere is altogether different. The informality of the Magistrate's Court, where both Bench and lawyers wear informal dress, vanishes. The Crown Courts, differing only in name from Quarter Sessions and Assizes, are places reeking of tradition and formality. In our fictional assault case, the same order of questioning would occur. The doctor witness will be sworn in, and led through his deposition by prosecuting counsel. In the Magistrate's Court, the legal representatives are usually solicitors, but in the Crown Courts they are barristers, wearing either the stuff gown of a junior barrister or the silk gown of a Queen's Counsel. After the 'evidence-in-chief' has been gone through step by step from the statement, cross-examination by counsel for the defence then takes place. This can be a far more rigorous and arduous matter than in the lower court and although the days of hectoring, shouting and bullying advocacy are thankfully past, the polite tones of an astute counsel can be no less damaging to pride, where the medical witness is concerned. This is no place to discuss the technique of the expert witness, but the old adage 'open one's mouth and put one's foot in it' is most apt. The medical witness should answer only what is asked and not volunteer any elaboration, as the expert defence counsel is adept at allowing, or indeed encouraging, the doctor to use sufficient rope to entangle himself. Tempers should not be lost, and any apparently unfair gambit should be referred to the Judge, who can be guaranteed to act as a just referee. As in preparing the original report, simple language with the minimum of medical terminology should be used and the doctor should not be afraid of admitting his ignorance of certain facts. So often, the amount of medical jargon and unwise elaboration is in inverse proportion to the experience of the medical witness.

After cross-examination, re-examination by the prosecution counsel will take place, and again the doctor will usually be released by the Judge if the case does not warrant the possibility of his future recall.

Unless the doctor is a specialist called to assist the defence, the above description will apply to instances where the doctor is called by the prosecution. Although it is often extremely difficult to avoid being partisan towards 'our side', the doctor must remember that he is there to assist the *court* and not to fight too valorously for the party who has called him. The truth is still the truth whether defendant or prosecution has caused the doctor to appear in the witness box, and excessive zeal in loyalty to one side or the other can only bring his evidence into disrepute, when bias is almost certain to be revealed by an astute barrister.

Fees

In criminal and coroner's courts, there is a statutory scale laid down for medical witnesses, who are giving evidence of fact. The actual amount is revised every few years. The fee for an expert witness giving an opinion, or fact combined with specialist interpretation and opinion, is based on a variable scale.

In civil cases, or where a doctor is called as an expert witness for the defence, the fee is negotiated with the solicitor and it is wise to reach a firm agreement beforehand that the solicitor will be responsible for the fee. The actual amount can rarely be agreed in advance, as the amount of work, research and time in court may only be calculable at the end of the trial.

8

The coroner system

The office of coroner is one of the most ancient in the English legal system and one which retains a considerable amount of power, though this has lessened over the years. The name derives from *custos placitorum coronas* – Keeper of the Crown Pleas, and possibly dates as far back as Saxon times. The office was certainly in existence at the end of the twelfth century, being revived by Richard Coeur de Lion, who so desperately required money for his ransom and foreign wars. One source of income was the confiscation of the property of felons and the appropriation to the Treasury of all articles involved in unnatural deaths. For example, if a cart ran over a man and killed him, it was forfeit to the Crown. This object was called the 'deodand' and as late as the mid-nineteenth century, even a steam locomotive was impounded after causing a fatal accident! At first, the coroner was appointed to check the corruptness of the county Sheriffs who diverted much revenue into their own pockets. The coroner investigated unnatural deaths, treasure trove, wrecks, fires and so on, all of which had a financial aspect. Over the years, many of these responsibilities have been shed, until the coroner of the present day is involved almost totally with the investigation of death, though some vestigial interests such as treasure trove still remain.

There about 180 coroners in England and Wales, the vast majority being practicing solicitors who carry out coroner's work on a part-time basis. A few large cities, including the area of Greater London Council, have full-time coroners who are both medical practitioners and barristers. In former days, many coroners were doctors only, but this is now extremely uncommon, except for some assistants and deputies. It has always been a matter of some controversy as to whether a medical or legal qualification is the most important requisite for a coroner, but the Brodrick Report (1971) made recommendations in favour of lawyers. The coroners are employed by the local authority, and are appointed for life or until voluntary retirement. Unlike the United States, the office of coroner is quite independent of any political election. Once appointed, a coroner enjoys a large degree of autonomy and cannot be dismissed except for a grave breach of behaviour. The ultimate authority over coroners is the Lord Chancellor, who himself has the powers of a coroner, as do all High Court judges.

Coroners have their own professional body, the Coroner's Society, and the everyday conduct of their business determined by various Coroner's Acts and Rules.

Following the partial implementation of the Brodrick Report (1971), a number of changes in coroner's procedure were made in the period 1977–1980, which are referred to later in the chapter. The major changes were the abolition of the coroner's power to commit a person for trial on a charge of criminally causing a death (Criminal Law Act 1977): the abolition of the need for the coroner to himself view the body before inquest (Coroner's Act 1980): the acceptance of written, instead of oral, evidence, which is of great advantage to doctors as they now attend the coroner's court much less frequently (Coroner's Rules, 1980): the referral of criminal deaths to the Director of Public Prosecutions (Coroner's Rules 1977): and the dispensing with the need for a jury in many inquests (Criminal Law Act 1977).

The relationship of the doctor to the coroner

At the moment of writing, doctors have no statutory obligation to report cases to the coroner, but such a duty has been recommended by the 1971 Report of the Home Office Interdepartmental Committee on Coroners and Death Certification (the 'Brodrick Report'). Though the general practitioner or hospital doctor have no special responsibility to report even the most obvious case to the coroner (this being the duty of the Registrar of Births and Deaths) in practice it is obviously both courteous and practicable for the practitioner to do so, as well as being the common law duty of every citizen. Though the Registrars are the only persons with a *statutory* obligation to report deaths to the coroner, in actual practice the vast majority of cases are reported by doctors and the police.

In cases of obvious violence whether criminal, accidental or suicidal, reporting will usually be done directly by the police force, though where death has been delayed and occurs in hospital, it may well be that a doctor first brings it to the notice of the coroner.

In most cases where natural disease or death associated with medical treatment is concerned, the doctor will report. In terms of numbers, this represents about 80 per cent of the coroner's case load. The relationship therefore, between the practitioner and the coroner needs to be efficient and amicable, both for the peace of mind of the doctor and for the welfare of the bereaved relatives, whose distress should not be further burdened by administrative difficulties.

The actual procedure for disposal of the dead is described elsewhere, but here we are concerned with the types of cases which concern the coroner.

Cases reportable to the coroner

Though there may be some minor local variation in practice between different coroners, the general principles remain the same over the whole of England and Wales.

According to the Coroner's Rules 1953–1980 (Consolidated), the following deaths should be reported to the coroner:

1. When no doctor has treated the deceased in his or her last illness.
2. When the doctor attending the patient did not see him or her within 14 days before the death or after death.
3. When the death occurred during an operation or before recovery from an anaesthetic.
4. When the death was sudden and unexplained or attended by suspicious circumstances.
5. When the death might be due to an industrial injury or disease or to accident, violence, neglect or abortion or to any kind of poisoning.

This 'official' list does not specifically mention other types of death which should invariably be reported, such as deaths in legal custody or any allegation of negligence, medical or otherwise.

It is broadly similar to the list of situations in which a Registrar of Births and Deaths must himself report cases to the coroner: in the latter instance, the Registrar reporting is *mandatory* whilst that above referring to doctors is *advisory*, though as the Registrar will query any doubtful death certificate sent by the doctor, the difference is largely academic, apart from the delay involved.

Obvious criminal deaths

Murder, manslaughter, infanticide, 'aiding, abetting, counselling or procuring a suicide' and causing death by reckless driving ('motor manslaughter') are reportable to the coroner (Fig. 4), usually by the police. In the case of the last mentioned, the report-

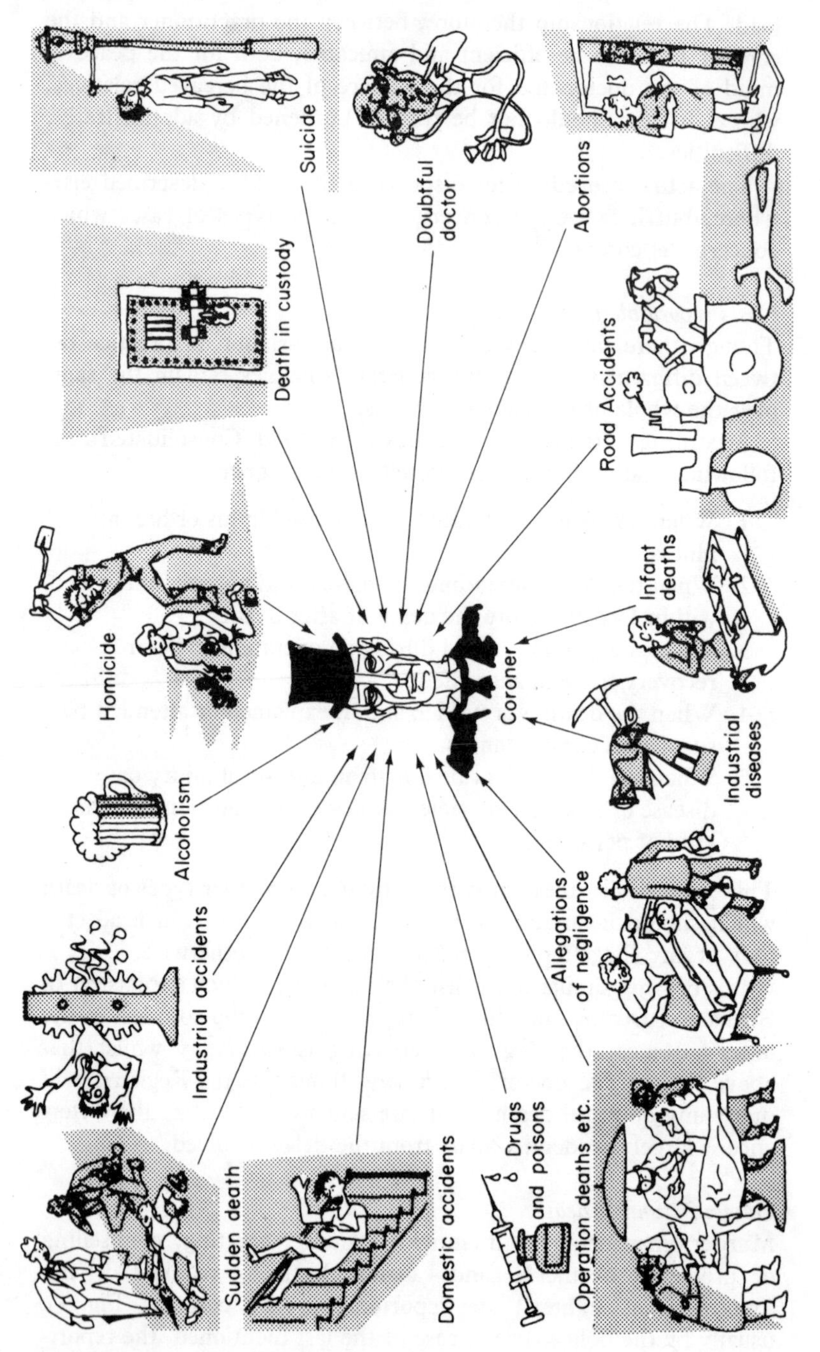

Fig. 4 Types of death which must be reported to the coroner

age may initially be as a case of accident, the decision to prosecute under Section 1 of the Road Traffic Act being taken by the police and Director of Public Prosecutions.

In all these cases, the jurisdiction of the coroner is severely curtailed, he merely being obliged to open an inquest to take evidence of identity and then adjourn for a period under Section 20 of the Coroner's (Amendment) Act, to allow time for criminal proceedings to take place. Whether the result be a conviction or an acquittal, the Clerk of the Crown Court will notify the coroner of the verdict, when there will then be no need for the inquest to be resumed. Only where no person is apprehended and charged with causing a criminal death, does the coroner have to hold a full inquest. Since 1978, the coroner and his jury have no power to frame a verdict in such a way that it alleges that a death was due to any criminal act or civil negligence on the part of any named person. Neither can the coroner now exercise his historic right to commit any person for trial on a charge of criminally causing death (Criminal Law Act 1977).

However, if the inquest reveals a possible criminal element in the death, the coroner must inform the Director of Public Prosecutions (Coroner's Rules 1977).

Suicide

All cases of suicide are reportable to the coroner. An inquest must be held and this forms one of the most serious criticisms against the coroner's system, as suicide is no longer an offence but properly considered as a manifestation of natural mental abnormality. To explore the family circumstances and cause witnesses to relive the unfortunate events in open court is a futile and often distressing experience, but as the law stands at present, there is no alternative. Again, the Brodrick Report recommends the discontinuance of public inquests in cases of suicide. Due to changes in procedure brought about by the Coroner's Rules (1980), an inquest may be conducted by means of documentary evidence only, if no interested party objects. This often avoids the unwelcome publicity surrounding suicide inquests, which number about 3500 per year.

Accidents

All accidents are reportable to the coroner, no matter how long a time has elapsed between the injury and the death. There is sometimes a mistaken impression amongst doctors that the 'year and a day rule' applies, but this is not so, being relevant only where delayed death occurs after a criminal assault.

Accidents fall into various categories: traffic accidents are extremely frequent (6000–7000 per annum), greatly exceeding the number of suicides investigated each year. Domestic accidents are almost as frequent (about 5000 per annum) and often involve old people who fall and fracture their femur, as well as domestic fires and poisonings.

Industrial accidents form an important part of the coroner's investigation, a jury inquest being held. Though not strictly an accident, industrial diseases are also reportable to the coroner, such as pneumoconiosis and numerous other industrial conditions.

Following the recent revision of the coroner's procedures, the coroner's jury can no longer add a 'rider' to a verdict of accidental death, to draw attention to some continuing public danger. However, the coroner is empowered to comunicate directly with the public department or individual officer concerned with such hazards.

Death in custody

Deaths in police custody or in prison are reportable to the coroner, mainly in order that a full and unbiased investigation may be held to exclude any suspicion of maltreatment by the custodians. One of the most common circumstances in which this occurs, is the detention of a presumed 'drunk' in the cells of the police station over night. Not infrequently, the prisoner dies during the night, either because of extreme drunkenness, with alcoholic poisoning or aspiration of vomit, or because drunkenness has masked or accentuated a head injury. A full enquiry into the facts is necessary to clear the police authorities of any suggestion of negligent or brutal actions. Following some adverse publicity surrounding deaths in custody in the period 1979–80, stricter attention is to be paid to the investigation of such fatalities.

Deaths associated with medical treatment

Where deaths occurs during medical or surgical procedures (which include diagnostic measures such as radiology etc.), the case must be reported to the coroner. This group includes a much wider-ranging set of circumstances than actual surgical operations. Death under anaesthetic is always reportable and usually coroners require any death taking place within 24 hours of recovery from an anaesthetic to be reported. Here there is some local variation in individual coroner's practice but the 24-hour rule is a convenient one in the absence of specific instructions from the coroner. Where the medical attendant suspects that any form of medical treatment, including drug therapy, may have caused, contributed to, or accelerated death, he is obliged to report. Such procedures as, for example intravenous pyelography, radiological air studies, minor operations under local anaesthetic, dental procedures, lumbar punctures, may all be suspected as having some relevance to the death. The onus falls upon the medical attendant as to whether he should report such a death, but if he does not, and the Registrar of Births and Deaths subsequently declines to register, the doctor risks censure from the coroner for his omission to report.

Alleged negligent treatment

Closely allied to the last groups is the allegation, express or implied, of improper or negligent treatment on the part of medical or nursing staff. Though the majority of cases are ill-founded, the slightest whisper of dissatisfaction from relatives should cause the doctor immediately to report the case to the coroner *and to his medical defence association*. The death may be linked, at least in the minds of the relatives, to some medical or surgical procedure or treatment, but other common causes of allegations of negligence arise when a patient in hospital falls from the bed, slips on a polished floor, or in general practice where the doctor omits or is late attending a call to a patient. From the doctor's point of view, this is the most important of all the circumstances reportable to the coroner, as an open, unbiased and exhaustive enquiry into the circumstances are the best means of clearing the doctor's reputation and restoring his peace of mind. As already mentioned, it cannot be too strongly emphasised that where any allegation of negligence is made, immediate contact should be made with the doctor's medical defence association before any verbal or written statement is given to the relatives.

Sudden death

Numerically, by far the largest group of cases reportable to the coroner are those natural deaths (or presumed natural deaths) which have occurred either suddenly and/or unexpectedly. Though a patient may be under the care of the medical attendant for a long period, the nature of his disease may not be such as to give to an expectation of sudden death. If a patient with, say osteoarthritis, has been seen weekly for some months and then suddenly dies, the doctor should report the case unless he is aware of other relevant disease. Similarly a sudden death in a patient whose medical condition has not recently given rise to any apprehension, must be reported to the coroner if the doctor is not prepared to be definite about the cause of death.

Though death certification is dealt with in Chapter 10 in greater detail, it is relevant here in that presumed natural death should be reported to the coroner if:

1. The doctor has not been in attendance during the last illness, which for the purposes of reporting to the coroner means during the last 14 days. Though legally he can satisfy the Registrar with a certificate if he sees the body after death, this is a most unsatisfactory alternative.
2. Even if he has attended recently, if he does not known the cause of death, then he must report to the coroner.
3. If he has any doubts about the natural causation, he must again report.

Until 1980, it was conventional for doctors not to issue death certificates in cases which they reported to the coroner. As will be described in Chapter 10, the Registrar General has now requested a stricter observance of the law as set out in the Births and Deaths Registration Acts, and wishes doctors to issue certificates wherever possible, even in cases which are reported to the coroner. However, if the doctor has no idea of the cause of death, then this is obviously futile and should not be attempted. Whether the doctor was 'in attendance during the last illness' is for the doctor to decide and has no time limit. The time limit of 14 days applies only to reporting to the coroner and not to the potential issue of death certificate.

Where a patient who presumably has died from a natural disease has been visited by another doctor, then the doctor attending the death cannot issue a death certificate on behalf of his colleague, even if the other doctor is a member of the same practice. However, when reporting to the coroner, that official will often be satisfied with the circumstances and direct the second doctor to certify, using the yellow Form A procedure.

Many coroners require all cases dying within 24 hours of admission to hospital to be reported to them. It is not a legal requirement, but a working rule established by many coroners on the principle that a diagnosis cannot be satisfactorily arrived at during the first day after an emergency admission and therefore there may well be some doubt as to the exact cause of death in newly-admitted patients.

Though the foregoing describes typical coroner's practice, there is considerable local variation. Many coroners will tell the reporting doctor to 'sign up' cases which appear to be natural. The autopsy rate amongst cases reported, varies from 95–99 per cent in large cities, down to 30–40 per cent in some rural areas. The Brodrick Report recommends reducing the '14-day rule' to seven days.

Miscellaneous deaths

Any death following abortion, unless definitely known to be a natural, spontaneous miscarriage, should be reported. Deaths from any form of neglect are reportable, whether self-neglect or neglect by other persons, usually in infants. It should be noted that alcoholism is reportable, if thought responsible for death.

Any death suspected of following drug addiction must be reported, as with any case of suspected poisoning, as these are obviously unnatural causes.

Persons receiving a 'war' pension (any disability pension following service in the Armed Forces) are reportable and it is wise to report all cases on an industrial disability pension where it is felt (or the relatives or responsible Trade Union official allege) that this was a possible factor in the death.

Infant deaths, including still-births, must be considered very carefully. 'Cot deaths' and suspected 'battered babies' must naturally be reported.

Formerly all inmates of mental hospitals and all foster children who died were reportable to the coroner, but recent changes in legislation have excluded these unless they became reportable on one of the other grounds detailed above. However, following cases of alleged ill-treatment of patients in some mental hospitals, the Brodrick Report recommends the re-introduction of automatic reporting to the coroner of deaths in such institutions. In general, the whole list of reportable cases is directed to bringing deaths, the cause of which is not absolutely straightfoward, to the notice of the coroner. Even if a doctor has attended a patient every day for a considerable period, but is still unsure of the cause of death, the case becomes reportable. In helping the doctor to decide which cases should be reportable after some accident or medical or surgical treatment in hospital, a good rule-of-thumb is 'would this patient have died at the time he did if there had been no accident, surgical operation, etc?'. If the answer is 'no!', then the case should be reported.

In passing it may be mentioned that though the doctor may be satisfied in his own mind as to the cause of death, he is frequently incorrect. Several surveys have been carried out, as recently as 1980, in which the cause of death as given by the clinician was compared with the cause of death obtained after autopsy. In several of these series the error was of the order of 50 per cent – that is, the clinician was as often wrong as he was correct! It must be admitted that the difference between the clinical and pathological diagnoses was often trivial e.g. coronary thrombosis as opposed to myocardial fibrosis, but in 25 per cent of the cases, the disparity was marked, often lying in a totally different anatomical system. Many a perforated peptic ulcer has been labelled coronary thrombosis and subarachnoid haemorrhage has even been called pulmonary embolism! In fact, pulmonary embolism is clinically the most under-diagnosed fatal condition, being forecast in less than half the actual instances. These errors may sometimes be of considerable medico-legal importance, especially in relation to insurance and compensation aspects: they also introduce a great error in mortality statistics.

Though there is probably a 5–10 per cent failure rate in autopsies (usually where no cause of death can be found in children and young persons), in general the post-mortem findings are greatly superior to the clinical diagnosis even when the latter is based on sophisticated diagnostic procedures in hospital.

Outline of coroner's procedure

The coroner's routine work is carried out by his 'coroner's officer', usually a police officer of maturity and considerable experience. In rural areas, this function is performed by the first police officer attending the death, though this is not such a satisfactory method.

The doctor, as well as the general public, usually contacts the coroner's officer for routine matters associated with deaths. The coroner studies the papers supplied by the officer and decides whether he wishes to dispose of it without ordering a post-mortem examination. This is uncommon in large cities, where the autopsy rate may approach 100 per cent, but if the coroner is satisfied that the medical attendant is confident that he knows the cause of death, he may dispose of the case on his pink Form A. This may be done, for instance, when a case is reported because of the '24-hour rule' after emergency admission to hospital, but the doctor is satisfied that he knows the cause of death. Form A notifies the Registrar that the coroner is taking no further action: the doctor must then issue a death certificate in the usual way.

Most commonly – almost invariably in large jurisdictions – a post-mortem examination will be ordered. Formerly, this could be done by any practitioner, but the coroner is now strongly recommended by his Rules only to employ a pathologist with access to laboratory facilities. The pathologist cannot be compelled to carry out an autopsy for the coroner, but the old power remains for the regular medical attendant during life to be ordered by the coroner to perform a post-mortem. As only specialist pathologists should now do this, the power is an anachronism.

In criminal or suspicious cases, the coroner is advised by the Coroner's Rules to accept the advice of the Chief Constable in choosing a pathologist of special experience, i.e. a forensic pathologist with experience in criminal matters. This is not always done, partly from the serious shortage of forensic pathologists in many areas and sometimes from non-compliance of the coroner with the recommendation.

When the post-mortem has been completed, the disposal of the case will depend partly on the determined cause of death and partly on the surrounding circumstances of the death (Fig. 5). The great majority of cases are due to natural death and can be signed up on the coroner's pink Form B, which notifies the Registrar of the medical cause of death and allows disposal without the necessity for an inquest. In former years, all cases reported to the coroner had to be the subject of an inquest, but thankfully, this practice has declined greatly due to a series of legislative reforms.

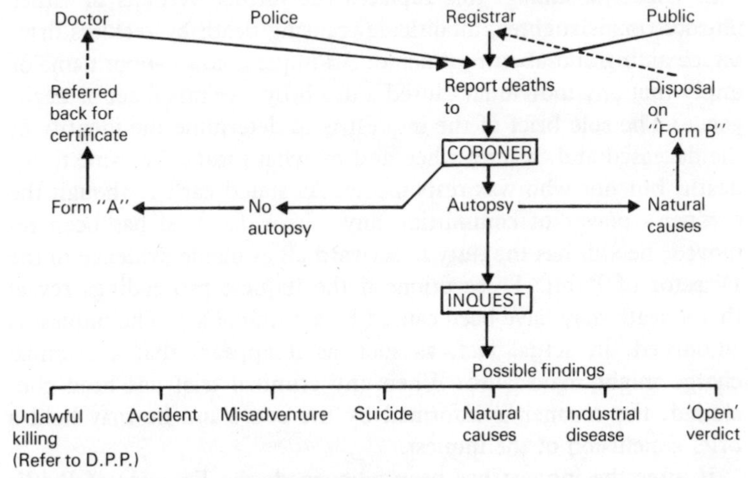

Fig. 5 Disposal of cases referred to the coroner

Certain types of case cannot be disposed of without an inquest. These comprise criminal cases (murder, manslaughter and infanticide), suicides, road, aviation, rail, domestic and other accidents, industrial accidents and diseases, deaths in prison or police custody, deaths where negligent medical treatment is alleged, deaths from neglect and any other case where the coroner feels that a public hearing would be beneficial.

Certain of these cases must be held with a jury, consisting of at least seven and not more than eleven persons. The coroner's jury has been the subject of much criticism, as another anachronistic part of the coroner's system. The Brodrick Report (1971) recommended its abolition as well as a reduction in the number of inquests, and the Criminal Law Act 1977 has reduced the range of deaths in which a jury is now required. The coroner now need only empanel a jury in cases where notice has to be given to a Government department e.g. deaths from accidents in industry, mines, quarries, railways, ships, aircraft (but not road accidents), where explosives, fires or petrol are concerned in an industrial context and also all deaths in prison or police custody. In all these instances, the coroner *must* sit with a jury, though he is entitled to summon one in any inquest if he thinks it expedient.

The jury can return a majority verdict, as long as no more than two members disagree.

The possible verdicts for a coroner to arrive at, following inquest proceedings are:

1. *Natural causes.*

2. *Unlawful killing*: this replaces the former verdicts of either murder, manslaughter, infanticide, causing death by reckless driving or aiding and abetting suicide. An inquest now cannot name or imply that any individual caused a death by a criminal act or negligence. The sole brief of the inquest is to determine the identity of the deceased and 'where, when and by what means' he came to his death, but not who was responsible. As stated earlier, though the coroner's power of committing any person for trial has been removed, he still has the duty to forward all available evidence to the Director of Public Prosecutions if the inquest proceedings reveal that a death may have been caused by a criminal act. The inquest is adjourned, in actual fact, as soon as it appears that a criminal charge might materialise. When any criminal trial has been concluded, the coroner is informed by the court and he may hold a brief conclusion of the inquest.

If after the inquest has been adjourned, the Director of Public Prosecutions declines to recommend criminal proceedings, then the inquest is resumed and a verdict reached, which might be 'unlawful killing', though the matter can then go no further.

Whilst possible criminal charges are pending, the coroner will delay issuing a disposal order for burial or cremation until the defence have had the opportunity to perform their own expert medical examination. Where no person has been charged with a criminal death, the coroner may be reluctant to allow cremation, as this will naturally remove the possibility of an exhumation and second examination if an arrest is made at a later date.

3. *Suicide*. The old phraseology 'whilst the balance of the mind was disturbed' is now falling into disuse. Since the Suicide Act 1961, suicide or attempted suicide is no longer a criminal offence, though it is still a crime to aid, abet, counsel or procure a suicide – and survivors of suicide pacts may find themselves charged with this offence.

4. *Accidental death* is naturally a very common verdict, due to a wide variety of road, rail, air, shipping, industrial and domestic tragedies. The distinction between 'accident' and 'misadventure' is rather vague and some coroners avoid the latter term. However, the distinction has been illustrated by the following example:– if a person walks along a river bank, trips over a stone and falls in and drowns, then that is an accident, as there was no intention to enter the water. However, if he dives voluntarily into the river, intending to swim, becomes tangles in weeds and drowns, then that is *misadventure*, as it arose from the consequences of a voluntary act. Similarly, someone dying of a broken neck in a rugby match would be considered to have suffered a misadventure, rather than an accident. The distinction is a fine one and is rarely of practical significance. Deaths during surgical operation or anaesthetic are usually termed 'misadventure', due to the element of consent on the part of the patient to undergo a potentially hazardous procedure.

5. *Misadventure* has been discussed, being a situation where the unlooked-for fatal outcome arose from some voluntary act of the deceased, rather than a pure mischance. Formerly, there were separate verdicts for self-neglect (malnutrition, hypothermia etc), acute and chronic alcoholism and drug addiction, but these are now usually included under *misadventure*, as again there is an element of self-exposure – even self-abuse – in these situations, though hypothermia might equally well be thought of as an accident.

6. *Industrial disease*. Where exposure to some industrial hazard has caused or contributed to death (other than a physical accident), then a verdict in those terms is returned.

7. *Open verdict*. Where insufficient evidence is available for a decision on the nature of the death to be made, an *open verdict* is returned. This means that the inquest is adjourned indefinitely, but could be resumed at any later date if further facts come to light. If the body remains unidentified (it might even be a skeleton) or if no cause of death can be found by the pathologist or if the circumstances of the death remain obscure, naturally no other verdict is available. A common reason for open verdicts arises in self-

poisonings when the evidence is insufficient to distinguish between accident or suicide.

The coroner has full powers to commit for contempt of court and to subpoena witnesses. Due to the recent wider acceptance of documentary evidence, doctors will be called to attend inquests far less frequently than in the past. As far as the medical witness is concerned, he is almost invariably treated with consideration and allowed, wherever possible, to leave the court after giving evidence, thus shortening the time taken from his practice. The rules of evidence are not applied with the stringency of criminal courts, no robes or wigs are worn and the whole atmosphere is less inimical than that of the Higher Courts. The doctor should read the facts of his case before attending and take the case notes or practice cards with him to refer to in the witness box. He will be sworn in, usually by the coroner's officer and be led through his previous statement in an informal way by the coroner.

Legal representatives, either for the deceased's family or other parties such as employer or motorist, may be present and are entitled to question any witness, including the doctor. They are not entitled to extract any incriminating admissions, however, and the coroner is there to see that no inadmissable practice takes place. Where the inquest concerns any hint of criticism of the medical treatment or allegations of medical negligence by the relatives of the deceased IT IS ABSOLUTELY IMPERATIVE THAT THE DOCTOR BE LEGALLY REPRESENTED BY HIS DEFENCE SOCIETY. If such allegations arise unexpectedly during the course of an inquest, the coroner should be asked to adjourn the case until such representation be obtained. Where such allegations are known or suspected beforehand, the defence society *must* be contacted, even if the doctor feels that the criticism is quite unfounded. Even the newspaper publicity surrounding an inquest can cause extreme distress to a doctor, though the subsequent legal proceedings show clearly that no fault lay at his door.

SCOTTISH PROCURATOR FISCAL

In many ways, the Procurator Fiscal is comparable to the Public Prosecutor in many continental legal systems, this being in part due to the close affinity of Scottish and continental law. Apart from his main function in initiating prosecutions, the Fiscal has the duty to investigate any sudden, violent, suspicious, accidental deaths or deaths from unknown causes, which are reported to him.

His interest in these deaths is closely linked with his criminal responsibility, in that his main concern is to establish whether or not there has been any criminality or possible negligence involved in the death. He is not obliged to establish the precise cause of death in the medical sense, once the possibility of criminal proceedings have been ruled out. Again this is an almost exact parallel to the continental system. Unlike the English coroner, the Procurator Fiscal cannot himself issue a death certificate.

The duties of the Procurator Fiscal in the investigation of sudden or suspicious deaths, differ from the English system in that there is no public inquest, though public enquiries take place in certain circumstances. The Fiscal's enquiry takes the form of 'precognition' of witnesses, both lay and medical. A precognition is an informal statement, not on oath, which could form the basis of the oral testimony to which a witness would give at any subsequent trial. This precognition is taken in person by a Procurator Fiscal or a Deputy at a private sitting and a person who fails to attend for the taking of such a precognition may be fined or imprisoned for contempt of court.

There is a Procurator Fiscal for each Sheriff Court District and his main responsibility is the initiation of prosecutions of criminal offences. Procurators Fiscal are appointed by the Lord Advocate and most of them are full-time officers, though in a few areas local solicitors act of Fiscals on a part-time basis.

The main difference between the English and Scots system of reporting deaths is that in Scotland, *any* doctor can certify a death if he feels competent to do so, whereas in England only a doctor who was in attendance during the last illness can do so. As in England and Wales, the Registrar of Births and Deaths, is the only person with a statutory obligation to report deaths to the Procurator Fiscal or coroner, though in fact, as in England and Wales, most cases are voluntarily reported by doctors and the police.

The Registrar of Births and Deaths and Marriages is obliged to notify the Procurator Fiscal of all deaths which fall into any one of nineteen categories. This list was established in 1966, before which there was a less comprehensive duty upon the Registrar to report particulars of sudden, violent, suspicious and accidental deaths and death due to unknown causes. The types of death which the Registrar must report are as follows:

1. Any uncertified death.
2. Any death which was caused by an accident arising out of the use of a vehicle, or which was caused by an aircraft or rail accident.

3. Any death arising out of industrial employment, by accident, industrial disease or industrial poisoning.
4. Any death due to poisoning (coal gas, barbiturate, etc.)
5. Any death where the circumstances would seem to indicate suicide.
6. Any death where there are indications that it occurred under an anaesthetic.
7. Any death resulting from an accident in the home, hospital, or institution or any public place.
8. Any death following abortion.
9. Any death apparently caused by neglect (malnutrition).
10. Any death occurring in prison or a police cell where the deceased was in custody at the time of death.
11. Any death of a newborn child whose body is found.
12. Any death (occurring not in a house) where deceased's residence is unknown.
13. Death by drowning.
14. Death of a child from suffocation (including overlaying).
15. Where the death occurred as a result of smallpox or typhoid.
16. Any death as a result of a fire or explosion.
17. Any sudden death.
18. Any other death due to violent, suspicious or unexplained cause.
19. Deaths of foster children.

These provisions are currently under review to bring them up to date e.g. the references to smallpox, typhoid, coal-gas, overlaying etc.

When apprised of a death, the Procurator Fiscal makes further enquiries via the police, his only form of investigative agency. There is no exact parallel to the English 'coroner's officer' but investigations are carried out on the Fiscal's behalf by uniformed or plain clothes officers, seconded for duty as 'sudden death officers'. The C.I.D. may be involved where necessary. The police make investigations in all cases except those concerning anaesthetic deaths, for which there is a special procedure.

When the available information is to hand, the Fiscal will decide whether or not an autopsy is necessary. The autopsy rate in Scotland is far lower than in England and Wales and again is often directed at the main necessity for confirming or excluding criminality or negligence. The police surgeons are more involved in the system than in England. The Fiscal will normally invite a police surgeon to make an external examination of the body. The police surgeon will, if he feels able after having seen the police report, certify the cause of death. If the Fiscal requires an autopsy or if the police surgeon cannot certify, the pathologist will issue a death certificate based on his findings. The Procurator Fiscal cannot himself issue a death certificate as can the English coroner, but he will issue a cremation certificate if required.

The Fiscal may also ask another doctor who has not previously seen the deceased to examine the body and if this doctor is willing to give a certificate, the investigation may go no further.

If the Fiscal considers that an autopsy is necessary, he must apply for authority for this from the Sheriff. This is almost invariably granted by the Sheriff, on the grounds of one of the following four reasons:

1. That his inquiries cannot be completed unless the cause of death is fully established.
2. That there are circumstances of suspicion:
3. That there are allegations of criminal conduct.
4. That death was associated with anaesthesia in connection with a surgical operation and the fact that all precautions were taken must be established.

Where a death has been reported to the Fiscal, but the latter does not require a post-mortem examination, a post-mortem for clinico-pathological reasons may be requested by the doctors treating the deceased during life if the Procurator raises no objection, as long as the relatives give their permission.

Certain categories of death are reportable by the Procurator Fiscal to the Crown Office, to whom he must communicate the result of the investigation. Outside these categories, the Fiscal can conclude the investigation with or without autopsy, without reference to other authorities.

Deaths which must be reported to the Crown Office are as follows:

1. Where there are any suspicious circumstances.
2. Where death was caused by an accident arising out of the use of a vehicle.
3. Where the circumstances point to suicide.
4. Where the death was caused by an accident, poison or disease, notice of which is required to be given to any government department or to any Inspector of other officer of a government department under or in pursuance of any Act.

5. Where the death occurs in circumstances continuance of which or possible recurrence of which is prejudicial to the health and safety of the public.
6. Where the death occurred in industrial employment.
7. Where the death occurred in any prison or police cells or where the deceased was in custody at the time of his death.
8. Where death occurred under an anaesthetic or in unusual circumstances or if there are features which suggest negligence.
9. Where death was due to gas poisoning.
10. Where death was directly or indirectly connected with the actions of a third party whether or not criminal responsibility rests on any person.
11. Where any desire has been expressed that a public enquiry should be held into the circumstances of the death or where the Procurator Fiscal is of the opinion that a public enquiry should be held under the Fatal Accidents and Sudden Deaths Enquiry (Scotland) Act, 1976.

The Crown Office may order further enquiries to be made if they are not satisfied with the conclusiveness of the Procurator Fiscal's investigation. Otherwise the Lord Advocate, acting through Crown counsel, may decide that no further action is necessary or he may initiate criminal proceedings against a third party or may order a Fatal Accident Inquiry to made in public. The latter is about the only parallel to the English inquest that exists in Scotland. A public enquiry must be held on deaths occurring due to industrial accidents or deaths occurring in legal custody. The Lord Advocate also has discretionary powers to order a public enquiry into the death if he considers it to be in the public interest or if the relatives request it.

Such accidents at places of employment are investigated under the Fatal Accidents Enquiries (Scotland) Act 1976 and no reference to the Crown Office need be made until the enquiry has been concluded. Such an enquiry must be preceded by a petition to the Sheriff, who appoints a date for the enquiry which is held in public after being advertised in the press. Since the 1976 Act, there is now no jury.

Witnesses can be compelled to attend and evidence is given on oath. Legal representation of the parties is allowed and questioning of the witnesses is permissible. There is no 'verdict' as in English inquests, the outcome being the 'Sheriff's determination' which may attribute the cause of the accident to negligent persons and defects in the systems of working may be pointed out.

The Lord Advocate can instruct the Procurator Fiscal to apply to the Sheriff for the holding of an enquiry in any case where he considers it expedient to do so in the public interest. Any type of death may form the basis for such an enquiry, and medical mishaps are included in this category.

It is a fundamental principle of Scots law that evidence in criminal cases must be corroborated. Therefore, where medical evidence upon a death is given to the courts, two doctors must have conducted an autopsy, again a parallel with certain European continental countries. There is no necessity for their opinions to be identical, but both are giving evidence on behalf of the Prosecution and should be distinguished from any other medical evidence called for the defence. The new Criminal Justice (Scotland) Act 1980 requires that only one of the two doctors need attend the trial unless the defence request that both be present.

The laws of Scotland naturally *constitute* the law, and are not merely alternatives to the English legislation. Due to public expediency and parallel legal evolution, it equally naturally happens that much new legislation is similar or almost identical in both countries, but statutes applicable to Scotland have '(Scotland)' included in the title. In other circumstances, sometimes with medical applications, the Scots law is markedly divergent. Also common law plays a somewhat greater role in Scotland than in England, though in both countries, statute law is gradually replacing common law.

THE CORONER SYSTEM IN IRELAND

Both in the Republic of Ireland and in Northern Ireland, the coroner's system operates, rather than the Scottish procedure. There are historical reasons for this, because as in the case of Wales, the law in Ireland was English law until the political changes earlier in this century. Thus the basic coroner's system is modelled on that of England, but various evolutionary changes have occurred since then.

In the Republic of Ireland, the Coroner's Acts place a statutory duty on doctors to report any suspicious circumstances to the Gardai or the coroner himself. The coroner has inquisitorial powers only, having no ability to commit persons for trial. He cannot return any verdict at an inquest which imputes any crime or civil liability against a third party. Thus verdicts of manslaughter and murder are not permitted, though verdicts of suicide or neglect are permitted though not common. The vague phraseology of a verdict 'in accordance with the medical evidence' is often given instead, and no attempt is made to categorize the motive where death was not natural or accidental. The coroner has powers to subpoena witness to give evidence on oath and failure to comply renders the witness liable to referral by the coroner to the High Court on a charge of contempt of court. The coroner, like the English official, can dispense with the jury in some cases but must summon a panel of between six and 12 persons in cases of (a) suspicious death or poisoning (b) traffic accidents (c) in matters prejudicial to public health or safety and in various other statutory circumstances, for example industrial deaths. The coroner does not have the overriding power of the English coroner to nominate a pathologist to carry out a particular post-mortem. The Minister of Justice has the power to do this in suspicious cases, a power which is vested in a Garda (Police) Officer of the rank of Inspector upwards, whereas the English coroner need only be 'advised' by the Chief Constable as the choice of the most suitable pathologist. Relatives or other parties dissatisfied with a Coroner's verdict may appeal to the High Court to have it quashed.

In *Northern Ireland* the system is very similar to that in England and Wales. Once again coroners are virtually all lawyers rather than doctors and in future only lawyers will be appointed to vacancies. They are currently appointed by the Lord Chancellor rather than by local government, since the suspension of the Stormont Parliament.

There is a statutory duty on doctors and funeral directors (amongst others) to report unnatural or suspicious deaths to the coroner. The Northern Ireland coroners did not have to view the body before inquest as was formerly done in England and Wales, but recent changes in mainland law have unified the procedure. A disposal certificate for burial of a body can be issued without the necessity for opening an inquest, as has to be done under English coroner's practice. The several reforms recently brought about in England and Wales following the Brodrick Report have not yet been implemented in Northern Ireland, but otherwise the procedure is very similar.

9

Medical reports and certificates

One of the most common areas in which the doctor comes into contact with legal matters is the provision of reports and certificates. These fall broadly into the following groups:

1. Reports on the medical state of persons, either the victim of, or accused of, a criminal action. When such reports are prepared in a form suitable for presentation as evidence, they are then called 'statements', and certain strict rules then apply.
2. Reports on fact and/or opinion for use in civil litigation.
3. Reports for non-litigious matters such as life insurance.
4. Certificates of health or illness required for a variety of causes including benefits under the National Health Service and Social Security, private employment, travel and emigration.

All these documents must be made with meticulous accuracy, especially the completion of statutory and other official certificates. False statements, either from negligent carelessness or from wilful intentions, may lead to disciplinary action by the General Medical Council. The provision of certificates on official matters is one of the privileges afforded by inclusion in the Register of the General Medical Council, and is one of the features which distinguish the Registered practitioner from his un-registered colleague.

Report and statements for the police
The initial obtaining of information on a matter of fact from a doctor by the police may be the less formal 'report', but if a case is to proceed to court, then this report will be recouched in a different form to constitute a 'statement', or an additional passage will be added in order to render the original report acceptable by the court. Thus a copy of a post-mortem report to the coroner may be re-written and a declaration added, or the report may be used as such, appended to a short 'declaration'. Since the Criminal Justice Act of 1967, it is thankfully much less common for a doctor to

attend the committal proceedings in magistrates' courts, and where no controversy exists over the medical facts, even his attendance at the higher court may not be required. To achieve this, the original statement must bear the words:

> 'This statement, consisting of X pages, each signed by me, is true to the best of my knowledge and belief and I make it knowing that if it is tendered in evidence, I shall be liable to prosecution if I have knowingly stated in it anything which I know to be false or do not believe to be true.'
>
> (*Criminal Justice Act, 1967*)

The report itself is signed, and this additional declaration is usually signed separately. It is also the usual practice to sign or initial the bottom of each page of a statement which exceeds one page in length.

The form of the report varies greatly with the nature of the case, but in general principle follows that as described for civil litigation. Certain points are particularly important where criminal matters are being dealt with. The time, place and persons present at the examination are extremely important. If the report refers to a deceased person, a careful note of who identified the body must be included. If the examination of a living person is performed at the specific request of the police, then his consent must be obtained, after fully explaining the reason for examination and the fact that the police will be informed of the result. His refusal is an absolute bar to examination.

In everyday medical practice, it is more usual for the police to request a report on a patient who his already been examined and treated: this especially concerns casualty officers, house officers, registrars and general practitioners. It is an abuse of professional ethics and might be the subject of an action for breach of confidence if the doctor provides such a report without obtaining the patient's permission. It must be said, however, that probably the majority of such reports are in fact given without reference to the patient, but this makes the practice no less hazardous if some litigation-minded patient becomes aware of the circumstances. As already pointed out in the section on 'Consent' the police have no authority to demand information on any patient, this compulsion being reserved for the court alone, but every effort is made to co-operate with the police, who are acting in the interests of the community at large. Following some deterioration in the relations between the police and some doctors, a mutual agreement was reached in 1980 between representatives of the police and the British Medical Association over the matter of medical information. The Association of Chief Police Officers (ACPO) had complained that doctors, especially casualty officers and general practitioners, were sheltering behind the Hippocratic Oath and hampering the police investigation of, for example, baby batterers. The present situation is still not entirely satisfactory and conflict still exists between a doctor's duty of professional confidence and his public duty to assist in the maintenance of law and order. No blanket guide can be given to cover every individual situation and the doctor is advised to consult his defence organisation when he is in serious doubt as to which direction his duty should lie. Also, where a report is being made on the injured victim of an assault, the legal proceedings are being made to bring retribution upon the assailant, so the victim is unlikely to offer objections.

Concerning the actual content of a report, it should follow that as described for civil matters, with particular attention to description of external injuries where present, and an assessment of their seriousness, especially in relation to danger of life, where applicable. Where facial injuries are concerned, for example, an opinion as to the permanence of the scars and disfigurement might be added, though too much should not be made of prognosis, as this may well be a matter for expert opinion.

Civil litigation

A request for a medical report on a patient may be requested by the patient himself or more often, his legal representative in the shape of a solicitor. In these cases, general consent to examination will be implied by the request itself, but if more intimate or complex examination is required, further specific permission must be obtained. Where a request for a medical report comes from another party, other than the patient or his representative (e.g. the defendant, his solicitor or some third party such as an insurance company), no report shall be rendered without the express permission of the patient, after he has been made aware of the circumstances.

In private practice, all medical records are the doctor's personal property, but in the National Health Service, whether in hospital or general practice, there is no legal right of use of the patient's documents by the doctor. In actual practice these are freely used, but their ownership is vested in the Area Health Authority who employs the doctor concerned. Similarly, patients and their solicitors have no legal right of access to medical records or other medical details such as X-rays, laboratory reports etc. Though, in fact, hospital authorities normally co-operate freely where the matter is advantageous to the patient, there is no right of access to these documents except on an order of the court or a judge in chambers enforcing 'discovery' of such documents, though recent changes in procedure have made it much easier for lawyers to obtain access to medical records, even where a civil action has not yet been formally begun. Where pending civil action involves a dispute between a patient and members of the medical or hospital staff or where any negligence is alleged, no statement, report, or offering of records would be made without first consulting the hospital administration and their legal advisers. Where such cases involve a member of the medical staff, the appropriate defence society must be notified without delay.

All medical reports made in good faith to a solicitor for the purpose of legal proceedings are privileged – that is, they cannot form grounds for an action for defamation, in the same way that statements made in the witness box are protected.

The content of such a report depends largely on the nature of the case being described, but some matters are common to all. There naturally must be a preamble containing a statement that the patient (identified by name and address) was examined on a certain date: the latter is very important, as the medical condition of a patient may change rapidly and it is the findings on a specific date which are material. The report should also be dated, this often varying from the date of the examination though it should ideally be on the same or subsequent day. The place of examination and the name of the person requesting the report should be given. This should be followed by a short summary of the nature of the case, and a short history as related by the patient. It does not matter if statements which are legally inadmissible are included, as these will be pruned out at a later stage. The history of the present complaint should precede the physical examination. Following this a summary of the findings should be offered and a brief opinion as to the prognosis. The relative weight given to the latter depends largely on the nature of the case and the status of the doctor making the report. A house officer would be ill-advised to elaborate on anything other than a recital of the facts, whereas a specialist may have been consulted with the main object of offering a prognosis and estimation of expectation and quality of life.

When a doctor other than the regular medical attendant is requested to see a patient and report, he normally arranges for the regular medical attendant to be present, to assist him with obtaining the facts and providing the medical records, X-rays, investigations and so on. For this facility it is customary to pay an 'attendance fee'.

Reports to insurance companies, etc.

Reports to insurance companies on the medical state of an applicant for a life policy, form a frequent addition to a doctor's income. There has been a tendency of latter years for insurance companies either to employ their own medical assessors or to use a single well-tried practitioner in each area. Even so, the personal medical attendant is frequently requested to complete a medical report on the 'life' of an applicant. It is particularly important that this matter be conducted with greatest attention to accuracy and detail. Contracts of insurance differ from other contracts in that they are *uberrimae fidei*, that it, all material facts must be disclosed to the other party (insurance company) whether disadvantageous or not. In a normal contract, there is no onus to disclose disadvantageous facts, short of misrepresentation or fraud. If such total disclosure is not made before a contract of insurance is made, any potential benefits under the policy will be void and the doctor will be doing a disservice to an applicant and his family by turning a blind eye to any matters which might lead to the application being turned down or the premium raised. Not only will there be no payment of benefit, but all premiums paid up to that point will be forfeit and therefore the dependants of the applicant will be worse off than if he had not attempted to obtain a policy at all.

The consent of the patient must be obtained before such reports are sent, though in the usual insurance case, consent is implied by the fact of the patient applying for a policy and presenting himself for examination. The form of report is usually set out on a printed proforma by the company, and must be followed meticulously. No short cuts can be made, for the reasons given above, especially as regards blood-pressure and urine testing.

Similar considerations apply to requests for examination from, for example, trade unions. Where no set form of examination is provided, a general physical examination following a history-taking and list of present complaints should be offered.

Civil actions about insurance claims are not infrequent, and unfortunately several cases are on record of medical practitioners being severely censured or worse, following irregularities in insurance medical examinations. The General Medical Council has issued specific warnings against such irregularities, which may lead to erasure from the Register.

Certificates of health and incapicity

Since the inception of the National Health Service, and the expansion of the Social Security Services, an increasing portion of the general practitioner's work is in the issuing of medical certificates enabling the patient to obtain sickness benefit. Though the pressures of everyday practice and the altering attitudes of many patients have made this an unenviable task, it is still a matter of considerable responsibility and numerous doctors have come to grief with either the Health Authorities or the General Medical Council over irregularities with certificates. Pressure from patients to issue or continue certificates may be great, and refusal may be difficult. However, the doctor's conscience and good sense must guide him, as the consequences of carelessness may be severe. The signing of blank forms is particularly dangerous, however convenient it may be in a busy practice.

10

The doctor and the dead body

When called to a dead body, the duty of the doctor varies according to the circumstances. As described in the section about the coroner, if the practitioner has little or no knowledge of the medical condition of the deceased before death, or if there are any unnatural or suspicious circumstances, the doctor's duty is confined to confirming that life is extinct and in notifying the coroner, unless this has already been done by the police.

In strict law, where the doctor attended the patient during the last illness, he is obliged to issue a medical certificate of the cause of death. However, it has been the convention for very many years for a doctor who intends to report a death to the coroner, to abstain from issuing a death certificate. In 1979, the Registrar-General of Births and Deaths requested that the strict requirements should be more closely adhered to, though the British Medical Association protested that this was impracticable in many cases. In the event, a compromise has been arrived at which may be summarized thus:

1. It is for the doctor to decide whether he was 'in attendance during the last illness'. If the mode of death is one which reasonably could be expected to arise from the illness for which the doctor was attending, then the Registrar General wishes the doctor to issue a certificate, even with a speculative cause of death. The fact that such a certificate is issued by no means inhibits the doctor from reporting to the coroner, in order that a coroner's autopsy might more exactly arrive at the cause of death.
2. If the doctor honestly has no idea as to the cause of death, even though he attended during the last illness, then there is obviously no point in him attempting to issue a certificate.
3. If he does issue a certificate in a case which he wishes to report to the coroner, he should initial 'Box A' on the back of the certificate, but also contact the coroner by telephone in the usual way. *He should not rely upon the delivery of the certificate to the Registrar of Births and Deaths as a means of notifying the coroner.*

4. Irrespective of whether the doctor attended the patient in his last illness (which has no particular time scale), if his last visit to the patient was more than 14 days before death and he has not seen the body after death, then the local Registrar of Births and Deaths has instructions to report the case to the coroner (Fig. 6). The doctor should anticipate this and if he realises that he had not seen the patient in the last fortnight before death, he should spontaneously report the case to the coroner, whether or not he sees fit to give a certificate. The alternative allowed by the Registrar of seeing the body after death is most unsatisfactory, as it merely excludes obvious trauma and is virtually useless as an aid to determining the cause of a natural death.

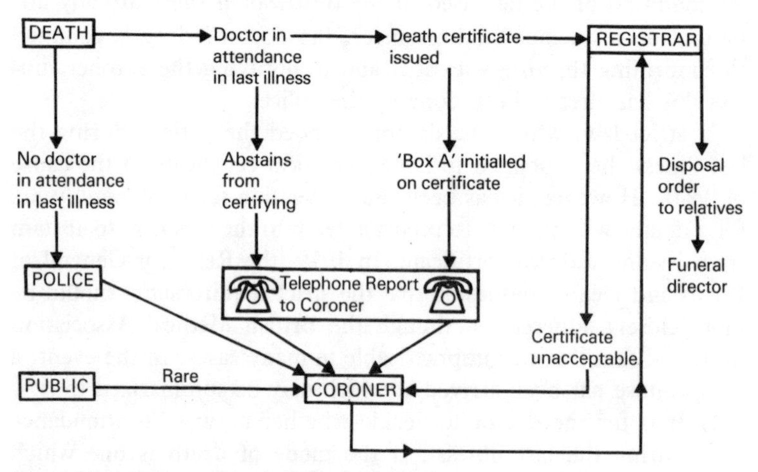

Fig. 6 Flow diagram of death disposal procedure

Regardless of the Registrar General's more recent requirements, the paramount consideration of the doctor is in reporting to the coroner all those cases which should come under his jurisdiction. This should be done directly as stated above, and not via an initial death certificate. When 'Box A' is initialled on the back of the certificate, the death cannot be entered in the Register until the coroner communicates the result of his enquiry to the Registrar.

Confirming the fact of death

Though this might appear to be a simple matter, it can sometimes be extremely difficult. Modern techniques in resuscitation and maintenance of cardio-respiratory function have in some way made the problem so difficult as to become more a matter of definitions and ethics than a straightforward medical decision. This is discussed more fully in the secion on organ transplantation.

However, in the usual case, the fact of death presents no problem. Sometimes in patients dying after a long illness, in coma or cachexia, there appears to be so little difference between the state of life and death that the moment of death may be hard to determine. For practical purposes, cessation of respiration and circulation are sufficient to assume somatic death. The radial pulse is unreliable, and prolonged ausculation of the praecordium forms the best test. Even here, in a long-enfeebled patient, heart sounds may be so faint as to be indistinguishable, and for a definite decision as to death, an ECG or even EEG tracing may be worth while. Even these can show surprising results, especially in barbiturate poisoning, as several sensational newspaper stories have proved. Examination of the optic fundi with an opthalmoscope is sometimes recommended, the columns of blood in the retinal veins breaking up into segments on cessation of the circulation. This examination is not always easy to make. In hospital cases, especially where relatives may be waiting outside screens, it is imperative for the clinician to definitely establish the fact of death before announcing this to the next of kin, as many doctors have had the embarrassing and distressing experience of having a 'dead' patient suddenly moving or groaning, albeit temporarily.

The duty of the doctor after death

Once the fact of death is definitely established, and there are no grounds for reporting the case to the coroner, the death certificate should be issued unless a post-mortem examination is requested on grounds of clinical interest. This is to display the *extent* of the disease and not its *nature*: if the nature was unknown, the case would then by definition be reportable to the coroner. Often, where relatives wish early disposal of the body, the death certificate is issued before the results of autopsy are available, so that registration formalities may be commenced. This is especially so with certain religious faiths, such as the Jewish. This practice should not be overemployed, as about half the clinical forecasts of cause of death is shown to differ from the subsequent autopsy findings. Box B can be initialled on the back of the certificate if necessary so that the final registration of the cause of death will be postponed until all data are made available, which may include bacteriology, virology, serology and histology etc.

The death certificate must be issued by a registered medical practitioner (which in hospital practice, includes a provisionally registered doctor working under supervision of his seniors) and as cannot be too often repeated, may only be issued if the doctor was in attendance upon the deceased during his last illness, though no time limit is laid down for this attendance. The '14 day rule' refers to reporting to the coroner, not to the issue of a death certificate, though formerly the two were inter-dependent. The doctor must also be satisfied as to the cause of death.

The statutory form of death certificate is divided into three detachable sections. In Wales, a much larger form in both the English and Welsh languages is issued, but the format is the same. The left hand part is the counterfoil for the doctor's own retention; the centre and largest part is the actual certificate, and the right hand slip is the 'Notice of Informant', which confirms that a certificate has, in fact, been issued to the relatives or other authorised persons. In theory, the centre part is sent by the doctor by post, in a sealed envelope to the local Registrar of Births and Deaths for the subdistrict in which the death occurred. Postage pre-paid envelopes may be obtained for the purpose from the Registrar, but in actual practice it is very common for the doctor to hand the sealed envelope to the informant, along with the right hand slip from the certificate. This saves time in that the relative may immediately attend the Registrar's Office and see that the death is registered, thus rapidly obtaining an order for disposal, which is required by the funeral director before burial or cremation can take place.

The books in which death certificates are issued to the doctor contain a wealth of information and directions as to the proper method of completion; unfortunately this advice is all too often ignored. Improper completion of certificates so frequently causes delays and further distress to the relatives, that considerable care should be employed by the doctor when writing them. The local Registrar is obliged to reject any certificate which shows facts incompatible with registration. On the certificate, the first three lines present no problem, the next states 'Last seen alive by me' – this should not indicate a date more than a fortnight before the date of death, unless the case has also been reported to the coroner or the body seen after death.

Below this are three cases, which require appropriate marking, indicating whether or not the body was seen after death. It is highly advisable for the doctor who completes the certificate to view the body after death though this is not a legal requirement at the moment. Numerous cases are on record where, either by fraud or accident, a certificate has been issued for a patient who was not dead, due to the doctor's omission to view the body. Even more frequent is inadequate viewing, where a distant view of the patient's head from the bedroom door, or even an examination of the soles of the feet inside the mortuary refrigerator has been deemed sufficient by the doctor to qualify as 'being seen after death'. Very many accidents, suicides and even a few criminal deaths have been missed by a visual examination so cursory as to be virtually negligent.

The most important part of the certificate is enclosed within a box and is the actual cause of death. This is divided into Part I and Part II, the former further sub-divided into (a), (b) and (c) (Fig. 7). Part I should indicate the disease or condition directly leading to death, the (a), (b), (c) providing a sequence of lesions all of which are causally related. Thus I(a) might be 'Haemopericardium' due to (b) 'Ruptured Myocardial Infarct' due to (c) 'Coronary Thrombosis'. There is no necessity to complete all three, and in the same case, using I(a) only, 'Coronary Artery Disease' would be quite acceptable, though of less value from the point of view of mortality statistics.

Part II is provided for other significant conditions, contributing to the death but not related to the disease or condition causing it. The degree of relation may be in doubt, as in the same hypothetical case, 'Diabetes Mellitus' might be thought to be yet another link in the chain leading to coronary artery disease or may be felt to be a separate condition contributing by virtue of some abnormal metabolic state. In a more clearly defined instance I(a) might be 'Chronic Bronchitis and Emphysema', whilst Part II might be 'Calcific Aortic Stenosis', which though in no way pathologically related, may be held to have accelerated death.

Unless the case has already been reported to the coroner, nothing must be written in the box which is in any way unacceptable to the Registrar, or the certificate will be rejected, causing delay and distress to the relatives, and possibly aggravating the coroner, who should have been notified at an earlier stage. A common mistake, especially amongst junior hospital doctors, is to include some condition which has a traumatic basis. Foremost amongst these is the fractured femur in old persons. A certificate which reads I(a) 'Massive Pulmonary Embolism', I(b) 'Leg Vein Thrombosis' and then, either in I(c) or Part II 'Fractured Neck of Left Femur' is bound to be rejected by the Registrar. This was from the first, not only a coroner's case, but one which will probably require an inquest. Other causes of confusion are mentions of diseases which may have a toxic background, either from drugs or alcohol. The unqualified use of 'Cirrhosis' is often queried by the Registrar, and should be specified as 'Non-alcoholic' if this is reasonable. Similarly, 'Pul-

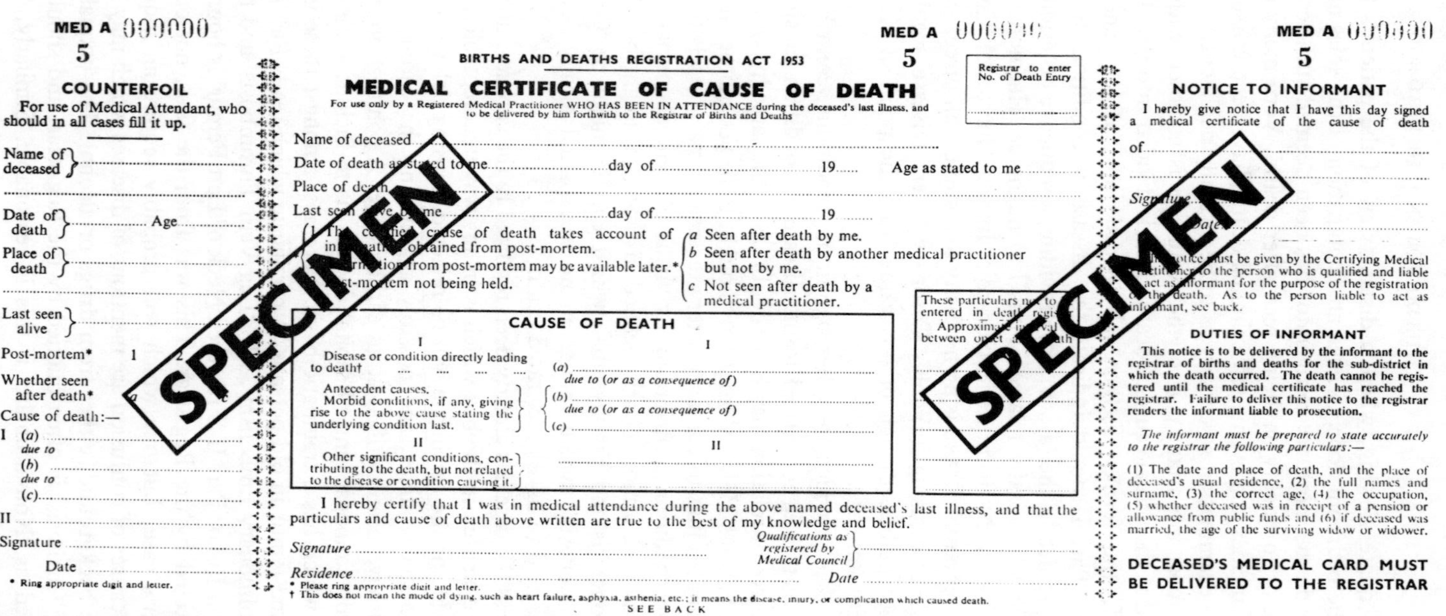

MED A 000000
5

COUNTERFOIL

For use of Medical Attendant, who should in all cases fill it up.

Name of deceased ....

Date of death .... Age ....

Place of death ....

Last seen alive ....

Post-mortem* 1 2 3

Whether seen after death* a b c

Cause of death:—

I (a) ....
due to
(b) ....
due to
(c) ....

II ....

Signature ....

Date ....

* Ring appropriate digit and letter.

MED A 000000
5

BIRTHS AND DEATHS REGISTRATION ACT 1953

MEDICAL CERTIFICATE OF CAUSE OF DEATH

For use only by a Registered Medical Practitioner WHO HAS BEEN IN ATTENDANCE during the deceased's last illness, and to be delivered by him forthwith to the Registrar of Births and Deaths

Registrar to enter No. of Death Entry ....

Name of deceased ....

Date of death as stated to me .... day of .... 19...... Age as stated to me ....

Place of death ....

Last seen alive by me .... day of .... 19 ......

1 The certified cause of death takes account of information obtained from post-mortem.
2 Information from post-mortem may be available later.*
3 Post-mortem not being held.

a Seen after death by me.
b Seen after death by another medical practitioner but not by me.
c Not seen after death by a medical practitioner.

CAUSE OF DEATH

I	I
Disease or condition directly leading to death†	(a) ....
Antecedent causes. Morbid conditions, if any, giving rise to the above cause stating the underlying condition last.	due to (or as a consequence of) (b) .... due to (or as a consequence of) (c) ....
II	II
Other significant conditions, contributing to the death, but not related to the disease or condition causing it.	....

These particulars not to be entered in death register
Approximate interval between onset and death

I hereby certify that I was in medical attendance during the above named deceased's last illness, and that the particulars and cause of death above written are true to the best of my knowledge and belief.

Signature .... Qualifications as registered by Medical Council ....

Residence .... Date ....

* Please ring appropriate digit and letter.
† This does not mean the mode of dying, such as heart failure, asphyxia, asthenia, etc.; it means the disease, injury, or complication which caused death.

SEE BACK

MED A 000000
5

NOTICE TO INFORMANT

I hereby give notice that I have this day signed a medical certificate of the cause of death

of ....

Signature ....

Date ....

This notice must be given by the Certifying Medical Practitioner to the person who is qualified and liable to act as informant for the purpose of the registration of the death. As to the person liable to act as informant, see back.

DUTIES OF INFORMANT

This notice is to be delivered by the informant to the registrar of births and deaths for the sub-district in which the death occurred. The death cannot be registered until the medical certificate has reached the registrar. Failure to deliver this notice to the registrar renders the informant liable to prosecution.

The informant must be prepared to state accurately to the registrar the following particulars:—

(1) The date and place of death, and the place of deceased's usual residence, (2) the full names and surname, (3) the correct age, (4) the occupation, (5) whether deceased was in receipt of a pension or allowance from public funds and (6) if deceased was married, the age of the surviving widow or widower.

DECEASED'S MEDICAL CARD MUST BE DELIVERED TO THE REGISTRAR

Fig. 7a Death certificate, front

PERSONS QUALIFIED AND LIABLE TO ACT AS INFORMANTS

The following persons are designated by the Births and Deaths Registration Act 1953 as qualified to give information concerning a death:—

DEATHS IN HOUSES AND PUBLIC INSTITUTIONS

(1) A relative of the deceased, present at the death.
(2) A relative of the deceased, in attendance during the last illness.
(3) A relative of the deceased, residing or being in the sub-district where the death occurred.
(4) A person present at the death.
(5) The occupier* if he knew of the happening of the death.
(6) Any inmate if he knew of the happening of the death.
(7) The person causing the disposal of the body.

DEATHS NOT IN HOUSES OR DEAD BODIES FOUND

(1) Any relative of the deceased having knowledge of any of the particulars required to be registered.
(2) Any person present at the death.
(3) Any person who found the body.
(4) Any person in charge of the body.
(5) The person causing the disposal of the body.

* "Occupier" in relation to a public institution includes the governor, keeper, master, matron, superintendent, or other chief resident officer.

Fill up where applicable

A

I have reported this case to the Coroner.

Initials of Certifying Medical Practitioner } ....

Fill up where applicable

B

I may be in a position later to give, on application by the Registrar General, additional information as to the cause of death for the purpose of more precise statistical classification.

Initials of Certifying Medical Practitioner } ....

NOTE.—The Practitioner, on signing the certificate, should fill up, sign and date the Notice to the Informant, which should be detached and handed to the Informant. The Practitioner should then, without delay, deliver the certificate itself to the Registrar of Births and Deaths for the sub-district in which the death occurred. Envelopes for enclosing the certificates are supplied by the Registrar.

A. Reported to Coroner ?

....

B. Further information offered ?

....

N.B.—If either Statement A or Statement B has been filled up, the fact should be noted in the appropriate place above.

Fig. 7b Death certificate, back

monary fibrosis' is sometimes suspect, especially in coal-mining districts, as this raises a suspicion of pneumoconiosis, and if unrelated to industrial disease, the fact should be stated on the certificate.

The rest of the certificate is straightforward, the small box requesting the approximate interval between onset of death being often impossible to answer accurately. At the lower part of the certificate, the qualifications are those *registered* by the General Medical Council and in most cases are confined to the qualifying degree, and not to a variety of post-graduate diplomas.

On the back of the certificate are the two spaces already mentioned, provided for special referral. Since 1980, when the Registrar General requested certificates to be issued in many cases even when reported to the coroner, Box A will be more frequently used, but again it must emphatically be repeated that the initialling of Box A should not be the sole means of reporting to the coroner This should not be done as hitherto, by a telephone call to the coroner's officer. The purpose of then initialling Box A is to tell the local Registrar of Births and Deaths that the cause of death must not be entered into the main Registrar until the coroner has concluded his enquiry. Box B has already been mentioned, as being a notification that further medical information will be forthcoming at a later date.

The informant to whom the doctor hands the certificate, is usually a relative of the deceased, though not necessarily the next of kin. The back of the 'Notice to Informant' provides an exhaustive list of informants: if not relative is available, any person present at the death, the occupier of premises in which death took place or the person responsible for the disposal of the body may act as the informant. In hospitals, where death occurs and no relatives are available, the function is assumed by the 'person in charge of the body' who is an administrator, usually the hospital secretary. The informant must take the Notice to the Registrar within five days of issue.

Once a case is reported to the coroner the above procedure is abrogated and all formalities are attended to by the coroner, who issues Form B if an autopsy has been held, or a certificate following inquest, if such an enquiry has occurred. This is then taken to the Registrar and registration completed in the usual way. If the coroner decides that the practitioner can certify, he will issue Form A, when the original procedure is recommenced.

Disposal of the body

Upon the informant attending the Registrar, (when in addition to the Notice to Informant, he must give up certain other documents such as the Medical Card, Pensions certificates etc.) death will be registered and the Registrar will issue a certificate for disposal. This is delivered to the undertaker and after burial formalities have been completed the Registrar is further notified by the funeral director that burial has been completed. It is a criminal offence to dispose of a body otherwise than via this Statutory procedure. The person responsible for seeing that the procedure is carried out is the executor or if the deceased was intestate, the next of kin. If no relatives can be traced, the local authority is obliged to both organise and pay for disposal of the body.

Cremation

Due to the almost complete destruction of the body following cremation, there were natural fears that all medico-legal evidence would be lost. About the only post-cremation evidence that has ever been obtained concerns thallium poisoning! In consequence, the regulations governing cremation are much more stringent than for burial, though in fact this is now rather an anachronism, as over 70 per cent of dead bodies are cremated, leaving burial to be the minority procedure. The legislation concerning cremation is thus archaic and overdue for radical reform. This has been discussed in the Brodrick Report but attempts to modify the procedure have not yet materialised.

Cremation in Great Britain became legal at the end of the last century, mainly due to the somewhat bizarre activities of a South Wales general practitioner, Dr William Price of Llantrisant. This eccentric family doctor, towards the end of a colourful career, became the father of a small son named Jesus Christ Price. When the infant died, his father publically cremated him in a field in full view of a departing chapel congregation. The public outrage caused him to be arrested, but he conducted his own defence at Cardiff Assizes and was acquitted. This became a precedent for cremation and the first Cremation Act was passed in 1902. The current outdated procedure basically stems from that time.

The cremation formalities are set out on no less than seven forms, distinguished by the letters, A, B, C, D, E, F, and G. Only two of these need concern the medical practitioner.

Form A is the application for cremation, completed by the relative or executor of the deceased. This is provided by the undertaker and must confirm that the deceased had no objection to cremation, and that the appellant has no reason to believe that death was due to any unnatural cause. The form must be countersigned by a person of repute known to the applicant.

Form B is a medical certificate given by the doctor who issued the death certificate (which must previously have been issued and the death registered). This doctor may be fully registered, or, if working in a hospital under supervision, be provisionally registered. He is obliged to disclose any relationship with the deceased person, and to reveal any interest he may have in the estate of the deceased. The body must have been viewed after death, this being a statutory obligation, unlike the requirements for the death certificate. Form B contains a large number of questions, including the doctor's enquiries amongst the attendants at the last illness, all of which are intended to assist the medical referee in assessing the application.

Form C is a confirmatory medical certificate given by a senior practitioner who has been registered at least five years. Statute Law does not state whether this five-year period runs from Provisional or Full registration, but after some confusion, the Home Office and General Medical Council indicated that they interpreted the period as running from the date of Full registration. This second doctor must not be a partner of the first, nor related to the first doctor, nor to the deceased. A direction from the Home Office to hospitals during recent years has also directed that the two certifying doctors should not belong to the same clinical 'firm', which is held to be similar to partnership in general practice. This ruling is by no means adhered to, but in some hospitals, the issuing of the confirmatory Form C is reserved to the medical superintendent of the institution.

The doctor issuing Form C must also examine the body after death, and see and question the doctor completing Form B. These points are important: though the viewing of the body is not mentioned as a statutory duty, as it is for Form B, it is expressly ordered in the Rubric to the Act. Questioning the doctor who completes Part B is also essential: some years ago, a doctor was convicted for nine offences of this nature. Very often, where a post-mortem is held, the pathologist will complete Form C, there being provision amongst the questions for indication that the certifier carried out an autopsy.

Form D is a certificate following a post-mortem examination requested by the medical referee of the crematorium where he requires further confirmation of the cause of death. As most doubtful cases are referred to the coroner, Form D is rarely used.

Form E is the certificate issued by the coroner and replaces Forms B and C.

Form F is the authority to cremate, issued by the Medical referee of the crematorium, almost always a community physician.

A recent addition to cremation procedure (though not part of the statutory requirements) is to safeguard crematoria and their employees from the risk of explosion and contamination from cardiac pacemakers. Pacemakers frequently have mercury-containing batteries and some modern types are even powered by nuclear fuel. The cremation of a body containing such a pacemaker may be hazardous, as mercury batteries explode.

Therefore most cremation medical forms have an addition requesting notification of whether a pacemaker is fitted and whether it has been removed. The procedure for removal is at present a matter of some doubt, but where there is an autopsy, it is removed by the pathologist. Where no post-mortem takes place, it may be removed by any doctor or possibly by an embalmer or funeral director, though the exact legal position of non-medically qualified removers is yet to be clarified.

An important postscript to this chapter is to emphasise two points which frequently give rise to trouble.

1. Where a death is to be notified to the coroner, *do not* issue a certificate and *do not* request permission for autopsy from the relatives.
2. In a case where it is not intended to notify the coroner, *do not* use the threat of such notification to obtain autopsy permission from reluctant relatives.

PROCEDURE IN SCOTLAND

Certification of death in Scotland can be carried out by any doctor, whether or not he was in attendance upon the deceased during life.

The Registration of Births, Deaths and Marriages (Scotland) Act 1965 provides that either the doctor in attendance upon the deceased (or if there was no such doctor, any other doctor) is able to issue a certificate. As in England and Wales, the doctor does not have to see the body after death in order to issue a certificate. Due to geographical difficulties, such as in the remote islands, it was necessary to provide for registration without viewing by a doctor, though in fact only a minute proportion of deaths are not actually seen by the certifying doctor.

Unlike England, it is possible for a body to be buried before the death has been registered, though in such a case, the Registrar must be notified of such an event. Cremation can only be carried out after registration: similar documentation exists as in the English system, though in Scotland there is a far lower proportion of cremations as opposed to burials compared to England, where over seventy per-cent of disposals are by cremation.

The death certificate is supposed to be issued by the doctor within seven days of the death, though no penalty is inflicted if this not done, unless the Registrar actually requests the information. In Scotland, the Act requires the doctor to 'transmit (the certificate) to any person who is a qualified informant in relation to the death, or to the Registrar'. This is official recognition of the usual practice in both England and Scotland of the relative personally conveying the certificate to the Registrar, rather than the theoretical provision in England and Wales for the certificate to be posted in a special envelope.

The Scottish certificate is very similar to that in England and Wales (Fig. 8), but has no separate 'Notice to Informant'. The usual international form of the cause of death is the most prominent part of the certificate, together with space for an approximate estimate of the interval between onset of the disease and death. It has an extra box requesting notification if the deceased was a married woman and death occurred during pregnancy or within six weeks thereafter.

The certificate requests information as to whether the body was seen after death by the certifying doctor, another doctor or no doctor at all. Unlike the English certificate, it does not require the doctor to state when the deceased was last seen alive. The Scottish certificate also requires the certifier to indicate whether the cause of death takes account of information derived from a post-mortem examination, or whether such information may be available later or whether a post-mortem examination is not proposed.

Unlike the English counterpart, the back of the certificate does not carry the boxes 'A' and 'B' which indicate whether the death was reported to the coroner nor whether further clinical information (other than that from a post-mortem) is likely to be available.

PROCEDURE IN NORTHERN IRELAND

Death certification in Northern Ireland is broadly similar to that in England, but has some of the features of the Scottish certificate. The doctor is statutorily obliged to issue a certificate of the cause of death. Like the Scottish certificate there is no Notice to Informant. The Informant, the categories of which are listed on the back of the certificate, must deliver the form within five days to the Registrar of Births and Deaths. The certificate does not require the age of the deceased to be stated nor whether a post-mortem examination was held. On the reverse there are spaces 'A' and 'B' as on the English certificate, but 'A' does *not* refer to notification to the coroner, but

Counterfoil

Name of deceased ____________________

Date of death ____________________

Place of death ____________________

Cause of death

1 a ____________________

b ____________________

c ____________________

11 ____________________

P – M *ring letter* A B C

Seen after death ring figure 1 2 3

Pregnancy ____________________

Date of certification ____________________

Medical Certificate of Cause of Death Form 11 *D2(R) Jul 75*

This certificate is intended for the use of the Registrar of Births, Deaths and Marriages, and all persons are warned against accepting or using this certificate for any other purpose.

To the Registrar of Births, Deaths and Marriages. *See note overleaf*

Registrar to enter
Dist no ________
Entry no ________
Year ________

I hereby certify that ____________________ died at ________ hours (*time*)

on ____________ (*date*) 19______, at ____________________ (*place of death*)

and that to the best of my knowledge and belief, the cause of death and duration of disease were as stated below.

Cause of death	Please PRINT CLEARLY
I	
Disease or condition directly leading to death*	a ____________________
	due to (or as a consequence of)
Antecedent causes Morbid conditions, if any, giving rise to the above cause, the underlying condition to be stated last.	b ____________________
	due to (or as a consequence of)
	c ____________________
II	II
Other significant conditions contributing to the death, but not related to the disease or condition causing it.	____________________

SPECIMEN

Not to be entered in register		
Approximate interval between onset and death.		
years	months	days

*This does not mean the mode of dying such as heart failure, asthenia, etc; it means the disease, injury or complication which caused death.

Please ring appropriate letter and appropriate figure:-

Certified cause takes account of post-mortem information ...	A
Information from post-mortem may be available later	B
Post-mortem not proposed	C
Seen after death by me	1
Seen after death by another medical practitioner but not by me	2
Not seen after death by a medical practitioner	3

If deceased was a married woman and death occurred during pregnancy, or within six weeks thereafter, write 'yes'. [ ]

Signature ____________ date ________ 197____

Name in BLOCK CAPITALS ____________________

Registered medical qualifications ____________________

Address ____________________

Fig. 8 Scottish death certificate

to whether the deceased was a married woman whose death occurred during pregnancy or within four weeks of delivery, similar to the Scottish certificate. It is lawful to dispose of a body by burial without obtaining a death certificate or registration of death certificate provided the Registrar of Births and Deaths is notified within the next seven days. It is unlikely that a burial would be permitted in an urban cemetery without the prior production of a registrar's certificate, or coroner's order.

Unlike England and Wales, especially since the 1980 instructions of the Registrar General, a doctor has a statutory obligation *not* to issue a death certificate and to refer the death to the coroner when the cause of death is unknown, whenever he has reason to believe that the death was due to unnatural causes, negligence or malpractice on the part of others or the administration of an anaesthetic and, where 'natural' deaths are concerned, whenever he has not seen and treated the patient for the fatal condition within 28 days of death.

PROCEDURE IN THE REPUBLIC OF IRELAND

In the Republic of Ireland, certification is very similar to that of the English procedure. However, a certificate of the cause of death is not statutorily required for registration and 3 per cent of registered deaths are uncertified as to the medical cause. No disposal note is required to the superintendent of cemeteries and in theory, relatives may bury without registration or certification. If a doctor refuses to issue a certificate to the relatives he should refer to the coroner and the Coroner's Act requires doctors and undertakers to report any suspicious circumstances to the *Gardai Siochana* (police) or to the coroner.

Still births are notifiable but do not require still birth certificates as in the rest of the British Isles.

Cremation is carried out in Belfast according to British law and certification. Bodies are accepted there from the Republic, only on receipt of a certificate from the relevant coroner that he sees no reason why cremation should not proceed.

A crematorium is being opened in Dublin in late 1981 without any specific disposal legislation. A voluntary code of certification is being drafted by the City Coroner and State Pathologist pending legislation on this matter.

The Medical Certificate of the Cause of Death in the Republic of Ireland is very similar to the English counterpart, except that there is no Notice to Informant. As in Scotland and Northern

Ireland, there is provision to record whether the deceased was a married women and the death was known to occur during pregnancy or within four weeks thereafter. The approximate interval between the onset of the fatal disease and death is also recorded, if known. The date of last attendance must be recorded, but not the fact that the body was seen after death or that a post-mortem examination was held.

11

The doctor at the scene of death

The details of legal procedure as regards certification and reporting to coroners are dealt with elsewhere: this section discusses the more medical aspects of a scene of death.

Circumstances under which a doctor is called
A practitioner may be called to the scene of death to render medical aid because lay bystanders may think that life is not completely extinct. He may be called merely to certify death; or he may be called to the scene because of his special experience, such as being a police surgeon or a forensic pathologist.

In the usual circumstances of a presumed or alleged natural death, the doctor is called by the family, either because the patient was *in extremis* or was known to be dead. Here the doctor must decide immediately whether he is entitled to issue a certificate or report the case to the coroner (or even directly to the police where obvious unusual circumstances exist). The latter need not be frankly criminal, but accidents and suicides are often notified direct to the police rather than to the coroner. If the death is natural, the cause known and the doctor has attended during the last 14 days, he must issue a death certificate as described in another chapter.

The body should be examined externally, this usually being done whilst confirming the presence of the signs of death, such as absent heart sounds. Though external examination of the body is of little use in determining the nature of internal disease or lesions, it at least can exclude many common conditions. The following should be looked for routinely:

1. Unusual discoloration of the skin, especially of the post-mortem lividity if present (Fig. 9). The cherry-pink of carbon monoxide poisoning has been missed on many occasions by practitioners, though admittedly, it is sometimes very faint or even absent, especially immediately after death. A somewhat similar colour is seen in cyanide poisoning. After the *Clostridium welchii* septicaemia of a septic abortion, the skin is often a greyish-bronze. A brownish tinge is also seen in methaemoglobinaemia, which occurs in poisoning by several substances including phenacetin and some nitro-compounds.

2. *Any external marks of injury*, especially around the neck under the chin or around the eyes or mouth.

3. *Petechial haemorrhages* in the lips, conjunctivae or facial skin, suggesting the presence of anoxic or asphyxial conditions.

4. *Any obvious injuries*, burns or blisters on the surface of trunk or limbs.

5. *Any signs* inconsistent with the stated time of death should be noted. This will be elaborated later, but obvious cooling or the presence of rigor and marked hypostatic lividity in a body alleged to have just died, indicates some inconsistency.

When called to the scene of some overtly unnatural or unusual death, greater care and a more thorough examination must be performed. If the case is frankly suspicious or criminal, then unless the practitioner is a police surgeon or pathologist, he would do well to limit his opinion to confirming that life is extinct. If there is to be delay in the arrival of a medico-legal expert, he should attempt to collect information that may be lost by the passage of time, but taking extreme care not to prejudice further investigation by disturbing the scene.

Where the doctor is to be the sole immediate examiner, the examination of a body in unnatural or suspicious circumstances should follow the routine set out below.

General view of the scene

The position of the body, especially in relation to adjacent objects such as furniture and any objects which could have caused injuries found upon the body should be noted. Though in any suspicious case, this aspect will be fully covered by the police and their photographers, they are frequently unaware of the nature of objects which could cause various skin trauma or deeper injuries.

The position of the clothing should be noted, especially if disarranged. The finding of a body wth trousers or underclothes down by no means indicates a sexual crime, as several spurious police investigations have been started after the finding of a trouserless body, where death has occurred from pulmonary embolism or cerebral haemorrhage during defaecation.

If no photography is available, the doctor would do well to make a rough sketch indicating the position of the body and the sur-

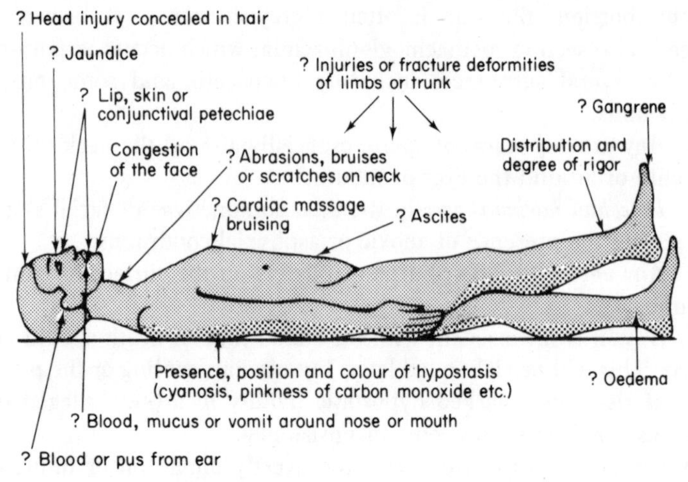

Fig. 9 Scheme for 60-second minimum examination of a corpse

roundings. The presence of vomit around the mouth and nostrils or on the front of the clothing should be noted, as well as the position of any blood-staining on the body or adjacent floor.

TIME OF DEATH

The time of death is sometimes extremely important. It is a question almost invariably asked by police officers, sometimes with a touching faith in the accuracy of the estimate. Determining the time of death is extremely difficult, and accuracy is impossible. It is unwise and unhelpful to offer a precise time of death, and a 'time bracket' should be worked out which reasonably includes the actual time of death. Should a case come to trial, a medical witness who has provided an absurdly accurate time will undoubtedly suffer at the hands of the opposing counsel and have the rest of his evidence discredited.

Methods of estimation vary according to the approximate period that has elapsed since death. This may be conveniently divided into (a) the first day, (b) the first couple of weeks and (c) more than a few weeks.

The first day after death

This is the only period during which any semblance of accuracy can be expected, though here errors of up to 100 per cent cannot be excluded. The only worthwhile method is estimation of body temperature (Fig. 10). Though in theory, there should be a steady

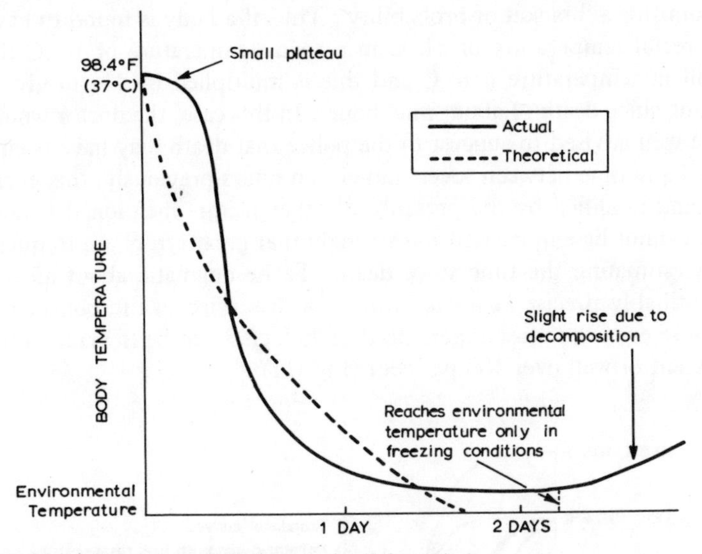

Fig. 10 Cooling curves of a body; actual and theoretical

fall from the original temperature at death to that of the environment, numerous interfering factors may exist.

Where access to the rectum can be gained without serious disturbance of the position of the body (and where no sexual element such as buggery is suspected, unless examination and swab-taking have already been completed) the insertion of a long chemical thermometer (not clinical) will give the most accurate temperature reading, which is usually of the order of one or two degrees higher than axillary or mouth temperature. The thermometer should read from 0–50° C or the equivalent Fahrenheit range. It has long been stated that the approximate fall in temperature during the first twelve hours after death is 1·5° F, often faster during the first six hours, when it may be as much as 2·5° F. There are so many exceptions to this rule of thumb, that great errors habitually arise. Account must be taken of the environmental temperature, even if this is known to have varied over the period since death.

A more practical way of arriving at a rough estimate is to use Centigrade measurements in the following way:

> The fall in temperature (37 minus observed thermometer reading) is multiplied by 1, 1¼, 1½, 1¾ or 2 for an air temperature of 0, 5, 10, 15 or 20° C respectively.

The answer to this simple calculation hopefully gives the number of hours since death, or more realistically, an approximate centre point for a 'bracket of probability'. Thus if a body is found to have a rectal temperature of 31° C in a room temperature of 10° C the fall in temperature is 6° C and this is multiplied by 1½ to give a time since death of about nine hours. In this case, the doctor would be well advised to suggest to the police that death may have occurred any time between seven and eleven hours previously, this guess being modified by the presence of other factors mentioned below. It cannot be emphasized too strongly that great errors are frequent in estimating the time since death. To be dogmatic about an unjustifiably precise estimate is to do a disservice to the police, because even the most experienced pathologists can be in error to the extent of well over 100 per cent (Fig. 11).

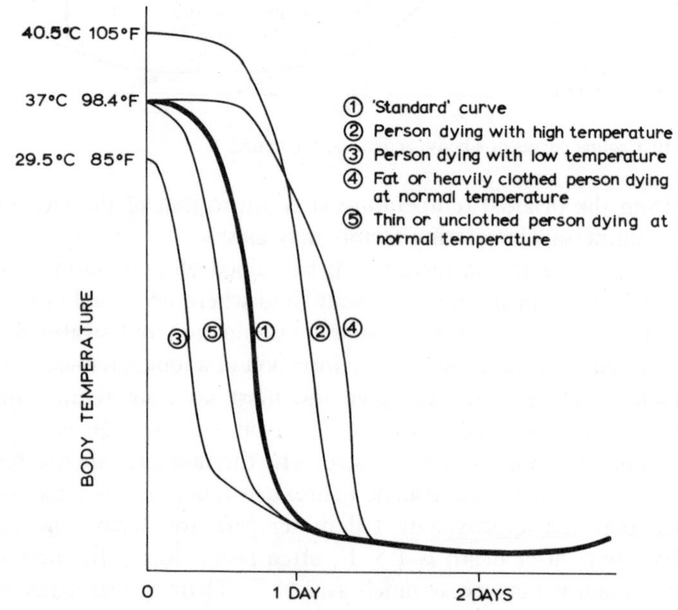

Fig. 11 Common variations from 'standard' cooling curves

Modifying factors in cadaver temperature estimations

Many factors distort the above straightforward reasoning when extrapolating time from temperature. One or more may be present simultaneously. In some cases (especially environmental conditions outdoors) the same factor varies from time to time, which cannot always be within the observer's knowledge.

1. Clothing

It is obvious that clothing will retard the rate of cooling, and a naked body will lose heat far faster than one wearing several layers of clothing. Bedclothes naturally come into this category, as well as artificial means of heating such as hot-water bottles and electric blankets, which are not infrequently found at scenes of death.

2. Body size and physique

Rate of cooling is dependent upon mass/surface-area ratios and thin persons and infants have a relatively larger surface area. In addition, a thick layer of fat beneath the skin in adipose people acts as an effective insulator, as well as causing the obese body to have a greater mass/surface-area relationship. The deep rectal temperature of an obese person will stay higher for very much longer than an emaciated corpse. Another factor which tends to retard cooling is oedema, and persons in congestive cardiac failure, especially with ascites, have been found to retain heat for a long period due to the large volume of water present with a high specific heat. Dehydration naturally has the opposite effect.

3. Environmental temperature

This is obviously a potent factor, and is allowed for in a simple calculation given earlier. However, marked changes in wind velocity, air temperature and humidity cannot be allowed for over the long period of the first day.

4. Body temperature at death

The calculation assumes that the body temperature at death was 37° C (98·4° F). This is a most unsure assumption, as numerous conditions can alter the temperature at death by many degrees either way.

In cases of cerebral haemorrhage (especially pontine), septic conditions, asphyxial deaths etc., the body temperature may be raised by as much as 5° C. Conversely, hypothermia due to exposure during life to low temperatures may reduce the temperature. Thus, as can be seen in the accompanying diagrams, the cooling curve may begin at a higher or lower point on the scale.

There are therefore numerous factors which will modify the interpretation of temperature estimations and it is patently impossible to allow correctly for each one. For example, one could hardly be expected to arrive at any satisfactory answer in an emaciated man with a pontine haemorrhage, who died naked in a wind-swept field in December. All that can be done is to extend the 'time-bracket' for the more difficult cases in order not to mislead investigating authorities. Many carefully-controlled series of temperature estimations (where the time of death was known) have been carried out, some including two separate estimations in order to attempt to gauge the slope of the cooling curve. These investigations have all succeeded mainly in demonstrating the extreme inaccuracy of the temperature method, but it remains the only one where errors can be measured in hours and not days. Numerous other more sophisticated techniques have been attempted, such as enzyme and biochemical analyses of various body fluids. The vitreous humour of the eye is probably the more promising of these techniques but they suffer from two defects:

1. They are specialised laboratory procedures which take considerable time to perform and are thus of no use in assisting detective officers in the middle of the night.
2. They are to a large extent temperature-dependent, as are almost all chemical reactions.

The results of these sophisticated methods vary according to the rate of cooling, so that the errors which distort thermometer readings are also likely to distort these more elegant methods. As a rough guide, the body will feel cool to the touch in four hours and uniformly cold in twelve hours.

Post-mortem staining

After death, the fluid blood settles to the dependent parts of the body, and in the usual circumstances where a death occurs with the body supine, the back of the trunk, neck, arms and legs will be discoloured a purplish-pink. In the early stages it is often blotchy due to uneven relaxation of superficial blood-vessels and variation in rigormortis from place to place causing uneven pressure on capillaries, but this blotchy appearance has no diagnostic significance. This post-mortem hypostasis (or lividity as it is commonly misnamed), is not always permanent and if the body is turned over after it has appeared, the colour will often gravitate slowly to the next most dependent areas.

As a means of estimating time since death, staining is almost useless. It tends to begin some 36 hours after death, but frequently can be seen earlier. Its main uses are in (a) indicating that a body has been moved after death by some outside interference, and (b) its colour may arouse suspicion of certain types of poisoning. The cherry-pink of carbon monoxide, the darker pink of cyanide and the brownish stains of methaemoglobin should cause further notice and analysis to be taken. The hypostasis of refrigerated bodies, of those recovered from cold water or cases of hypothermia, may be a bright pink due to undissociated oxyhaemoglobin in the superficial vessels.

Rigor mortis

Like post-mortem staining, rigor mortis is virtually useless as a means of estimating time since death. Rigor is the stiffening of the muscles which occurs as the result of protein changes in the muscle caused by the action of acid metabolites. It is thus dependent upon the activity immediately before death and also upon temperature. Where extreme exertion has been indulged in immediately up to the point of death, rigor comes on extremely rapidly and conversely, in cachetic patients dying after a lingering illness, rigor may be slight. In children, rigor is slight or even absent in many cases. The stiffening first occurs in the small muscles of the eyelid and jaw and spreads to the major groups, mainly the flexors of the limbs. Though the time of onset may be anything between four and eight hours, the appearance of rigor is extremely variable. A well-established, though highly inaccurate, rule-of-thumb is that rigor commences in six hours, takes another six to become fully established, remains for 12 hours and passes off during the succeeding 12 hours. This takes us roughly to 36 hours after death when rigor is vanishing because of the onset of post-mortem autolysis of muscle protein. However, the only reliable aspect of this rule is that it is usually *un*reliable. A more practical dictum is that if a body is *warm* and *flaccid*, it has probably been dead less than half a day: if it is *cold* and *flaccid*, it has probably been dead for more than two days.

Extreme cold may delay the onset of rigor, which then occurs when the body is allowed to warm up. Very hot conditions may cause rapid onset of rigor, apart from the actual muscle contraction that occurs in burrning from the direct heat effect.

It is extremely unsafe to use rigor at all in the estimation of time since death. The only possible use is in the period around the second day, when body temperature may have dropped to environmental but putrefaction has not yet occurred. If full rigor is present, then one might assume that this is about the second day following death.

Cadaveric spasm is an oddity seen rarely in civil practice, in which instantaneous rigor occurs immediately on death, usually being manifest by the gripping of objects in the fingers. This usually happens in sudden violent deaths (especially falls into water) where objects may be clutched in a desperate attempt to save life. It has been reported as an apparently common phenomenon on battle-fields.

Post-mortem decomposition

This again is extraordinarily variable in the time of onset. In the average unrefrigerated body left in domestic surroundings without extremes of temperature, early post-mortem discoloration of the abdomen is normally seen around the third day. The nature of the death affects this considerably, and ante-mortem infective changes may cause rapid advancement of decomposition. For instance, definite post-mortem discoloration is frequently seen in South Wales coal miners early on the second day, a large number of these bodies having had acute-on-chronic chest infection in the terminal illness, together with tissue oedema from congestive cardiac failure, which facilitates the growth of putrefactive bacteria.

The progress of decomposition depends largely on environment. Putrefaction is usually first seen over the right lilac fossa where the caecum is near the skin. It then spreads over the whole abdomen, which becomes a greenish colour. Rapid spread along the superficial veins may cause a 'marbling' of the abdomen, thoracic, neck and proximal limb veins. This is well advanced by the fifth or sixth day in average conditions. At the end of the first week, the face will be discoloured and gas formation present in the abdomen, genitals and softer tissues around the neck and face. This gas formation proceeds during the second week with distortion of the features, protrusion of the tongue and eyes and sometimes evacuation of the rectum and even the gravid uterus. The skin surface begins to break down at the end of the first week, with loosening of the epidermis, fluid-filled blisters, generalised sliminess and loosening of hair. Continuous advance of these changes occurs over the next few weeks, though they are not constant enough to act as anything like a reliable indication of time since death.

The above changes occur in air, and are delayed by immersion in water or burial in ground. The speed of decomposition in water is again extremely variable and depends upon water temperature and the amount of contamination from, e.g., sewage. Post-mortem injuries are extremely common in bodies recovered from water, either from collision with underwater obstructions or active damage from passing vessels.

Estimation of time of death after a prolonged interrval

The processes of putrefaction go on for some months, depending upon the environment and season. A body dying outdoors in the summer months may be reduced to a skeleton within a matter of weeks, the action of maggots and larger animal predators assisting in the dispersal of the soft tissues. If a body dies in late autumn or winter, it may remain largely intact until the following warm season. Usually, a body is reduced to a skeleton within one year if outdoors, though periosteum, ligaments and tendon tags may survive for several years. Again environment is extremely important and the body left in a dry cave or buried in well-drained sandy soil will survive better than one in wet loam or exposed in an open ditch to animal predators.

Once all soft tissue has vanished, then estimation of date of death becomes virtually impossible. The appearance of the bones gives a rough guide to the antiquity or otherwise of the remains, though even this can be fraught with difficulties – again, the environment is all important. Bodies buried in waterlogged peaty soil may vanish, bones and all, within a few decades, whilst it is common knowledge that archaeological specimens many thousands of years old can survive in an excellent state of preservation. The dating of bones is an extremely specialised task, and it is usually sufficient (though often difficult) to decide whether human skeletal remains are more or less than 50–100 years since death. If in excess of this period, there will be obviously no medico-legal significance and the matter will pass into the hands of antiquarians or archaeologists. Even this simple decision is fraught with difficulties: the general appearance of the bones, their friability, apparent porosity must be compared with recent bones. The basic criterion is the apparent loss of collagenous stroma which makes the bone surface soft and powdery when tested with a thumb nail. In any case where obvious antiquity is not immediately apparent, they should be referred to a forensic laboratory for expert opinion.

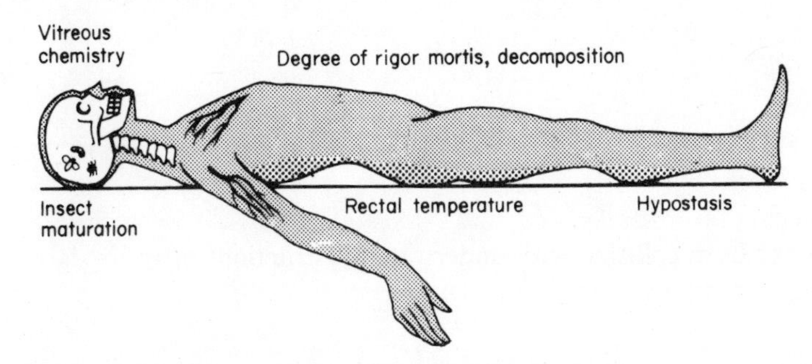

Fig. 12 Summary of factors useful in estimating time of death

Summary of methods for estimating time of death (Fig. 12)

1. Take rectal temperature with a long chemical thermometer. Take adjacent air temperature. Subtract indicated body tempera-

ture from 37 and multiply by a factor of 1, 1¼, 1½, 1¾ or 2 for air temperature of 0, 5, 10, 15 or 20° C.

2. Use the figure obtained as the centre of a range of probable times in hours, in which death was most likely to have occurred. During the previous 12 hours, this should be not less than one hour either side of the indicated time. Modify your calculation for obvious variations in body size, clothing, environmental factors etc.

3. Check that this time is not incompatible with the observed state of post-mortem lividity and rigor mortis.

4. Where putrefaction is present, the range given should be in days or even weeks according to the stage of putrefaction reached.

5. If the body is skeletalised, and no tendon tags remain, death probably occurred more than one year previously. Further expert opinion should be sought.

12

Identification

The identification of both living and dead is something in which medical evidence may play an important part, sometimes constituting the only evidence which establishes the identity of a person. Identifying the dead body, especially in criminal or suspicious cases, is a highly specialised task. It may be beyond the capabilities of the forensic pathologist alone, requiring other experts such as anatomists, radiologists and dentists to be co-opted into a team.

For the purposes of this book, as relevant to the more general aspects of medical practice, identity is of minor importance, but the doctor may sometimes be requested to assist in identification of the living and occasionally be involved in the early stages of identification of a dead body.

Identification of the living becomes necessary when through debility, illness, mental confusion, unconsciousness or true amnesia, evidence of identity is not forthcoming from a person who has no relatives or friends immediately available and who carries no documentary evidence of identity. Such cases are sometimes seen in vagrants, residents in lodging houses, victims of accidents, fires and mass tragedies, such as a rail or air crash.

With the increased immigrant population in Britain, estimation of age has become more important in the living. Matters of immigration, claims for pensions and other family matters depending upon the reaching of a certain age might be needed, especially where no adequate documentation is available in immigrants from countries where certification is less accurate or not readily available. There has been considerable recent controversy about the X-raying of immigrant children for estimation of age from epiphyseal fusion. However, this might be the only practical way, together with dental development, of reaching any accurate estimate of age.

Unidentified corpses are commonplace, especially after recovery from the water or rural surroundings. Decomposition is here the main obstacle to recognition.

A systematic and logical sequence of observations will greatly assist the authorities in establishing identity.

Height, weight and general nourishment

These are obvious steps in identification, though they may be impossible in dead bodies where advanced decomposition or skeletalisation has occurred. In measuring cadavers, up to 1½ inches either way is an acceptable margin of error, compared to the known live height, due to changes which take place after death. In decomposed bodies, putrefactive bloating may distort the general impression of nourishment.

Race, pigmentation, hair colour, eye colour, beard, moustache

These again are obvious features which can be recorded without trouble, though the eye colour is often extremely difficult to distinguish when death has occurred more than a few days previous. In decomposing bodies, much of this evidence may be difficult or impossible to recover. In bodies recovered from the water, the hair often peels off and where present, a sample may have to be washed free of to reveal the true colour.

Sex

Though this is usually obvious in all but the most decomposed bodies, occasional cases of pseudohermaphroditism may be encountered, and also the facial appearance of some elderly people is extremely ambiguous, especially where some degree of hypothyroidism is present. In skeletal material, specialised examination and measurements are required to establish the sex. Sex determination by microscopic examination of nuclear chromatin has so far found little forensic application.

Age estimation

As mentioned above, estimation of age in both the living and dead may be of considerable importance. In the fetus, age estimation may be necessary to determine whether the subject has attained the age of 28 weeks or is at full term. Here length, weight and other features of maturity give a fairly accurate guide. In infants, again dimensions may assist, though there is marked variation. Radiologically, ossification centres and epiphyseal union in older children given an accuracy to within a few per cent, though the advisability of radiation for such purposes in the living may have to be weighed against the importance of the result.

The state of development of the dentition, either deciduous or permanent teeth, can be an excellent guide up to the late teens (and into the early twenties as far as the third molar is concerned)

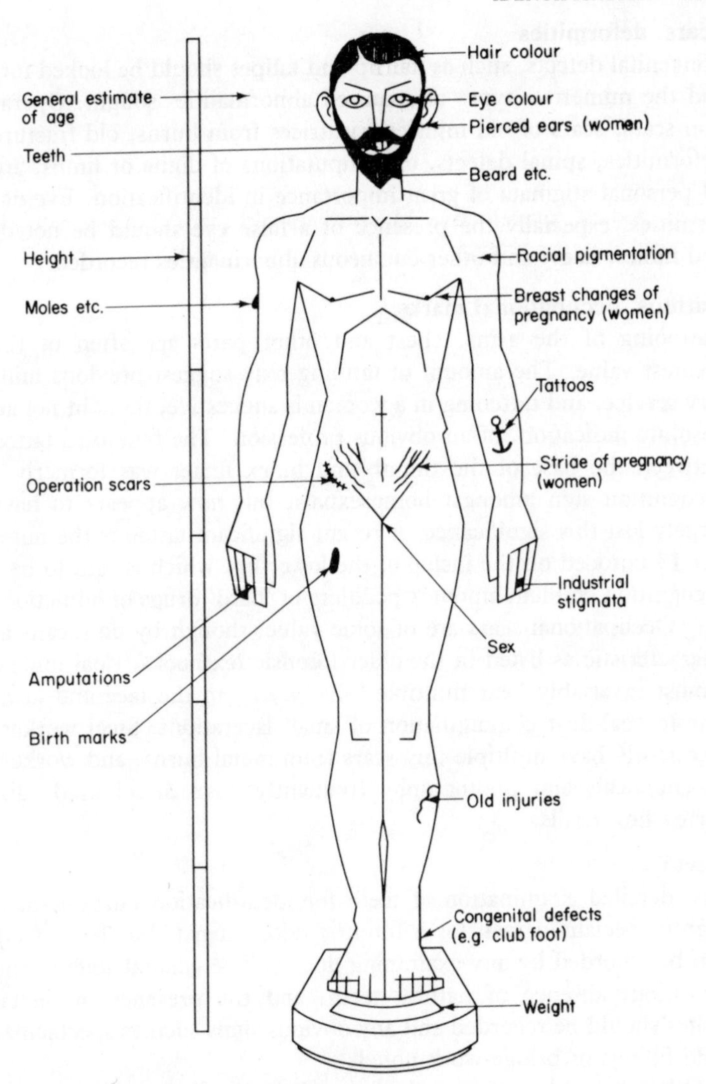

Fig. 13 External features useful in establishing identity

(Fig. 13). After the age of about 25 years all epiphyses are fused and in the living there is little except a general impression of the appearance of age to given any exact time marker. In the dead, several skeletal and dental techniques can give a fairly accurate age estimation though as middle age is passed, the errors become larger. These matters are for the specialist anthropologist or forensic pathologist.

Scars, deformities

Congenital defects, such as hairlip and talipes should be looked for, and the numerous types of acquired abnormalities sought. Operation scars, scars of old injuries, cicatrices from burns, old fracture deformities, spinal defects, old amputations of digits or limbs, are all personal stigmata of great importance in identification. Eye deformities, especially the presence of a false eye should be noted, and moles, naevi and other cutaneous abnormalities recorded.

Tattoos, occupational marks

Tattooing of the arms, chest and other parts are often of the greatest value. The amount of tattoing may suggest previous military service, and tattooing in a women is suggestive, thought not an absolute indication, of an obvious profession. The blue-bird tattoo between the base of the thumb and index finger was formerly a recognition sign amongst homosexuals, but now appears to have largely lost this significance. A recent significant tattoo is the number 13 tattooed on the inside of the lower lip, which is said to be a recognition emblem amongst peddlers of 'hard' drugs of addiction.

Occupational scars are of some value, though by no means as characteristic as listed in the older forensic textbooks. Coal miners almost invariably bear multiple 'blue scars' on the face and arms due to coal-dust contamination of small lacerations. Steel workers frequently have multiple tiny scars from metal burns, and workers in chemicals and photography frequently have discoloured, distorted fingernails.

Teeth

The detailed examination of teeth for identification purposes is a highly specialised task for a forensic odontologist, but basic facts can be recorded by any examining doctor. The general state of the dentition, absence of natural teeth, and the presence of dental plates should be recorded and any obvious signs such as spectacular gold fillings or bridge-work noted.

Other general matters, which can be as well described by lay persons and police, include the presence of spectacles, wedding rings, type and state of clothing and the general air of care or neglect. Otherwise, the doctor's function is limited to measurement of body dimensions, interpretation of artefacts such as operation scars, recognition of acquired or congenital physical defects and the superficial examination of the dental state.

Where skeletal material is concerned, the recognition of bones as being of human origin is an important first step in elimination of unnecessary work for police or specialist medical opinion.

13

Sudden natural death

This topic has an important medico-legal aspect in respect of reporting deaths to the coroner and also in the proper completion of a death certificate.

When a sudden death must be reported to the coroner
Though this topic has been discussed in more detail in the section on Coroner's procedure (Chapter 9), it is of such basic importance that a summary is given here. Where the patient had not been seen for more than two weeks before death (excluding the terminal visit at, or immediately before death) then the case must be reported.

However, a patient with long-standing serious disease, which might have a fatal outcome at any time (for example serious coronary artery disease) might legitimately be signed up if he dies suddenly on the day following a routine visit. This, of course, is only applicable if the doctor has no doubt that the chronic disease was the cause of death, and that no other factors operate.

A patient may suffer from a serious chronic disease, but still not be a candidate for sudden unexpected death. Examples are numerous, but a sufferer from, say, multiple sclerosis or rheumatoid arthritis, should be reported to the coroner if sudden, unexpected death occurs. In borderline cases where the practitioner is in doubt, he should at least communicate with the coroner (or his officer) by telephone, and ask his opinion. There has been some legal argument in the past as to whether this informal approach actually constitutes 'notification', but most coroners will gladly offer their opinion. They will either instruct the doctor to sign the death certificate or they will take over the case and dispose of it speedily either by Form A (no autopsy and referral back to the doctor for a death certificate) or Form B (certificate after autopsy, but without inquest). In certain areas, coroners may issue more specific directions as to the range of cases which they wish to have reported, apart from those deaths such as accidents, suicides and so on, where there is no choice. These directions are often given to hospital doctors, but often not to general practitioners unless specifically requested.

Whatever the nature of the disease, if any other factor operates, such as a previous injury, a war pension, a relevant industrial background or, most important to the doctor, the slightest breath of dissatisfaction with the medical treatment as voiced by relatives, then the case should always be notified to the coroner. In addition, it is always wise to report sudden infant deaths and any death following abortion, even if natural disease is thought to be the cause. A more comprehensive list will be found in the chapter under Coroner's Procedure, but in the context of sudden death, it is always wiser to contact the coroner rather than try to push the case through the normal registration channels, with the consequent risk of censure from the coroner, and, more important, distress to the bereaved relatives by possible administrative complications and delay of the funeral arrangements.

Causes of sudden death (Fig. 14)

Considerable errors are constantly made in the certification of causes of death, particularly sudden death, where no autopsy is performed. This does not mean to say that autopsy is the final arbiter, but it certainly greatly reduces the errors produced by clinical opinion only. Though between five and ten per cent of autopsies reveal no satisfactory cause of death, several surveys have shown a 45 to 55 per cent discrepancy between clinical forecasts of the cause of death and the results of the subsequent autopsy. It must be admitted that in the majority of cases the discrepancy is relatively slight, but a significant proportion of causes of death are wildly inaccurate, frequently being not even in the correct anatomical system. For a clinician to certify 'coronary thrombosis' when autopsy reveals a subintimal haemorrhage in a coronary artery, is of no great moment; often, coronary thrombosis is diagnosed, where in fact the cause of death it a ruptured aortic aneurysm, this being excusable if no autopsy is held. But quite commonly, in a case which has been written up as 'coronary thrombosis', autopsy reveals the cause of death is actually cerebral haemorrhage, pulmonary embolus from leg vein thrombosis, mesenteric thrombosis or one of a host of other quite unrelated disease processes. In the medico-legal sphere, a number of barbiturate poisonings, carbon monoxide poisonings and post-traumatic lesions have been missed by clinicians who offer a natural cause of death with little clinical foundation. Some of these are due to frank negligence in examining the body after death, especially carbon monoxide poisoning. Others are impossi-

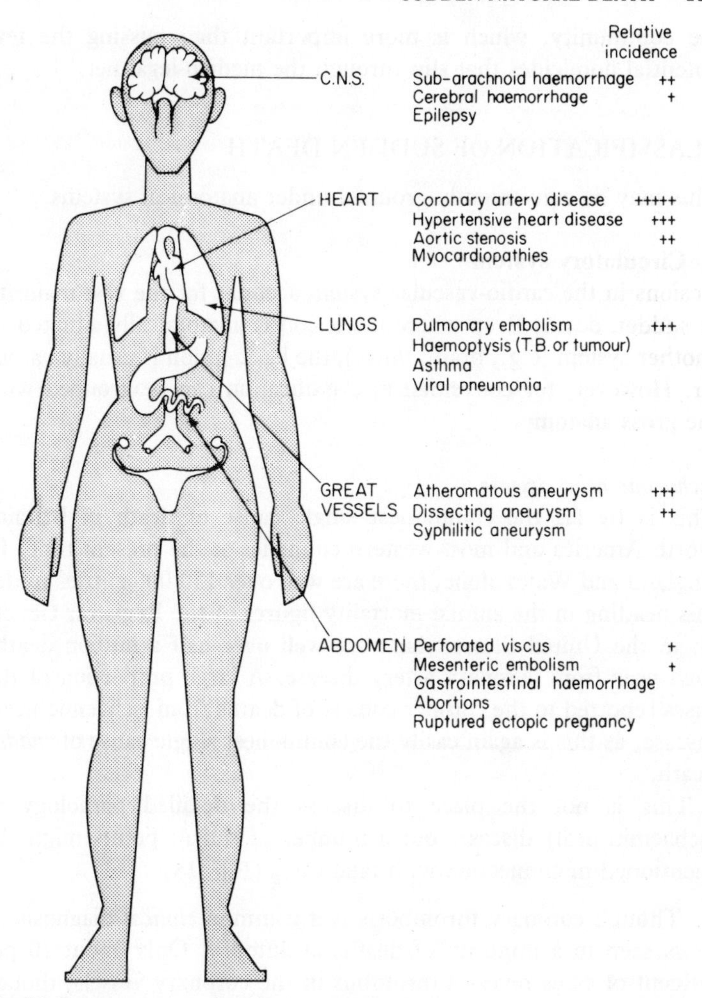

Fig. 14 Common causes of sudden or rapid death

ble to recognise without autopsy. The practice which is common on the continent, of external scrutiny of the body as a means to diagnosis of internal pathology, is to be deprecated, as very few natural diseases can be identified by looking at the skin surface. Indeed, the cause of death may be difficult or even impossible to determine after a full autopsy with microscopic and biochemical investigations, so it follows that superficial external examination is virtually valueless in establishing the true cause of death. This attitude may be countered by the opinion that a high post-mortem rate is socially and ethically undesirable. This may well be so, but we cannot then expect accurate knowledge about the pattern of mortality in the community, which is more important than missing the few potential homicides that slip through the medico-legal net.

CLASSIFICATION OF SUDDEN DEATH

This may be conveniently grouped under anatomical systems.

1. Circulatory system

Lesions in the cardio-vascular system account for the vast majority of sudden death. Even where the lesion is anatomically situated in another system (e.g., brain, lungs), the basic lesion is usually vascular. However, for convenience, classification can be grouped with the gross anatomy.

Ischaemic heart disease

This is by far the commonest single cause of death in Britain, North America and most western countries at the present time. In England and Wales alone, there are well over 150 000 entries under this heading in the annual mortality figures of the Registrar General: in the United States, there are well over half a million deaths each year from coronary artery disease. A large proportion of the cases reported to the coroner consist of deaths from ischaemic heart disease, as this is again easily the commonest single cause of *sudden* death.

This is not the place to discuss the detailed pathology of ischaemic heart disease, but a number of salient points might be mentioned in connection with fatal cases (Fig. 15):

1. Though coronary thrombosis is a common *clinical* diagnosis, it is seen in a minority of deaths at autopsy. Only about 20 per cent of cases reveal a thrombus in the coronary vessels, though it must be admitted that the frequency of finding it is directly proportional to the diligence of the search. Even so, most sudden deaths occur as the result of stenotic coronary atheroma, rather than fresh thrombus. In certifying death where the benefit of an autopsy has not been available, it is better to use one of the terms *coronary atheroma, atherosclerosis* or *coronary artery disease* rather than assume that thrombosis must have occurred.
2. In the sudden deaths reportable to the coroner, fresh myocardial infarction is also the exception rather than the rule. After a recent coronary occlusion, infarction of the distal myocardial may or may not occur, according to the efficiency of the collateral circulation. Even where the blood supply is cut off, infarction

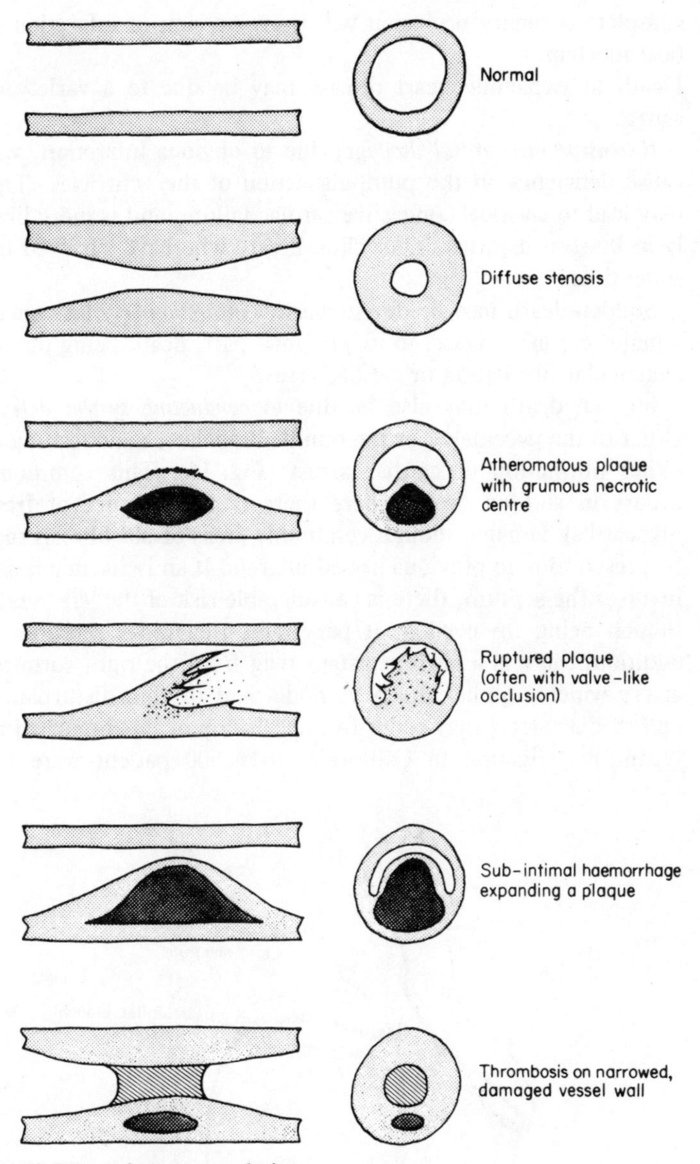

Fig. 15 Types of coronary occlusion

cannot be recognised naked-eye for at least 12–18 hours following occlusion, and even histological changes are not visible in less than 8–12 hours. By histochemical methods, infarcts can be detected after four hours, but this technique is not commonly employed. Thus any person dying in the first few hours after a complete coronary occlusion will show no sign of infarction at post-mortem.

3. Death in ischaemic heart disease may be due to a variety of causes.

Extensive myocardial damage, due to obvious infarction, will cause deficiency in the pumping action of the ventricles. This may lead to classical congestive cardiac failure, and is more likely to be seen in cases under clinical care who have survived for some time.

Sudden death may be due to *massive infarction* by blockage of a major coronary vessel in its proximal part, death being due to ventricular fibrillation or cardiac arrest.

Sudden death may also be due to *conducting system defects*, either of the pacemaker or the bundle branches, again leading to either fibrillation or cardiac arrest (Fig. 16). This commonly occurs in sudden death where there is no evidence of fresh myocardial damage, though commonly areas of old fibrosis may be present due to previous healed infarcts. If an ischaemic lesion involves the septum, there is considerable risk of the left bundle branch being involved as it penetrates the upper septum. In addition, there is a fairly constant twig from the right coronary artery which supplies the A.V. node, and rhythm disturbances and cardiac arrest may occur from occlusion of this branch. In a recent investigation in California, over 600 patient were fol-

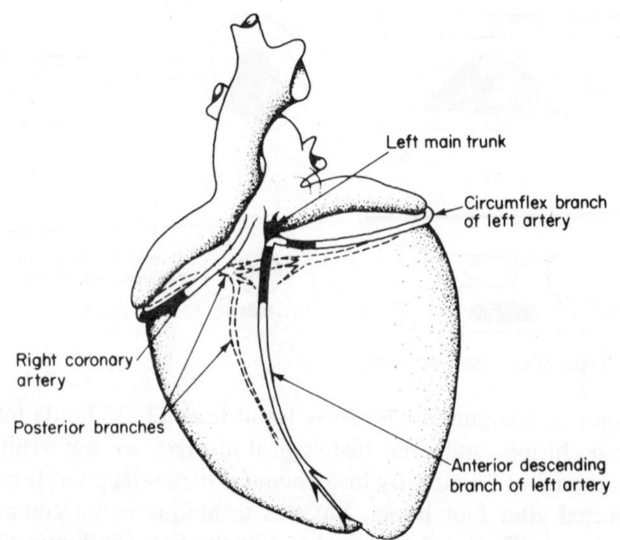

Fig. 16 Anatomy of coronary arteries, with most frequent sites of occlusion

lowed up who had been resuscitated after a cardiac arrest. The survival rate was better in those with a proven myocardial infarct, as opposed to those with diffuse myocardial ischaemia without an infarct.

Rupture of the heart may occur through a recent infarct causing a haemopericardium and fatal tamponade. This almost invariably occurs in the left ventricle, a ruptured right ventricle being so rare as to be a pathological curiosity. Rupture does not occur on the first day as sometimes stated, but is more usual on the second or third day and is commonest in senile hearts, especially in females. Occasionally, rupture of the septum may occur with striking clinical features due to left-right shunt.

Infarction of the papillary muscles is common, as they are at the termination of the coronary supply and suffer badly from reduced blood flow. Occasionally a papillary muscle may rupture, again leading to classical clinical signs.

Fibrotic plaques in the myocardium may lead to *cardiac aneurysms* but these almost never rupture, due to their tensile strength (Fig. 17).

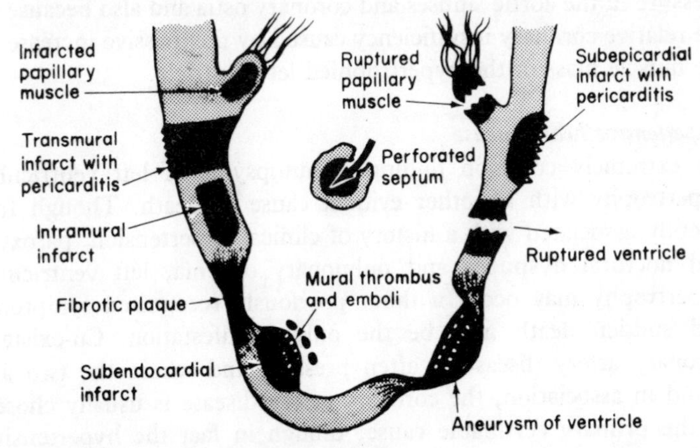

Fig. 17 Possible sequelae of coronary occlusion

Infarcts involving the endocardium almost invariably cause *mural thrombus*, parts of which may become detached and cause embolic infarcts in other organs, especially kidneys.

Where death is absolutely instantaneous, as opposed to a rapid death occupying a moment or two, the causes are almost always due to coronary artery disease, hypertensive heart disease or aortic stenosis. The mode of death is a cardiac arrest with sudden complete loss of pressure in the cerebral arteries, which causes the 'pole-axing' effect. Other rapidly fatal conditions, such as pulmonary embolism, massive cerebral haemorrhage etc., do not display the same instantaneous nature, where the person is 'dead' on hitting the ground. Exceptions naturally occur, but as a diagnostic aid in identifying the cause of death, these extremely rapid deaths can usually be confidently attributed to one of the three causes mentioned.

Aortic valve disease

Another frequent cause of sudden death, often instantaneous as mentioned above, is calcific aortic stenosis (Fig. 18). This is not related to rheumatic aortic valve disease but is a primary degenerative condition affecting the aortic valve, usually in men over the age of 60. Sometimes the valve is bicuspid, and it appears that a congenitally bicuspid valve has a considerable risk of calcific disease. Sometimes this bicuspid appearance is spurious, due to the fact that the degenerative process has destroyed one of the commissures of an originally tricuspid valve, leading to a bicuspid appearance. Sudden death is common in these cases, partly because of the low pressure in the aortic sinuses and coronary ostia and also because of the relative coronary insufficiency caused by the massive increase in the muscle mass of the hypertrophied left ventricle.

Hypertensive heart disease

An extremely common finding at autopsy is of left ventricular hypertrophy with no other evident cause of death. Though frequently associated with a history of clinical hypertension, paroxysmal noctural dyspnoea and pulmonary oedema, left ventricular hypertrophy may occur without previously recognised symptoms and sudden death may be the only manifestation. Co-existent coronary artery disease is often present, and where the two are found in association, the coronary artery disease is usually chosen as the primary certifiable cause, though in fact the hypertensive element may be either as important, or even pre-eminent. Pathologically, this was formerly a somewhat unsatisfactory diagnosis, but recently, gross enzyme deficiencies have been found in the myocardium in victims of sudden death from pure hypertensive heart disease. It would appear that a patient with an enlarged left ventricle and normal coronary arteries is in the same relative state of myocardial ischaemia as a patient with a normal sized left ventricle and stenosed coronary arteries. The frequent association of both conditions naturally makes the prognosis more serious.

The fact remains that a patient with hypertensive cardiac hyper-

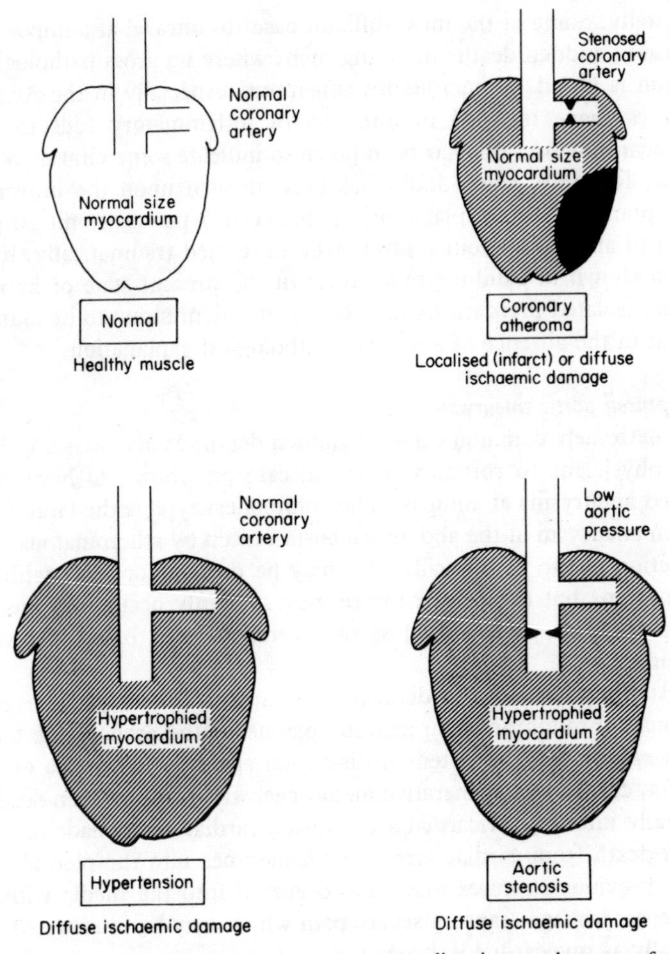

Fig. 18 Mechanisms of ischaemic damage to myocardium in several common fatal conditions

trophy is always a candidate for sudden death, either from the direct effect on the myocardium just described, or from a cerebrovascular accident.

Myocarditis

In spite of the misuse in the past of this term for the late results of ischaemic lesions in the myocardium, myocarditis is now recognised as a mixed bag of pathological conditions either arising as a sequel to specific infections, such as diphtheria or as a separate entity known as 'isolated, Fiedler's or Saphir's myocarditis'. It is usually found in young adults who have died suddenly and unexpectedly. Some of the most difficult cases to unravel at autopsy are those of sudden deaths in young men, where no gross pathological lesion is found. Numerous investigations, especially in the Armed Forces, have revealed minute foci of inflammatory cells in the myocardium and this has been taken to indicate some viral myocarditis. Recently, some doubt has been thrown upon the universal acceptance of this explanation, as between 5 per cent and 20 per cent of all healthy young adults who have died traumatically, have been shown to exhibit similar foci. In the present state of knowledge, isolated myocarditis may be a convenient straw to be clutched at in the absence of any other pathological explanation.

Ruptured aortic aneurysm

An extremely common cause of sudden death. Many cases ascribed by physicians to coronary artery disease are shown to have ruptured aneurysms at autopsy. The commonest type is the large fusiform aneurysm of the abdominal aorta caused by atheromatous destruction of the vessel wall. This may be present for years without symptoms but explosive rupture may suddenly occur into the retroperitoneal space, with loss of several litres of blood and very rapid death.

Another form is the dissecting aneurysm, which usually commences through an atheromatous plaque in the arch of the aorta and splits open the potential dissecting space in the media of the aorta, caused by degenerative medio-necrosis. Rupture then occurs, usually into the pericardial sac (causing cardiac tamponade or sudden death from cardiac arrest), or sometimes into the pleural cavity. Previous ruptures may have occurred into the media without external leakage, causing severe pain which may be interpreted clinically as myocardial ischaemia.

Syphilitic aneurysms are relatively rare, and have more chance of being diagnosed clinically before death by rupture. They almost always involved the aortic arch and may rupture into the pleural cavity or even the bronchus.

Pulmonary embolism

An extremely common cause of death, more frequent in women. There are certain features in many cases of pulmonary embolism which make diagnosis possible, even over the telephone. Death is not instantaneous as with ventricular fibrillation, but rapid, often accompanied by intense cyanosis and breathlessness. An important feature from the point of view of diagnosis, is the frequency with which pulmonary embolism occurs during defaecation. In an analysis of a large series, no less than 20 per cent were found to have occurred either in the toilet or on a bed-pan. Though pulmonary embolism classically occurs after trauma, surgical intervention or prolonged confinement to bed, a large proportion (about one-third of cases) occur in ambulant, otherwise healthy patients. In spite of what is said in some textbooks, varicose veins are rarely a significant predisposing factor. The peak incidence of embolism following fracture, soft tissue injury or surgical operation is about 14 days, but this is merely a mid-point of a wide range: cases can be expected from the first day after trauma, up to several months, though the longer periods may be associated with venous stasis due to bed rest or immobility. As part of a useful rule of thumb, death in a middle-aged woman is most frequently due to either a complication of pregnancy, subarachnoid haemorrhage or pulmonary embolism. Pulmonary embolism is the condition most unsuspected by clinicians when certifying death without the benefit of autopsy. A Birmingham investigation in 1977 revealed that less than half the deaths from pulmonary embolism were diagnosed before autopsy.

2. Central nervous system

As already stated, lesions in the central nervous system are themselves usually vascular.

Intracerebral haemorrhage

This is a frequent cause of rapid unexpected death, possibly heralded by previous 'strokes' or a history of hypertension. Death may occur within minutes or survival may be prolonged for months or even years. The acute deaths are almost never as spectacularly abrupt as those heart lesions causing cardiac arrest or fibrillation. The clinical spectrum of pre-mortal symptoms and signs in cerebral haemorrhage is very wide.

Subarachnoid haemorrhage

This is an important cause of death in the younger adult and middle-aged group, before coronary artery disease becomes the 'captain of the men of death'. Though there is little sex variation throughout the overall range of subarachnoid haemorrhage, the ones which appear to lead to sudden unexpected death without previous clinical symptoms tend to be more common in women. In fact, where a death is reported in a woman of child-bearing age, it is a useful maxim to assume that death is due to some complication of pregnancy until proved otherwise. Once an abortion or ectopic pregnancy etc., is eliminated (and numerically these are in the minority) the next most probable condition is subarachnoid haemorrhage from a ruptured berry aneurysm. Though cases which come to surgical notice often have had a previous bleed, the ones which are seen first at autopsy usually have had no recognised premonitory episode, though this may have occurred in a minor fashion and been dismissed as a severe headache or migraine. The cause is almost always a rupture of a berry aneurysm on the basal cerebral vessels, usually on the circle of Willis at the junction of one of the major vessels with a communicating vessel. Death may be very rapid, but is certainly not of the instantaneous variety associated with cardiac arrest. There is often a latent period of neurological signs and possibly coma, though some are extremely rapid in their course.

Other C.N.S. lesions

Other C.N.S. lesions may be associated with sudden death if an acute complication arises, such as haemorrhage into a cerebral tumour. These are undiagnosable without autopsy, unless previous clinical diagnosis has been made visible. One other important C.N.S. condition can give rise to sudden death, viz. epilepsy. It was formerly taught that death from epilepsy was always associated with severe and prolonged status epilepticus. This is not so, and epileptics, like asthmatics, appear to be able to drop dead for no demonstrable reason. Some epileptics die because they have a fit whilst lying on their face during sleep, when classically asphyxial changes may be found. However, numerous cases come to coroner's autopsy where nothing but a history of grand mal is available, and no visible pathological lesions are found, though bitten tongues and lips should be sought and the possibility of either barbiturate overdose or withdrawal convulsions borne in mind.

Other systems

Again miscellaneous conditions leading to sudden unexpected death are almost always vascular in origin. Massive intra-abdominal haemorrhage either from a bleeding peptic ulcer or from an ectopic pregnancy may cause death in a few minutes, though usually there is time for removal to hospital and attempted treatment.

A ruptured viscus may occasionally cause rapid death, sometimes clinically undiagnosed. Perforated peptic ulcer (usually duodenal) may cause a widespread chemical peritonitis and rupture of a colonic tumour or diverticulitis may again give rise to a fulminating faecal peritonitis. Other conditions in the abdomen which lead to death are massive infarction of the intestine due to mesenteric embolism or thrombosis. Supra-renal haemorrhage (frequently bilateral) is not uncommon and most often follows trauma or stress, usually a few days after some injury or surgical intervention. Meningococcal infection is well-known to precipitate supra-renal haemorrhage (Waterhouse-Friedrichsen syndrome). Sometimes a volvulus or even strangulated hernia may lead to death before a clinical diagnosis is made. These are hardly sudden, unexpected deaths, but may occur in persons who do not seek medical aid and are found dead at home.

Sudden death in asthmatics is by no means unknown, and like epilepsy need not be a sequel to prolonged severe status asthmaticus. A marked rise in deaths amongst asthmatics occurred twenty years ago, and suspicion has been directed towards the over-use of broncho-dilator inhalants, which, if used to excess, may cause cardio-vascular toxicity due to their adrenergic properties. Probably many of the unexplained sudden deaths in asthmatics were due to this cause, and recent recognition and publicity of the dangers of over-indulgence in such aerosols, seems to have reduced the number of fatalities.

Apart from asthma (and probably the 'cot death syndrome') sudden death from respiratory disease is not common, though some fulminating virus pneumonias may cause rapid death within a matter of hours. The autopsy findings reveal an intensely bluish-black, congested, oedematous lung, often with frank haemorrhages. Massive haemoptysis from pulmonary lesions is not a common cause of death at the present day, but occasionally is still seen due to cavitating tuberculosis or bronchial carcinomas.

14

Injury and death from physical agents

Once again, though the detailed examination of fatal cases due to extremes of temperature, electricity, and so on, are the province of the forensic pathologist, every practitioner should have knowledge of the basic facts for reporting on non-fatal cases and on external appearances where death has occurred.

TEMPERATURE

Hypothermia

A not uncommon condition, even in the relatively mild climate of Britain. Recognition of this entity has increased greatly over the past few years. The extremes of life tend to be more affected, babies, children and aged persons being more at risk. However, in particularly severe winters, cases of young adults are reported, especially in those of subnormal or schizoid tendencies who may live alone in circumstances of self-neglect. Externally, the only significant feature may be an abnormal brownish-pink colour of the skin, especially over extensor surfaces and large joints such as the knees, elbows and hips. This redness is due to oxygenated blood remaining in the surface capillaries, there having been no metabolic activity at the low temperature to reduce the oxyhaemoglobin. There may sometimes be actual necrosis of the skin and sometimes blistering, but the characteristic brownish-pink colour is most commonly seen. Unfortunately, fatal hypothermia can occur without any post-mortem indication whatsoever.

This pink colour may also be seen in bodies exposed to cold *after* death, and is a notable feature of bodies recoverd from cold water or after refrigeration. The colour may sometimes be confused with that of carbon monoxide poisoning, but the tint is different and spectroscopy of blood will differentiate the two. Frost-bite of the fingers or toes is occasionally seen in this country, not only in mountaineers, cavers etc., exposed to extremes of weather, but also in babies and old persons exposed at home. The 'sudden death in infancy syndrome' has sometimes been acribed to hypothermia, though the facts of most cases are incompatible. Several cases of frank necrosis of the extremities have been described in infants in this country, who were neglected and lay in damp, urine-soaked cots in unheated rooms, usually in rural surroundings.

Generalised hypothermia is usually seen in old, often emaciated persons suffering from self-neglect. Progressive apathy, stupor, coma and the above-mentioned skin changes may be seen during life and the temperature drop to 80–85° F (26–29° C) or less. Recovery is rare when the temperature falls to 75° F (23° C).

Internal appearances include gastric ulceration, patches of fat necrosis, pulmonary oedema with diffuse lung haemorrhages and sometimes a pancreatitis associated with local abdominal fat necrosis. In the case of elderly persons, there may sometimes be evidence of pre-existing myxoedema.

Hyperthermia

This is even more rare in temperate climates than hypothermia, and is usually confined to working spaces which are abnormally overheated, such as boiler-rooms. Two forms exist, *heat exhaustion* – a less serious condition due to excessive sweat loss and chloride depletion, leading to faintness, muscle cramps and collapse with circulatory failure, and *heat stroke* – where breakdown of the physiological heat controlling systems occur and hyperpyrexia up to 108° F (42° C) or more may occur. This latter condition is virtually confined to tropical climates, and is closely related to humidity as well as temperature, being heralded by delirium, photophobia and convulsions. Suppression of sweat is a feature and this may be precipitated or worsened by use of drugs such as atropine or phenothiazine. 'Malignant hyperthermia' is a relatively recently described condition, which usually occurs during anaesthesia due to the action of certain drugs (such as halothane or suxamethonium) upon patients who suffer from some congenital muscle disorders.

BURNS

The following features are of importance in the examination and reporting of external burns.

1. An estimate of the total body surface involved. Recovery can occur after a considerable area has been involved even by second degree burns, but this area is related to age, the prognosis becoming worse with advance in years. Children may survive having half their body surface burnt, but in old age, 10–20 per cent may prove fatal. As a general rule (in adults), the outlook is very poor if a third or more of the body surface in involved. A rough estimate of the area involved may be arrived at by 'the Rule of Nine', i.e. assessing each limb as 9 per cent and the front and back of the trunk as 18 per cent each of total surface area, the remainder being made up of head, neck, perineum etc.

2. *The severity of the burns in various areas.* Though the older surgical classification gave six degrees of burning, it is sufficient for description purposes to employ the following:

First degree – erythema and vesiculation.

Second degree – full thickness burning of the skin with exposure of underlying tissue.

Third degree – complete destruction with carbonisation, exposing muscle and possibly bone.

3. *Differentiation between ante-mortem and post-mortem burns.* Though both are commonly present, it is the absence of ante-mortem burns that raises the presumption that death was due to other causes, possibly criminal. Where death occurs very soon after the burning, it may be impossible to state definitely that a burn is ante-mortem, and various sophisticated histological techniques, including enzymes, have been developed to assist in this differention. For practical purposes, the presence of a bright marginal zone of reddening is the most useful sign. Blisters may be present on either ante-mortem or post-mortem burns and the distribution of the burns relative to the circumstances at the scene may be or may not be compatible with having been received before death. It has been said that it is possible to distinguish ante-mortem blisters from post-mortem bullae by the chemical content of their contained fluid. The ante-mortem blisters are alleged to have a highly proteinaceous fluid as opposed to the more serous post-mortem lesions, but in practice this differentiation is almost never useful. In fact, where the burns occurred perimortally i.e. within minutes of death, there is no satisfactory method of differentiation and even the most sophisticated histochemical techniques are rarely of assistance.

4. *Signs of injury other than burns* must be looked for, not only potential marks of foul play, but injuries from the falling fabric of a building or furniture, etc.

5. *The colour of the skin* may give some indication that carbon monoxide has been inhaled in considerable quantities, again pointing to the fact of the person being alive during the fire. These points will be further clarified by post-mortem examination, when chemical examination of the blood for carbon monoxide and

examination of the air passages for soot will confirm the fact of life during the conflagration. It should be appreciated that though the presence of carbon monoxide in the blood and tissues is firm evidence that the victim was alive during the fire, the converse is certainly not true. Numerous cases are on record where undisputed evidence of ante-mortem burning was present, with a complete absence of monoxide or bronchial soot. House fires with burning furniture, upholstery, carpets and curtains etc., produce large volumes of sooty smoke and carbon monoxide which are frequently the cause of death rather than burning, the bodies being either unburnt on recovery or having post-mortem burns. In flash fires such as vehicles involving petrol conflagrations, the amount of monoxide produced may be less and they are also usually in outdoor surroundings. In addition, the fierceness of the fire usually causes very rapid death, so that a low or even absent monoxide and soot content may be found at autopsy.

In addition to carbon monoxide, the victims of fires may die wholly or partly as the result of the inhalation of other poisonous fumes. Burning plastic in particular gives rise to very toxic substances, including cyanide and other nitrogen-containing gases which may be rapidly fatal when inhaled.

6. *Certain apparent injuries* must be recognised as being the effects of heat. Where a body suffers third degree burns, there is often tearing of the body surface at joints such as elbows and shoulders, and commonly tearing of the scalp due to contraction of the skin through heat. The tissues may be very brittle and may be severely damaged post-mortem from movement by firemen or undertakers; these injuries must not be misinterpreted. Similarly, internal artefacts may occur, notably a spurious 'extra-dural haematoma', which is common where heat has been applied to the outside of the head. The limbs are frequently drawn up into flexure contractures, the classical 'pugilistic attitude'.

7. *Alcohol*. Where an adult is found dead in a burned bed or where there are other features suggestive of alcoholic intoxication, examination of the blood for alcohol should be performed. A common cause of death by burning follows from an inebriated person going to bed whilst smoking, then dropping a lighted cigarette into the bedclothes. He may die either of burns, carbon monoxide poisoning or a combination of both.

The distribution of the burns may be suggestive, as when the pyjamas or nightdress of a person (all too often a child) catches alight whilst standing near a hearth. Burns will then be on the front of the thighs, abdomen, face and possibly hair.

8. The possibility of natural death before burning must be considered. A not uncommon occurrence is of a person in middle or old age collapsing forwards on to a lighted fire, sometimes whilst in the act of putting on the kettle or poking the fire. As discovery may be delayed for some time, the most gross burning can occur in an already dead victim, but in favourable circumstances, an autopsy will still reveal the presence of natural disease sufficient to explain sudden death.

9. Certain burns are suggestive of various circumstances. Slight burns on the inner sides of the thighs of a woman less than 50, should raise the suspicion of attempted resuscitation after abortion, a hot water bottle having been used in a desperate attempt to revive the collapsed victim. Another frequent burn with a hot water bottle is seen between the elbow and the side of the chest (sometimes obviously post-mortem) where an effort has been made to resuscitate a dying patient. Burns from hot water bottles and electric blankets can be severe, in that although the temperature is relatively low, the time of application may be prolonged. This has particular medico-legal aspects in negligence actions against hospital nursing staffs.

10. Suicide by burning is now no longer a rare curiosity. The circumstances will usually be obvious, and if paraffin or petrol is used, there may be typical distribution of burning due to trickling of fluid and the sparing of certain areas, such as the cleft of the buttocks and between the thighs. The same applies to burning by corrosives such as acids and alkalis, which again will show gravitational trickling effects, with sparing of areas inaccessible to the corrosive fluid.

11. Scalding by hot liquids is particularly common in children, and is by no means unknown as a deliberate act as part of the 'battered child' syndrome. Even dipping of children into very hot water as a deliberate act is on record, and the presence of a horizontal margin to the burns may be of considerable significance.

Deaths from burns may be due to a variety of causes. Massive tissue destruction with associated shock is common, and the combination of carbon monoxide poisoning is a potent factor in house fires. Here it may be of some comfort to relatives to emphasise that unconsciousness, due to carbon monoxide poisoning, may mercifully have reduced or obliterated the painful effects of the burns.

Later fatal sequelae of burns include sepsis of the skin area, tubular necrosis leading to anuria, gross fluid and electrolyte disturbances due to exudation from the burnt areas and bronchopneumonias and respiratory-passage damage from flame or irritant gases (sometimes leading to laryngeal oedema). Adrenal failure and haemorrhage may occur several days later, and gastric and pulmonary haemorrhages may take place. The defibrination syndrome is also a well-known sequel to burns.

A very localised form of fire which may present difficulties in interpretation is that of almost total destruction of a body which is lying near a hearth of other source of draught. Under these circumstances, the body fat may burn, sometimes with the clothing as a 'wick', and almost complete destruction of the body may occur with minimal damage to the premises, though penetration of the carpet and even floor boards is not uncommon. The victim is usually an obese woman, who either collapses into a hearth or ignites her clothing in a similar position.

ELECTROCUTION

Electrical considerations

The domestic supply in Britain is about the most lethal combination that could have been devised. The voltage of around 240 volts is sufficient to cause muscle spasm and thus a 'hold-on' effect, so that a live conductor may not be able to be released. At the same time, it is too low to cause a 'throw-off', a phenomenon which accounts for the survival of many persons who have come into contact with high tension conductors. Similarly, the frequency of the cycle of the alternating current, viz. 50, is in the middle of the most lethal range for causing cardiac fibrillation. The Continental and American voltage of 110 at 60 cycles is much safer, though still potentially fatal.

Electrocution is rare at less than 100 volts, and most fatal cases occur at more than 200 volts. The lethal factor is the current flowing through the body at the existing voltage, and this in turn depends upon skin resistance and earthing.

Where earthing of the body is poor, as with dry or rubber-soled shoes, carpets, wooden floors and upstairs premises, then fatal electrocution is unlikely. The converse is true where damp conditions, metal-studded shoes, damp concrete floors or metal plating is present, especially out-of-doors (Fig. 19). This also explains the dangerous nature of the bathroom, where metal baths, copper and lead piping all constitute an almost perfect 'earth'. The resistance of the skin varies greatly, according to its dryness. Again, wet skin in the bathroom may have a ten-fold reduction in resistance compared to dry skin, and even the presence of perspiration may increase the hazard. The thick skin of palms and soles if dry, may have a resistance as much as 1 000 000 ohms, but wet skin may offer resistance of as little as 300 ohms. The current passing from entry to earthing point will be dangerous to life if more than 50 milliamperes, but prolonged contact allowing even much lower current to pass, may still be extremely dangerous.

60 mA for more than a second is very dangerous and the critical current very likely to cause death is anything in excess of 100 mA at 50 cycles A.C. for only one-fifth of a second.

Direct current is much less dangerous, the critical amperage being about 200 mA. With a current above 4 A, it may in fact cause a fibrillating heart to revert to normal rhythym.

The direction of the current is also important, as if the contact point is in one upper limb, and the earthing point in the opposite foot, then the current will pass across the chest in a diagonal direction and be most likely to produce myocardial fibrillation. Slightly less dangerous are currents from one arm to the other, and contacts in the lower part of the body may not cause fibrillation at all. Currents across the head without earthing lower in the body may not affect the heart, but may cause brain stem effects with central respiratory paralysis.

Nature of the electrical lesion on the skin

The appearances of the contact points on the body will vary according to the nature of the contact and of the current.

1. Where domestic voltage is applied by means of firm contact (such as a finger gripping a flat conductor with considerable pressure, possibly due to spasmodic muscle contraction), the commonest lesion is a raised blister, containing either gas or a little fluid. This *firm contact lesion* is characteristic, and often seen on the pads of the fingers or thumb.

2. A poor or intermittent contact will produce the *spark burn*, which is a dry pitted lesion (often very tiny) due to arcing of current from the conductor to the skin. A yellowish parchment-like scab may form with a surrounding ring of pallor due to capillary contraction forming an areola around the centre dimple. These lesions may be multiple but still extremely hard to find, especially on the calloused hands of a workman. The presence of rigor mortis makes them even more difficult to find on hands, as they may frequently be in the skin creases on the flexor surface of firmly contracted fingers. Similar lesions may be seen on the soles of the feet where metal studs in the boots have arced to the skin.

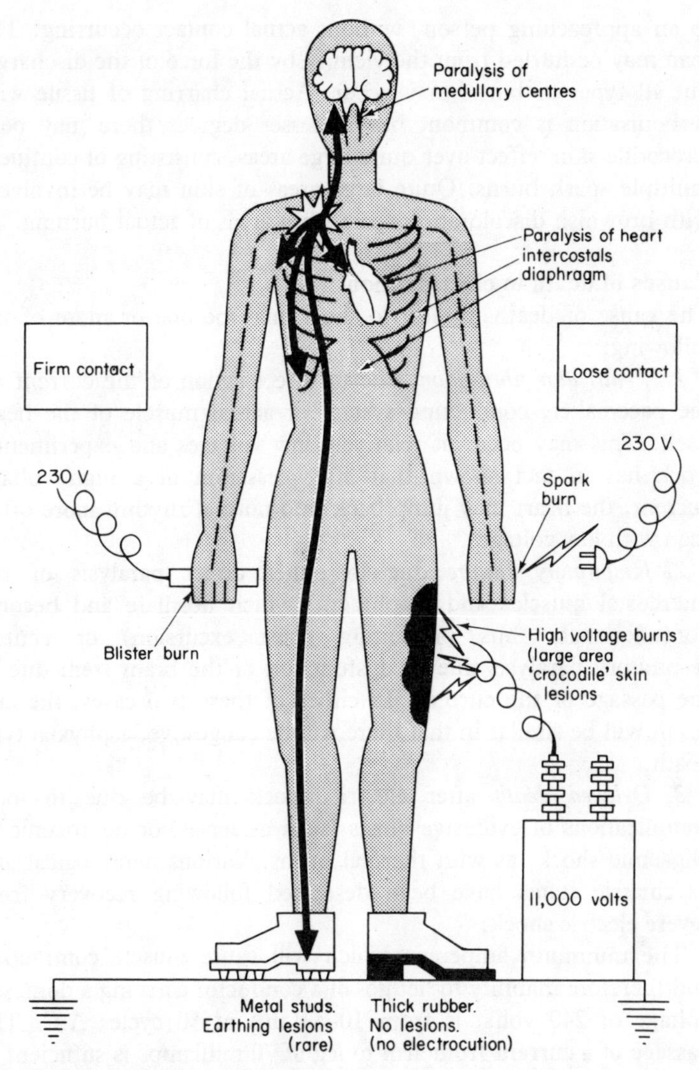

Fig. 19 Essential features of electrocution

Commonly, however, there is no earthing point visible, as the sole of the foot, often dampened by perspiration, conducts over a large area.

3. With high voltages, the main feature may be actual *thermal burns*, sometimes involving a large area of the body. These are seen in lines-men working on the Grid system and sometimes in thieves who are stealing copper high-voltage overhead lines. With very high voltages, such as 33 000, there may be actual arcing of current

to an approaching person, without actual contact occurring. The man may be hurled from the vicinity by the force of the discharge, but all types of burns may occur. Actual charring of tissue with carbonisation is common, but in lesser degrees there may be a 'crocodile skin' effect over quite large areas, consisting of confluent multiple spark burns. Quite large areas of skin may be involved, with brownish discoloration apart from areas of actual burning.

Causes of death in electrocution

The cause of death in electric shock may be one or more of the following:

1. *Ventricular fibrillation*, due to direct action of the current on the pacemaker, conducting system or actual muscle of the heart itself. This may occur at relatively low voltages and experimental work has in fact shown that after cessation of a high voltage current, the heart may jump back into normal rhythm more often than with low voltages.

2. *Respiratory failure* due to either direct paralysis of the intercostal muscles and diaphragm (which fibrillate and become nonfunctional, thus preventing chest excursion) or central respiratory paralysis due to dysfunction of the brain stem due to the passage of the current. In either of these two cases, the end result will be similar in that there will be congestive, asphyxial type death.

3. *Delayed death* after electric shock may be due to local complications of extensive burns (such as sepsis) or neurogenic or oligaemic shock, as with thermal burns. Various neurological and psychiatric states have been described following recovery from severe electric shock.

The minimum amperage which will cause muscle contraction and therefore inability to 'let go' of a conductor carrying a domestic voltage of 240 volts, is from 10–60 mA at 50 cycles A.C. The passage of a current from arm to leg of 70 milliamps is sufficient to cause fatal ventricular fibrillation.

The differentiation on external appearances of the various types of fatal electrocution, is confined to distinction between asphyxial and nonasphyxial deaths. Where ventricular fibrillation occurs, there may be relative pallor or normal coloration of the body, but with the respiratory paralysis, either of the muscles or the respiratory centre, there may be a gross cyanosis, sometimes petechial haemorrhages in the skin and eyes and extreme congestion of all organs at autopsy.

Electrocution in one condition in which autopsy provides very little additional information to external examination. Although extremely minute and subtle histological changes have been described, especially in electron microscopy, in general there is little to see internally, apart from gross congestion in the asphyxial type cases. Some of the older histological descriptions are fallacious.

From the clinical point of view, one of the most important things to remember about electrocution is the surprisingly long periods of apnoea or fibrillation which may be consistent with eventual recovery. Artificial respiration and cardiac massage are probably nowhere so useful and potentially successful as in electrocution. Recovery has been reported after several hours' artificial respiration following apparent fatal collapse from an electric shock.

15

Wounding

Wounds may be seen either upon the living patient presenting for treatment or upon the dead body. Examination of the latter is almost always the concern of the pathologist, and the minute description of the pathology of trauma is a specialist subject outside the aims of this book. However, practitioners and especially hospital casualty officers are not infrequently faced with a wounded patient, and may later be requested to write a report or to give evidence in court. Where a patient subsequently dies, the clinician may be called upon to assist the coroner in his enquires, or even proceed to a Crown Court if a criminal charge is brought.

However expert the clinical diagnosis and treatment may be, the doctor frequently fails to describe the injuries adequately or fails to make a proper (or any) record. These deficiencies may later be all too obvious, sometimes to the doctor's acute discomfort in court.

Preparing the report on a wounded patient

Naturally, the doctor should first obtain consent to examine and treat, though naturally the emergency situation of most woundings means that the consent is either implied or the patient is in no fit condition to be bothered with legal niceties – indeed, not infrequently, he is unconscious.

Consent to the submission of the report itself should also be obtained from the patient, but in actual practice, he has often been long discharged from hospital by the time the report is requested. It then has to be constructed from the clinical record, which is a powerful argument for the prompt writing-up of every case immediately it is dealt with by the doctor.

As the patient is usually the aggrieved party in an assault case, it is often assumed that he will be only too glad to assist in bringing the assailant to justice, so express consent to the making of report is not sought. Theory and practice often diverge, but the risks of failing to obtain such consent must be pointed out.

No further measures than examination, diagnosis and treatment must be taken without explanation and further consent. Foremost in this connection is the taking of blood for alcohol analysis. As with vehicle accidents, blood should not be taken for alcohol analysis without the patient's express permission, and if an analysis is conducted on a sample of blood taken for other clinical tests, the result should not in any circumstances be communicated to the police, without the patient's permission. In instances where this has been done, the defence counsel has successfully applied for the evidence to be rejected in court.

Where an injured patient (usually from a traffic accident) has been admitted to hospital, the police may request a blood sample for alcohol estimation. This should not be taken by the treating doctor, but if he considers that his patient's condition would not be adversely affected, he can give his consent to the police, calling a police surgeon to take the sample. Naturally, it is the responsibility of the police surgeon to obtain consent for this from the patient.

Where the wounds appear to have been caused by some criminal action, particular care should be taken in the report. The number of wounds (trivial and otherwise) should be carefully listed and described both as to size, position and appearance. The best method is to mark them on an outline sketch of the body, either on a printed form used for clinical purposes, or upon a rough sketch. The apparent age of the lesions should be noted, as there may be mixed injuries of different ages.

A general assessment of the severity of major injuries should be made, especially as to their potential danger to life or to permanent maiming, though detailed opinions of this nature are usually left to an expert consultant.

The general clinical condition of the patient should be evaluated, and any pre-existing natural disease noted. Where practicable, photographs of lesions should be taken as with transient injuries, this is the only way of recording the true appearance soon after infliction.

TYPES OF EXTERNAL INJURY

Many of the appearances described below apply equally to accidental and suicidal injuries, as well as deliberate wounding.

1. Abrasions

An abrasion is a superficial wound of the body surface which does not penetrate the full thickness of the skin. Though rarely a danger to life, large areas of abraded skin can cause extreme pain and severe bleeding. Abrasions are seen at their worst in the 'brush' abrasions of traffic accidents, where a body is projected across the rough gravel surface of a road, causing linear 'skid' grazes, sometimes over an extensive area of skin, especially buttock, thigh and chest.

Abrasions may be caused by a limitless variety of objects. The direction of impact can often be defined by noting the small skin tags which are found at the further end, where the striking object left the skin surface. When a weapon strikes the body, the skin tags will indicate the direction and angle of the blow. Where, as in the traffic injury described above, the body itself is moving across a stationary surface, the direction of movement will be equally obvious, this sometimes being of use in reconstructing the circumstances of an accident.

Abrasions frequently take a fairly detailed impression of the shape of the object causing them, more so than with a diffuse lesion like a bruise. Some very characteristic marks may be imprinted as abrasions, especially the tread of motor tyres, the weave of coarse fabrics, the spiral of electric cables and ropes, the honeycomb pattern of the older-type vehicle radiator and numerous other easily recognisable objects. Shattered wind-screen glass leaves characteristic abrasions on the faces of those sitting in the front seats of a motor vehicle. Numerous Y and V shaped cuts, as well as linear scratches and square or triangular pits are left on the skin, often with blunt fragments of glass embedded. These features may be of vital importance in a criminal case, and as the lesions are not permanent, should be recorded by a faithful drawing or preferably a photograph.

Foreign bodies are more usually found in deeper wounds, but abrasions may contain small particles of matter which might assist in interpretation. Traffic injuries often contain road dirt, grease, and even fragments of glass. In a case with medico-legal implications, any foreign body removed either during surgical toilet or operative cleansing, should be retained for possible forensic examination. Due attention should be given to the 'continuity of evidence' mentioned elsewhere, and such objects should be properly labelled and handed to an identified police officer with no intermediary messengers to confuse the chain of evidence. The same considerations apply to blood samples sent for blood grouping etc.

Once more, it should be remembered that the patient's consent is necessary before handing any such material or reports to the police or solicitors: though this is strictly the case in law, it is not carried out in practice. In some hospitals, internal regulations require the permission of the consultant before such disclosures are made, but this is not a legally valid alternative to the consent of the patient.

Abrasions seen on the surface of a dead body often differ from those of the live patient, in that, after death, the abraded epidermis becomes leathery and dark in colour. The pattern of any object is still retained, for example, the woven or spiral pattern of a rope seen in a suicidal hanging. Abrasions and bruises frequently become much more apparent following the first day after death, especially when the body is refrigerated. The appearance of a body when seen fresh may be totally different to that when seen the next day for identification purposes before the police. Due allowance must be made for this post-mortem accentuation of surface lesions.

2. Bruises (contusions)

Bruising is the subcutaneous escape of blood from small vessels, due to a blunt impact which may not rupture the skin. Bruises may be seen in association with abrasions or lacerations, when the skin lesion often obscures the underlying bruise.

Due to the intervention of surface tissues, the bruise does not follow faithfully the shape of the wounding weapon, though sometimes a rough approximation can be discerned. Bruises vary in severity according to the site and nature of the tissue struck, even when the force of the impact is the same. Thus it is virtually impossible to bruise the palm of the hand or the sole of the foot, where there is thick skin and dense fibrotic stroma beneath. Conversely, lax tissues such as the orbit, cheek, neck and abdominal wall, bruise readily. The orbit is the most vulnerable, giving rise to the common 'black eye'.

Where skin is tightly stretched across bone, bruising may be very prominent. Bruises are then seen on the scalp, the cheek bones, the temple, jaw and over the ribs. In such sites, the subcutaneous tissues can be easily compressed against unyielding bone beneath.

The shape of some bruises is characteristic; on the chest, a row of small disc-shaped bruises may indicate a knuckle impact. Parallel 'tram-line' bruises on the trunk, arms or legs may indicate impact of a rod-shaped weapon, especially one of circular section such as a broom-handle.

For a given impact, there may be a vastly different degree of bruising. Children and senile victims bruise most easily, the bruising of old persons often being grossly disproportionate to the force inflicted. In senile purpuric conditions, even finger pressure may produce ugly and long-persistent bruising. Similarly, in patients with blood-clotting disorders, the dermal haemorrhages may be severe.

When writing a report on bruises, some estimate of the age should be made, though this is an extremly inaccurate exercise. A fresh bruise is pink or purple depending on the amount of blood visible through the semi-translucent epidermis. The progression of colour changes is usually from purple to brown to greenish-yellow, the time taken for these changes depending both on the amount of extravasated blood and upon the general physical state of the victims. Again, old people tend to be extremely slow in dispersing their bruises, and in really senile patients, large bruises may persist indefinitely. In the 'average' bruise caused by a fist upon a healthy adult, the full range of colour changes may be seen within the first week, and the bruise may well fade completely within a couple of weeks, though this generalisation is so vague as to be virtually useless.

Bruising, as well as abrasions, may have special significance when found in certain sites. Bruising upon the neck, especially small disc-shaped bruises suggestive of fingers, may be indicative of attempted strangulation. In children, the so-called 'six-penny' bruises are characteristic of gripping by an adult hand, multiple bruises of about 1–2 cm diameter being caused by the finger-tips, usually in a group of 3–5. These are situated around the large joints, such as elbow and knee. In adults, especially women, they may be seen on the upper arm or forearm, from forcible gripping by an assailant. Bruises between the thighs and upon the lower abdomen and perineum may be seen in rape or attempted rape, and some similar bruises are not infrequent during attempts at criminal abortion. Bruises and abrasions (often contaminated with earth or vegetation) are classically seen upon the buttocks and back of the genuine sexual assaults taking place outdoors. In general, the examination of alleged sexual assaults provides one of the most important occasions upon which bruises and abrasions should be searched for and recorded with meticulous care.

Some controversy has arisen in the past as to whether bruises can be produced post-mortem. They most certainly can, though a more severe degree of injury is needed to produce a visible bruise. The ministrations of heavy-handed undertakers and removal of bodies from awkward places can certainly cause abrasions and bruises on the cadaver. These may not be distinguishable from ante-mortem bruises without sophisticated techniques such as enzyme histochemistry; even these are useless if the injuries occurred less than about one hour before death.

3. Lacerations

These are wounds which penetrate the full thickness of the skin and have been caused by a relatively blunt injury as opposed to a sharp slash with a knife-like weapon. Lacerations of all varieties are seen both in criminal assaults and in accidental injuries, notably traffic accidents. The description in a report is straightforward, again bearing in mind the special circumstances of every case and the need for the retention of any foreign bodies removed by surgical debridement.

Certain types of laceration need particular mention: the skin on a limb may sometimes be 'flayed', that is, stripped off a large area of muscle by the rolling action of a rotating wheel. In criminal assaults especially, some lacerations may closely resemble the clean-cut wound produced by a knife, though in fact it is the result of a blunt injury. This usually happens where the skin in stretched over a bony surface, especially the scalp, cheek bone, shin, etc. Close examination will always distinguish these from an incised wound, as there is invariably crushing of the wound margins, though it may be very narrow. In its usual site, on the scalp, hairs will be forced into the wound, and examination with a lens will reveal inversion of the wound edges with bruising in the immediate vicinity, which does not happen with an incised wound. Though such lacerations may bleed profusely, the haemorrhage is often noticeably less than with an incised wound, as the blunt trauma tends to retract and occlude the ends of torn vessels, rather than slice through them cleanly.

4. Incised wounds

These are of two varieties, the slashed wound and the stab wound, which differ basically only in that the latter is deeper than it is long and *vice versa*.

The dangerous properties of a slashed wound depend upon the site and the depth. Injuries to the neck and where large blood vessels are near the surface, such as the groin, front of the elbow and wrist are especially dangerous. The wound gapes according to its relation to skin creases, muscle planes and other features. When reporting on such slashes, it is of particular importance to measure the length, the direction and the angle, as this assists in reconstructing the traumatic event. The direction of travel of the knife is not always easy to decide, but usually the deeper part of the wound is near the end which was inflicted first, the knife or other weapon tending to rise more superficially as it leaves the body. Very little can be deduced about the nature of the weapon causing a slash, apart from its probable sharpness or bluntness, which may be determined by the raggedness or otherwise of the wound edges.

The stab wound offers much more to be learned about the weapon, though much of this comes from the deep inspection of the wound at autopsy, rather than an examination of the superficial appearances. The inspection of the wound is a poor guide to the width of the knife blade, for two reasons: (a) the skin tends to retract after withdrawal of the blade, so that the length of the wound shortens and the lateral width slightly increases: (b) a knife is rarely plunged in and removed in a perfectly perpendicular way, so that there is some rocking of the blade which tends to make the wound wider than the weapon. The shape of the blade may sometimes be deduced by the extremities of the wound. A blade with a single cutting edge and a blunt back may show corresponding appearances in the wound, whereas a two-edged dagger may cause very sharply cut edges at either end. Some knives, such as a scout's sheath-knife, may have serrations at the top of the blunt edge, which may leave a wide ragged margin at one end. However, even a one-edged blade may leave a wound with sharp extremities at either end, as the skin may split at the blunt end.

When such a wound is seen in the casualty department, any foreign material removed during cleansing must be preserved. In the case of a dead person seen by a doctor, though the matter will soon be one for the forensic pathologist, the police may proffer a suspect weapon and ask for a quick opinion as to whether it was consistent with the knife used. Any temptation to put the weapon in close proximity to the wound must be resisted, as this might ruin any forensic examination for blood stains.

5. Other objects which can cause injury

Almost any object can be used to produce an abrasion, bruise or laceration, but some leave characteristic marks. The head of a hammer, especially when applied to the scalp may leave a characteristically round impression; broken glass can inflict injuries identical with those of knives, and the multiple lesions caused by a shattered windscreen are easily recognisable.

Murder, suicide or accident?

Though most injuries could have been inflicted in one of several ways, there are certain characteristic patterns. Easily the most recognisable is the suicidal injury, where tentative preliminary cuts are extremely common. Both cutting of the throat and the wrists is almost invariably preceded by experimental superficial cuts, sometimes very numerous. A suicidal cut-throat may exhibit numbers of parallel scratches on either side of the eventual main wound, and if the person is right-handed, will normally be deeper on the left side of the neck and tend to slope downwards towards the right. Similarly, there may be several superficial scratches or slashes upon the wrists with or without a major deeper wound. Though homicidal cut-throats are rare in Britain, they seldom show multiple incisions, there being a single deep slash.

In addition to linear incised wounds in suicide, self-stabbing is not uncommon, and certain sites of predilection exist. These include the neck and wrists, the front of the chest (especially over the imagined heart area on the left) and on the abdomen. Multiple severe stab wounds are common in suicide, even though more than one wound would appear to be instantly fatal. Several definite suicides have recently been reported where stab wounds have been deliberately made through the upper part of the neck near the angle of the jaw, but these are uncommon. Stab wounds on the right side of the chest, lateral or posterior parts of the thorax, and in the obviously inaccessible sites such as the neck of centre of the back, arouse grave suspicion of foul play. The same applies to suicidal shooting, the favoured areas being the temple, mouth, and front of chest. As will be mentioned in the section on fire-arm injuries, it is extremely uncommon for a female to shoot herself, and such a case should be viewed with suspicion until any alternative to suicide is excluded. Though suicides tend to favour the above-mentioned areas, there may occasionally be injuries to the genitals (often gross in character) where some masochistic element exists.

Attention should always be directed to the rest of the body as well as the obvious wounds. Defence cuts on the front and back of the fingers, forearms and bruising of the arms may indicate resistance to an assailant. The clothing should be carefully retained in such a way that the orientation of any cuts is preserved.

HEAD INJURIES

Head injuries constitute one of the most difficult realms of accident medicine, both from the technical and medico-legal points of view. Many actions for negligence have arisen from failure to view head injuries with sufficient concern and the doctor's procedure when dealing with a head injury must be coloured by his regard for possible medico-legal complications at a later date. Even if he considers that the clinical state does not warrant further investigation, it is most unwise to proceed other than with the greatest caution.

In hospital practice, one of the most important facts to elicit on admission is whether a period of unconsciousness took place, however short. Where concussion seems definite or likely, it would appear most unwise to discharge the patient home. Wherever possible he should be admitted for 24 hours in order to be kept under observation for the insidious onset of an extra-dural haemorrhage.

Formerly, it was virtually a sacrosanct rule that all but the most trivial head injuries should have a skull X-ray. The reason for this defensive-style medicine was that numerous cases of litigation were brought where radiology was omitted and a subsequent fatal or serious complication of the head injury was alleged to have been compounded by the doctor's negligence in failing to order a radiograph. In recent years, this defensive concept has been challenged. Both on grounds of cost and radiation hazard, the necessity for such X-rays has been queried, it being pointed out that in a high proportion of skull fractures, the treatment would be identical whether or not X-rays were taken.

As with the prophylactic anti-tetanuus injection and 'blunderbuss' antibiotic cover this criticism may well be valid, but until such time as the majority of medical opinion comes to stand solidly behind the individual doctor, it is he alone who has to decide what degree of risk he is willing to accept. However, in the field of emergency radiology, a substantial weight of opinion is now opposing the former defensive attitude established because of the fear of medico-legal consequences.

Extra-dural haemorrhage

Fractures of the temporal bone which cross one of the branches of the middle meningeal artery, may produce slow bleeding between the skull and the dura. In the period immediately after the head injury (where usually a period of concussion has occurred), there may be perfectly normal cerebration with no neurological signs or clouding of consciousness. After the classical 'lucid interval', blood begins to accumulate outside the dura and compresses the brain, leading to raised intracranial pressure and local disturbances beneath the swelling. This may occur up to many hours or even a day after the injury. The onset of coma may be insidious and not noticed until an advanced stage has been reached, especially if the patient has been discharged from hospital. Though the results of surgical intervention in extra-dural haemorrhage are not so favourable as was once thought, the medico-legal consequences of an undiagnosed haemorrhage may be profound in that the attending doctor may be accused of negligent behaviour. A frequent cause for missing extra-dural haemorrhage is the combination of alcohol intoxication and head injury. Many cases have died during police custody and there is also the risk of sending such a patient home after treating the scalp injury, under the impression that drunkenness is the main condition present. The affects of alcohol may closely resemble post-concussional states and the two cannot legitimately be separated. The only answer is to keep the patient under observation until the possible effects of drink have worn off. Admittedly, this practice may be easier in theory than fact in a busy surgery or casualty department, but the effort must be made.

Subarachnoid and sub-dural haemorrhage

These are usually caused at the same time as the head injury, there being no lucid interval. Sub-dural haemorrhage is particularly common in children and old people, and arises from rupture of cortical veins on the surface of the brain. In old persons, they may be extremely chronic, the effects being insidious over a long period – and indeed many are found incidentally at post-mortem having caused apparently no neurological defects. Almost any form of head injury, with or without skull fracture may give rise to a subdural haemorrhage.

Subarachnoid haemorrhage, though a common natural disease from a ruptured aneurysm of the circle of Willis, may also occur as a complication of cerebral contusion and also in injuries to the upper neck region. It has recently been recognised that damage to the vertebral arteries can produce basal subarachnoid haemorrhage with fatal effects. This lesion is not uncommon, even from relatively minor trauma, the vertebral arteries being damaged during fracture of the upper cervical vertebrae.

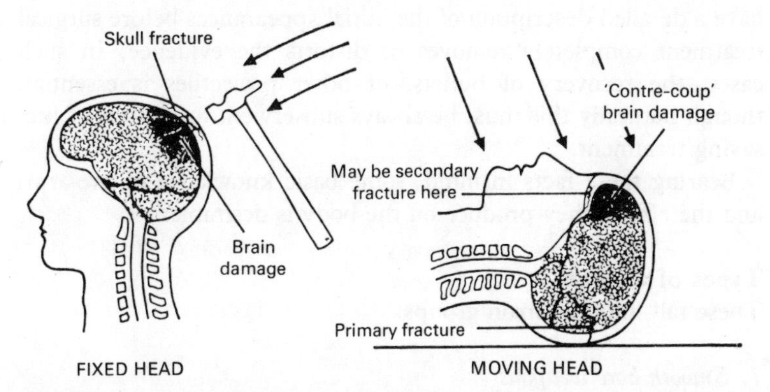

Fig. 20 Use of '*contre-coup*' lesion to differentiate fixed from moving head injuries

Interpretation of the intra-cranial lesions following fatal head injury is a matter of applied pathology, but it worth mentioning that the differentiation between injuries to a *fixed* head and injuries following arrest of a *moving* head, can be an extremely useful exercise (Fig. 20). When a fixed head is struck, e.g., with a blunt weapon, the fracture and underlying brain damage tend to be in the same place. When, however, a moving head hits the ground, then, though the fracture may be at contact point, the brain damage is usually diametrically opposite on the other side of the skull. Thus when a person is knocked backwards and strikes the occiput on the ground as during a fight or road accident, there may be an occipital fracture, but no occipital brain damage. The frontal lobes may be pulped, and the force transmitted across the cranium may be sufficient to fracture the thin bony plates above the orbit.

The recognition of this classical *contre-coup* injury either by clinical or surgical diagnosis or at autopsy, may have profound medico-legal significance, in helping to clarify the circumstances of an unwitnessed event. *Contre-coup* is seen in impacts on the back of the head or on either side, but virtually never when a fall occurs on to the front of the head. This is due to the configuration of the interior of the skull.

FIRE-ARM INJURIES

Though the examination of fatal fire-arm injuries is a matter for a pathologist, medical reports on non-fatal shootings, whether they be attempted murder or accidents, may sometimes be required. Where a person seriously injured by a fire-arm is admitted to hospital and there is a possibility of a murder or manslaughter charge being brought when the patient eventually dies, it is essential to have a detailed description of the initial appearances before surgical treatment completely removes or distorts the evidence. In such cases, the recovery of bullets, or other projectiles is essential, though naturally this must be always subservient to matters of life-saving treatment.

Bearing these facts in mind, some basic knowledge of fire-arms and the effects they produce on the body is desirable.

Types of weapon

These fall into two main groups:

1. Smooth bore weapons

Smooth bore weapons, which usually fire a large number of small projectiles such as lead shot, are by far the most common weapons in Britain, comprising 12-bore and .410 shot-guns. These weapons are used in sporting and agricultural activities, many shot-gun injuries being seen as accidental events in these circumstances. The 12-bore is often double-barrelled, one barrel having a slightly converging taper, which affects the pathological appearances in respect of range. The ammunition for smooth bore weapons is the cartridge, consisting of a paper or plastic tube with a brass base containing a percussion cap. Inside, there is a layer of powder, one or more felt or cardboard washers and a mass of lead pellets. All these components may contribute towards the wound, and may be vital in estimating direction and range.

2. Rifled weapons
These are guns in which a single missile is fired, being projected through a barrel possessing a shallow spiral pattern, which imparts a spin to the bullet and also leaves characteristic rifling marks upon it. The common types of rifled weapon are the *revolver*, where fresh shells are brought into position by means of a rotating cylinder; the *automatic pistol* (more accurately described as 'self loading' as new shells are inserted into the firing position by means of a gas operated system); and the *rifle*, a military or sporting weapon with a long barrel. In Britain, the most common rifled weapon legitimately available is the .22 light sporting rifle, though revolvers and pistols are still available either as war souvenirs or thorough illegal purchase.

Types of wounds

1. Smooth bore weapons
When a smooth bore weapon is fired, the mass of lead shot emerges from the muzzle as a solid mass and then progressively diverges as its distance from the weapon increases. Thus, a cone-shaped cloud of shot is formed, with clumping of the pellets during the early stages of the flight. The effects on a body, especially the pattern on the skin, will naturally depend on the position in the cone at which contact occurred. Many factors influence the shape of the cone of shot, and even the same weapon will not produce exactly the same pattern on two separate occasions, unless the ammunition used is identical in type and condition. With a double-barrelled weapon, the divergence of the standard 'cylinder' barrel will be greater than that of the 'choke' barrel, which tends to constrict the shot as it leaves the muzzle. A long-established but very approximate rule of

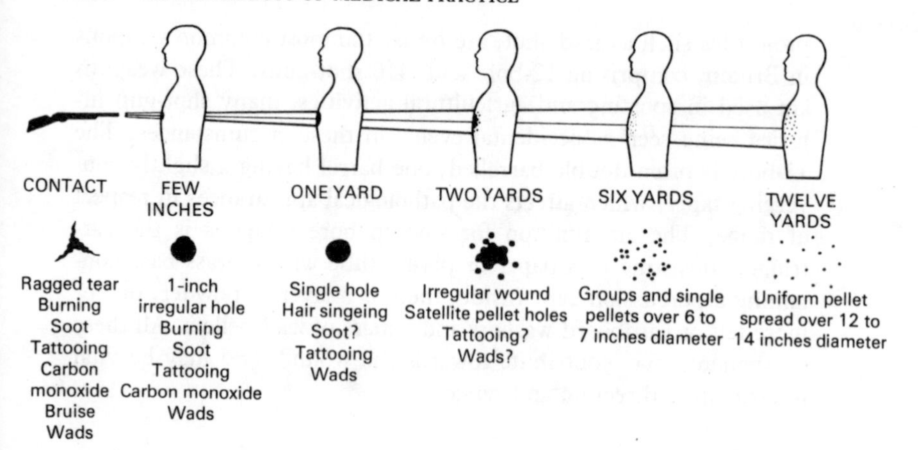

Fig. 21 Characteristics of shot-gun wounds at varying ranges

thumb for estimating range is that *the maximum diameter of the skin wound in inches is equal to the range in yards minus one*. It must be emphasised that this is extremely approximate and that test-firing by an expert forensic scientist must be performed to achieve any hope of accuracy.

At close range, the undiverged shot leaving the muzzle will enter the body as a single mass. As the range increases, satellite pellet holes will appear at the periphery, gradually increasing until the centre mass vanishes. At very close range, other factors will assist in determining the range. A contact wound, with the muzzle touching the skin, may produce any or all of the following features (Fig. 21):

1. a *circular bruise* upon the skin due to impact of the muzzle, especially if no clothing is interposed.
2. *gas* will be forced into the wound, causing cruciate or stellate tearing of the wound margins. Introduction of gases containing carbon monoxide may stain the surrounding tissues pink due to the production of carboxyhaemoglobin.
3. *powder blackening* of the wound margins and surrounding skin by soot and unburnt propellant may be present. This is less commonly seen nowadays, due to the use of cleaner 'smokeless' propellant mixtures. Unburnt flakes of propellant may be recoverable by skin-scraping and may be identified by forensic scientists as belonging to one particular brand of cartridge.
4. *burning* of the skin and *singeing* of hairs. This may be severe at point-blank range, but even at a foot or so, there may be singeing of hairs with clubbing of the ends (Fig. 22).

Gross tissue destruction may occur with contact or very close range discharges, but with a shot-gun it is unusual for an exit wound to appear in the chest or thorax, as the shot is dispersed in the tissues. They may, however, penetrate the neck or a limb, and secondary exit wounds, often multiple, may occur due to fragmented bone emerging from the opposite side. Shot-gun discharges into the mouth, a common suicidal method, may also produce a very large exit wound, with disruption of the cranium and projection of brain tissue for some distance.

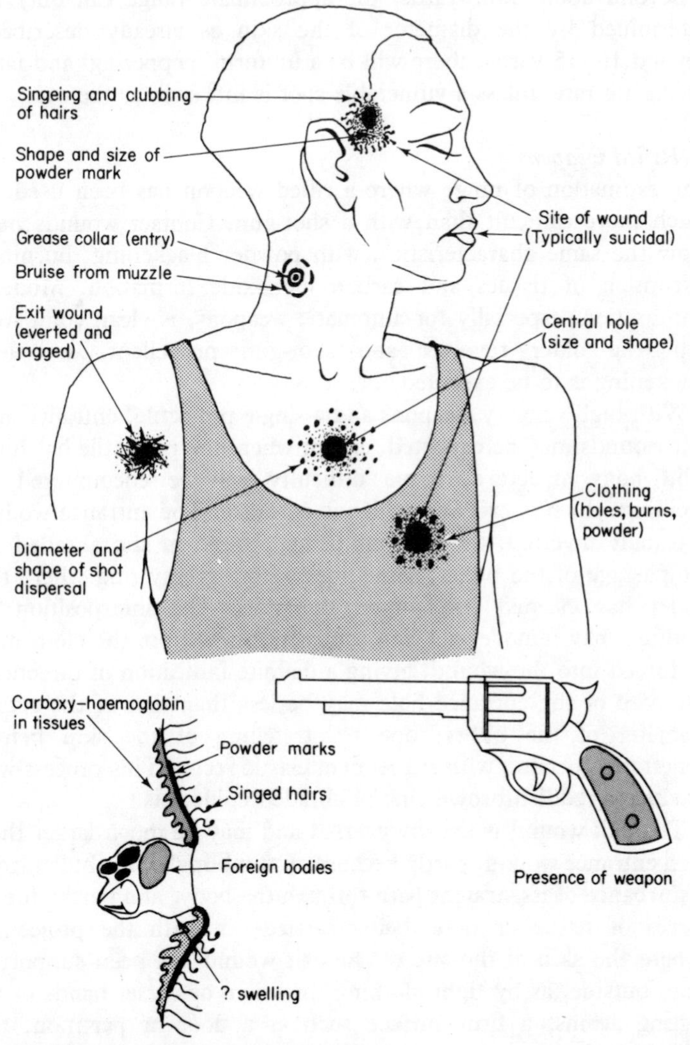

Fig. 22 What to look for in shot-gun wounds

Non-contact, but close-range discharges will still cause powder blackening, singeing and carbon monoxide formation, all decreasing as the range increases. Beyond one yard, these effects virtually disappear, though microscopic evidence of power residues may be found on scrapings from the skin surface. The cardboard and/or felt wad from the cartridge can penetrate the wound up to about 2–3 yards and may travel in free flight up to six yards. The finding of wads deep inside the wound, indicates that the range was probably not more than six feet.

Beyond about four yards, the approximate range can only be determined by the diameter of the skin as already described. Beyond 10–15 yards, there will be a uniform 'peppering' and fatal effects are rare unless a vulnerable spot is hit, such as the eye.

2. Rifled weapons

The estimation of range where a rifled weapon has been used, is much more difficult than with a shot-gun. Contact wounds may show the same characteristics, with powder blackening, burning, disruption of tissues and carbon monoxide formation. Modern ammunition, especially for automatic weapons, is clean compared with the older revolver and shot-gun propellant, and less blackening is to be expected.

With high velocity weapons and a single projectile, entrance and exit wounds may be expected, except where the projectile has hit a solid bony structure. Little difficulty will be encountered in deciding which is exit and which is entrance. The entrance wound is usually inverted, the margins being pressed in and abraded by the passage of the bullet, sometimes with a greasy ring where the bullet has cleaned itself upon the skin. The interposition of clothing may remove this sign, but here fibres from the cloth may be forced into the wound, giving a definite indication of direction. The size of the entrance hole may be less than that of the actual diameter of the bullet, due to stretching of the skin before penetration occurs, with subsequent elastic recoil. This process will produce a reddish-brown ring of abraded epidermis.

The exit wound is usually everted and may be much larger than then entrance wound, partly because of 'tumbling' of the bullet from disturbance of its straight path through the body, and partly due to pieces of tissue or bone being carried out with the projectile. Where the skin at the site of the exit wound has been supported from outside, as by tight clothing, brassiere or corset bands or by resting against a firm surface such as a door or partition, the eversion of the wound will be lessened or even prevented. This may cause difficulties in distinguishing it from an entrance wound, unless other criteria are taken into account. This enlargement of the exit wound may be extreme and the wounds may be multiple, due to fragments of bone being expelled. Where a high velocity bullet has been fired from a distance, and has acquired a steady gyroscopic spin, the entrance and exit wounds may be almost identical, but the edges will almost invariably be inverted and everted respectively unless the skin has been supported as described above.

The internal appearances of fire-arm injuries are matters for forensic pathologists, but it is usually the skin wounds which provide the most information about direction and range. The direction may often be determined from the shape of the entrance wound or the pattern of powder blackening. Where the angle of discharge was perpendicular to the body surface, the wound and surrounding zone of blackening will be circular. Where the discharge was oblique, they will be more or less elliptical according to the acuteness of the angle of the axis of the weapon to the skin. The depth of the wound may be undercut, giving an obvious indication or direction.

The range of discharge, even if not accurately determinable without test-firing, may be of considerable use. Naturally, a discharge from beyond arm's length at once rules out self-infliction. Wounds anywhere but in the favoured sites for suicide (chest, mouth, temple) mean that accident or homicide is almost certainly the explanation. Fatal gun-shot wounds in women are almost never suicidal.

16

Examination of motor vehicle injuries

In view of the frequency of road accidents, reports to police and coroner on the victims of traffic injuries are of particular importance to doctors. The detailed interpretation of fatal injuries is the task of the coroner's pathologist, but where death does not occur or has been delayed, the casualty officer or general practitioner may be in the best position to describe the original injury. The same applies when extensive surgery has been carried out, which then radically alters the original appearances, which might be vital for reconstruction of the accident. Medical reports on traffic injuries may also be required in civil litigation for claims against third parties and both solicitors and insurance companies may request such reports from hospital and family doctors.

The type of injury sustained varies considerably according to the situation of the victim in the accident, i.e. whether he was a car driver, a passenger, a motor cyclist or cyclist or a pedestrian. In some multiple fatalities, medical evidence may be the only means of indicating which of the deceased was the driver and which was the passenger.

The driver of a motor vehicle

Though circumstances vary greatly in individual incidents, the driver tends to receive a different pattern of injury to either the front-seat or rear-seat passengers. He may receive momentary warning of impending collision, and brace himself against the steering-wheel. Fractures of the wrists and arms may thus occur, as well as fractures of the legs and pelvis from pressure against the foot pedals on impact. Though much attention has been given to steering-wheel injuries to the chest, these are relatively uncommon. However, fractured steering-wheel spokes may penetrate the chest and lacerate the heart or lungs. Due to the grip on the wheel and its presence as an obstruction, the driver commonly sustains less injury than the front seat passenger from being driven through the windscreen and whiplash injuries to the spine are also less fre-

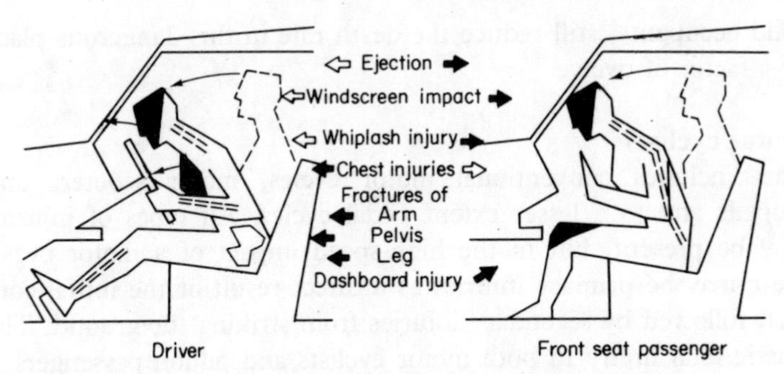

Fig. 23 Typical injuries to the driver and front seat passenger of a vehicle

quent. The same pattern of multiple small cuts upon the face from shattering of safety glass may be seen, and ejection on to the roadway and secondary injuries from other vehicles are a common cause of fatalities.

Passengers in a motor vehicle

The most dangerous place in the car is the front passenger seat (Fig. 23), though safety belts and harnesses have reduced mortality, mainly from preventing ejection into the road which is probably the commonest single cause of death. The front seat passenger may suffer injuries to the knee region from contact with the fascia, but most noticeable is the tendency to projection through the windscreen with attendant lacerations of the face. Severe 'whiplash' injury to the cervical and thoracic spine may occur, due to rapid acceleration or deceleration. Both driver and front-seat passenger may sustain severe frontal or parietal head injuries from contact with the windscreen pillar.

Passengers in the rear seats often escape such severe injury due to the absence of the windscreen and fascia, and the cushioning effect of the front seats. However, experiments with dummies in simulated crashes have shown that the occupants may be thrown about violently within the passenger compartment, and that many injuries may occur as a result of contact with projections such as door handles, interior lights, etc. Again expulsion through bursting doors may give rise to severe secondary injuries due to striking the road and being hit by other vehicles.

Injuries to children in the front passenger seat are distressingly common, there having been no less than 102 deaths and over 10 000 injuries within a recent three-year period. These are all the more tragic as the children are often allowed to travel in the front position as an act of indulgence. Seat-belts, though designed for child occupants, still reduce the death rate in this dangerous place by a factor of twelve.

Motor cyclists

This includes conventional motor cycles, motor scooters and mopeds and to a lesser extent pedal cycles. All types of injuries may be present, but in the high-speed impact of a motor cycle, there may be primary injuries as a direct result of the initial contact, followed by secondary injuries from striking the ground. The classic fatal injury in both motor cyclists and pillion passengers is fracture of the skull, usually from secondary impact with the ground. The use of crash helmets has reduced fatalities, though at sufficiently high speeds, no protection will avail. A crash helmet is designed to reduce friction of the head against the ground and make deceleration less drastic, by allowing the protected head to skid across the ground rather than come to an abrupt halt. To attain this end, the helmet should be free from projections, and those with a peak tend to defeat their own object. Fractures of the temporo-parietal region are common, often with *contre-coup* brain injury. Extension of the fracture across the base of the skull through the pituitary fossa, is commonly seen in such accidents. Externally, as in other types of motor vehicle accident, skid marks on the skin due to contact with road gravel may be seen, and the direction of travel may be easily identified by the presence of skin tags at the rear-most end of the grazes. Fractures of the cervical spine are also common in secondary impact from a motor cycle. In moped and pedal cycles where the speed is lower, the usual fatal injury is due to another motor vehicle striking the rider, and primary injuries of the legs, with secondary impact injuries to the head, shoulder and trunk are commonly seen.

Pedestrian injuries (Fig. 24)

Older people and children are more at risk than active adults as pedestrian victims, commonly as a result of moving into the roadway after alighting from buses or moving out between parked vehicles. Again the pattern of injuries can vary greatly, but are conveniently divided into primary injuries from impact of the vehicle and secondary injuries from contact with the ground or other stationary objects.

Pedestrians are most commonly struck from the side, but the pattern of injuries best illustrated by describing an impact from the rear. Though the design of vehicles is constantly changing, usually the furthermost projecting part is the bumper bar and this strikes

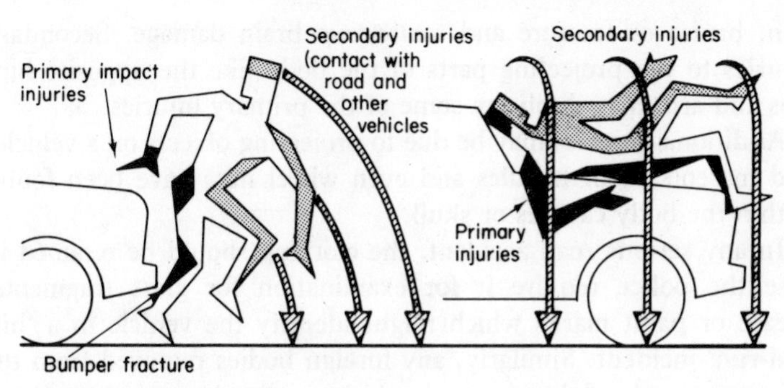

Fig. 24 General pattern of pedestrian injuries

the pedestrian first, usually on the lower leg somewhere beneath the knee. It is important when describing injuries, to measure the distance from the heel so that injuries may be related to the dimensions of any suspect vehicle. When struck from behind, such impact may fracture one or both legs at this level, and in the blunt-nosed vehicles of current fashion, there may be an almost simultaneous impact on the buttocks or lower lumbar region. Projecting mascots or lights may cause specific penetrating injuries, and in some countries these projections have been banned by legislation. The primary impact tends to lift the pedestrian up on to the bonnet where further primary injuries may occur from contact with the windscreen (particularly the windscreen pillars, as contact is rarely midline). There may be severe head injuries from striking the windscreen pillar or lacerations from penetration of the windscreen itself. More commonly, the body is thrown sideways, and may be run over by a passing vehicle. Where the trunk or a limb passes under a revolving motor wheel, the pattern of the tyre may be imprinted upon it, or the skin may even be rolled off in a flaying-type injury, revealing the muscle beneath over a wide area.

Secondary injuries occur from contact with the ground, and vary according to the nature of the impact. If, instead of being lifted upon the bonnet, the pedestrian is knocked forward by the impact, there will be further secondary injuries on the knees, hands and face and elsewhere. If thrown into the air, the contact with the ground may cause any injury including fractured skull and multiple bruises, abrasions and lacerations.

Where the pedestrian is hit from the side, there may be unilateral fracturing of the nearest leg, and certainly bruising in the absence of a fracture. There may be other areas of primary contact on the same side, including arms, ribs and hip. Secondary injuries will occur on the other side, especially head injury with a lateral laceration, bruise or fracture and *contre-coup* brain damage. Secondary injuries to the projecting parts of the body like the opposite hip, ribs and arm may duplicate some of the primary injuries.

Additional injuries may be due to projecting objects on a vehicle, and mascots, door handles and even wheel nuts have been found within the body cavities or skull.

In any serious road accident, the clothing should be retained in case the police require it for examination for glass fragments, grease or paint marks which might identify the vehicle in a 'hit-and-run' incident. Similarly, any foreign bodies removed from the skin or wounds of the victim should be retained.

The medical report on such a case has no special characteristics, apart from measuring the position, size and distance of the wounds from the ground. It is often helpful to make a pictorial representation of injuries on a printed body outline such as those commonly available for neurological purposes. If this is prepared soon after the patient is first seen, its value is far greater than a diffuse verbal description of hazily-remembered injuries some days or weeks later.

In connection with patients admitted to hospital after a road accident, it should be remembered that no blood sample nor result of any hospital analysis for blood alcohol, should be given to the police without the consent of the patient (after he has been informed of the significance of such tests).

If the police request a blood alcohol test on a driver who has been admitted as an in-patient, the hospital doctor has the right to agree or decline, according to his assessment of the clinical state of the victim. If he agrees, then the local police surgeon should attend to take the sample not the clinician in charge of the case.

17

Asphyxia

Many types of death and occasionally non-fatal clinical syndromes, may be asphyxial in nature. The physio-pathology of asphyxia has been the subject of extensive discussion and controversy, but from the practical medico-legal aspect, most of these complexities can be disregarded.

MECHANISMS OF ASPHYXIA

The accompanying diagram shows the levels at which asphyxia may occur (Fig. 25). As commonly employed, the term means 'deprivation of oxygen', and this can occur at any point along a long chain from deficient oxygen in the atmosphere to impaired utilisation by the distant tissue cells. However, in the context of the present discussion *mechanical* asphyxia is the form to be considered.

Certain general features are common to most forms of asphyxia, though they may be minimal or even absent in many cases. The three cardinal signs are *congestion, cyanosis and petechiae*.

These are all due to raised venous pressure, anoxia of capillary walls and reduction of oxyhaemoglobin following failure of gaseous interchange in the lungs.

Where asphyxia is due to pressure on the neck or chest, there is an added mechanical obstruction to return of the venous flow from the head and neck. This causes accentuation of the congestion, cyanosis and haemorrhages in that area, which may be sharply demarcated by the line of constriction.

Though congestion and cyanosis may appear in a variety of other conditions (especially cardiac and pulmonary disease) the multiple small haemorrhages are a most significant feature. Again, they are usually best seen in the head region, particularly where the tissues are lax, such as the eyelids and lips. Petechiae should be looked for on the outer aspect of the upper lids, on the conjuctival surface of both lids and on the sclera. In more severe degrees, they will be clearly apparent on the general skin surface.

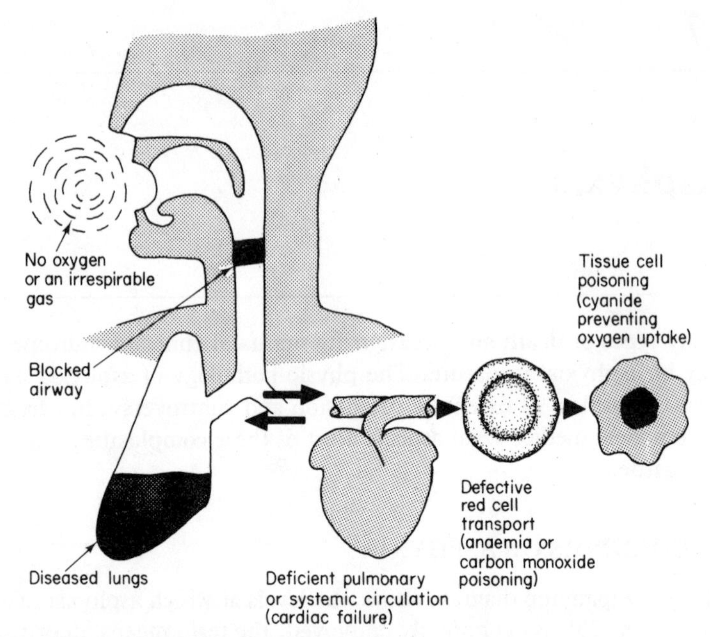

Fig. 25 Pathway of oxygen utilization with common causes of asphyxia

Internally, petechial haemorrhages may be seen on the pleural surfaces of the lungs, on the visceral pericardium and in the thymic remnants of young adults. Pulmonary oedema may also be a noticeable post-mortem finding, also bleeding from ear and nose.

However, it must be emphasised that all petechiae do not indicate asphyxia – they may be seen in many haemorrhagic diatheses, in poisonings of certain types (such as aspirin) and due to micro-embolism. Any gross congestive condition with right-sided heart failure may produce them. For instance, the well-marked petechiae seen in the internal organs of the typical 'cot death' are an agonal manifestation of the gross congestive phase of central respiratory failure, not to mechanical asphyxia.

Several apparently asphyxial conditions are due to other causes, and these will be included in the following list.

Obstruction of the nose and mouth

Asphyxia due to obstruction at this level is often called 'suffocation', though this term may be applied to any blockage in the main respiratory passages.

Suffocation may also be applied to absence of oxygen in the surrounding atmosphere. This may occur in a variety of conditions, both industrial and domestic. Entry of workmen into tanks, wells, ship compartments etc., where oxygen is lacking, may cause acute asphyxial death. Iron tanks which have been sealed for some time and are damp, may be oxygen-deficient due to the formation of rust; this is seen especially in the deep tanks of ships. Other situations where oxygen is absent, may be due to replacement by other gases, notably carbon dioxide which sinks to a low level and replaces oxygen. Wells and shafts sometimes are filled with carbon dioxide, a notable example being the shaft in a zoo which killed both a workman and the doctor who attempted to rescue him. High concentrations of carbon dioxide appear to have a special effect in that they can cause rapid, almost instantaneous death which cannot be explained on asphyxial grounds only. There seems to be some immediate toxic action, possibly on the respiratory chemo-receptors.

Carbon monoxide has a specific action, replacing oxygen in the red cells. This will be discussed in a separate section.

In domestic circumstances, suffocation may be seen in rooms

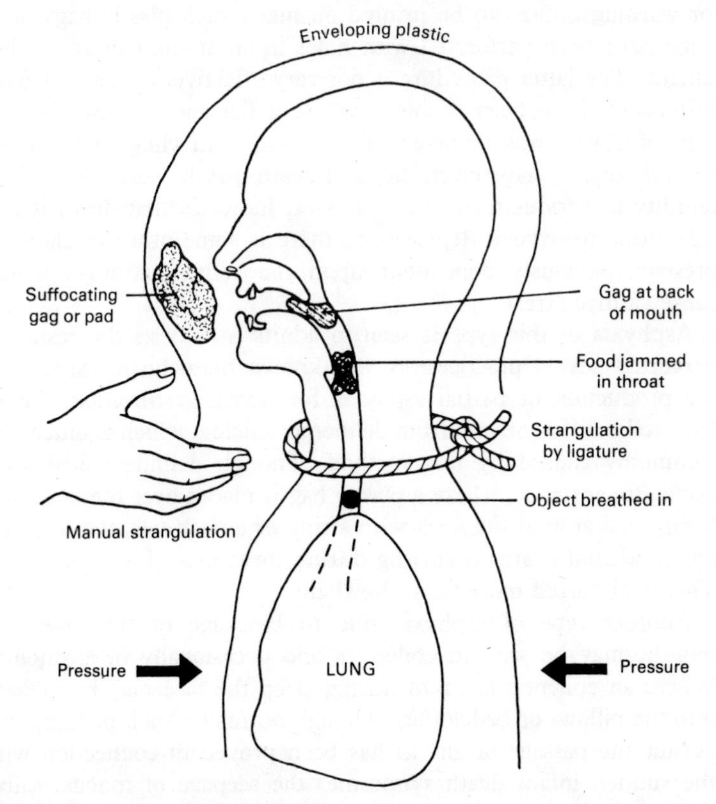

Fig. 26 Causes of mechanical asphyxia

where some heating appliance has used up all the oxygen and draught exclusion has prevented replacement. Though in similar circumstances carbon monoxide poisoning is a frequent offender, pure oxygen lack certainly can occur and a autopsy, only the circumstances and lack of other causes of death indicate the true explanation.

Suffocation from obstruction of the nose and mouth may be seen in adults and children. There has been much erroneous theorising about the role of suffocation in the 'sudden infant death syndrome', but there is no evidence to support it. Although true suffocation occasionally does occur in children, due to blockage of the breathing apertures, this is an entirely different phenomenon to the 'cot death'. Very occasionally, an infant may become entangled or covered with an impervious plastic or rubber sheet, sometimes in a perambulator or cot. More clear-cut cases occur in older infants and young children, who may be found definitely suffocated by a plastic bag or plastic sheet. Sufficient of these cases have occured for warning notices to be printed on many such plastic bags, and some have been perforated with holes in an attempt to avoid this danger. The latter procedure is not very effective, as cases of fatal suffocation have been reported where a flat sheet, rather than a bag, of plastic was involved. Thin plastic can cling to the face, possibly due to static electricity and death may be very rapid. This rapidity in various forms of asphyxias, indicates that death is not solely due to oxygen deprivation: there is some other mechanism present, obviously dependent upon the reflex pathways which cause cardiac arrest.

Asphyxia of this type is seen in adults usually as the result of perverted sexual practices. A well-known masochistic exercise is the production of partial asphyxia for sexual gratification. These have to be differentiated from deliberate suicide, which is much less commonly caused by this method. Though definite suicides do occur (for instance, where a plastic bag is placed over the head and firmly tied around the neck with string or a neck-tie), the majority are accidental deaths occurring during these masochistic activities. This is discussed more fully elsewhere.

Another type of asphyxia due to blockage of the nose and mouth, may be seen in epileptics and occasionally in alcoholics. Where an epileptic has a fit during sleep the face may be pressed into the pillows or bedclothes. Though normally, such bedding will permit the passage of air (as has been proved in connection with the sudden infant death syndrome) the seepage of mucus, saliva and sometimes vomit may cause the fabric to become impervious for long enough for asphyxia to take place. Sudden death in epilepsy may occur, of course, without asphyxia and without indeed, status epilepticus. Epileptics, like asthmatics, appear able to die suddenly for no reason discernible at autopsy, though it is always worth while performing a screening test for barbiturate on a blood sample. Similarly, persons in an advanced stage of drunkenness, may turn upon their face and suffocate in either vomit, or mouth and nasal secretions.

Blockage of internal air passages

Progressing inwards from the external orifices, asphyxia may next be due to 'gagging' (Fig. 26). Gagging is unusual, and the fatalities which have occurred are mostly in connection with robbery, where a caretaker or nightwatchman has been silenced by having his mouth stuffed with a cloth. Though he may be able to breath through his nose immediately afterwards, when left for some time, the collection of nasal secretions, oedema of the pharynx etc., may block the posterior nares and cause asphyxia.

Asphyxia or severe hypoxia frequently occurs after accidents and in narcotic poisoning etc., due to blockage of the airway by the tongue falling back into the pharynx. The use of metal or plastic airways and better instruction of first-aid teams has reduced this danger, but much damage to cerebral function and to life itself has been caused in the past by respiratory obstruction in cases which otherwise might have completely recovered.

Foreign bodies may cause asphyxia by obstructing the airway at any level from the pharynx to the bifurcation of the trachea. As with so many traumaic events, the extremes of life are most affected. Infants may aspirate all manner of objects, especially toys, plastic balls, etc. Elderly people and mental defectives may block their air passages by avidly cramming down food. Complete swamping of the glottis and lower air passages has frequently been seen in senile and demented persons, and a large food bolus, including such things as pancakes, masses of meat etc., may be recovered at autopsy.

The significance of gastric contents in the air passages is doubtful. Though often given as a cause of death, this is rarely justifiable. Unless an active cellular reaction in the air passages or lungs is discovered, when aspiration has been present for some time, the diagnosis of 'aspiration of vomit' as cause of death should rest only on clinical evidence of someone seeing the person aspirate before the agonal period. The only exception to this rule is the finding of objects which by their nature of gross size, could not have come from the stomach and must be a primary inhalation. If such evidence is not available, gastric contents in the trachea and main bronchi should be interpreted as an agonal phenomenon. Its use in the 'sudden death in infancy syndrome' is to be deprecated, as are all other spurious explanations of suffocation, which cannot be proved and can be definitely excluded in the vast majority of instances.

Blockage of a main or subsidiary bronchus rarely causes fatal asphyxia, though it a common surgical problem especially in children, when all manner of plastic or metal objects have to be removed. A special danger is the peanut, which has a specific irritant action upon the mucosa and can lead to chronic localised lung disease unless identified and removed by bronchoscopy.

Death due to external pressure upon the neck

This is not synonynous with '*asphyxia* due to external pressure on the neck'. It was formerly accepted that strangulation, hanging etc., were purely asphyxial processes, but this is now known to be far from the truth. Death from hypoxia following obstruction of the air passages takes at least several minutes, but it is well known that a fatal outcome can be far more rapid than this. Death may be virtually instantaneous, as the statements of accused in many criminal trials has shown. Mere grasping or prodding of the neck may cause sudden death from reflex cardiac arrest. Cases are on record of death occurring from even a playful tweak upon the neck. During the war, combat troops were specially trained to kill by a 'commando' punch in the sensitive areas of the neck, namely the area of the bifurcation of the carotid arteries, where the carotid sinus lies. This extremely pressure-sensitive zone can produce inhibition of cardiac function by a direct reflex.

Strangulation by hand, ligature or hanging may all produce this rapid cardiac-arrest type of death. Pure asphyxia certainly occurs in many instances of pressure on the neck, and sometimes there appears to be a mixed causation, possibly due to intermittent pressure and release. Occlusion of the carotid vessels may also lead to rapid loss of consciousness from cerebral ischaemia. This in itself is not rapidly fatal, but can explain the frequent absence of asphyxial struggling: it also may lead to cardiac arrest if the carotid pressure is maintained. In the cases where rapid cardiac arrest occurs, there will be none of the classical signs of asphyxia, with congestion and petechial haemorrhages. In fact, there may be nothing visible at autopsy, except perhaps signs of local damage in the neck, such as haemorrhage beneath the muscle, fracturing of parts of the larynx and sometimes tearing of the intima of the carotid vessels.

Manual strangulation

This is almost invariably homicidal in nature, though a very few cases have been recorded where determined suicides have succeeded in throttling themselves without the aid of a ligature.

Manual strangulation, where fatal, is the province of the forensic pathologist, though the external appearances where the victim survives may be even more florid than in the cadaver. Whether dead or alive, recognition of these appearances may be of importance to any practitioner initially called to see the body.

Essential features are marks upon the neck, often disc-shaped bruises 1 or 2 cm in size, scattered around the front of the neck, beneath the angles of the jaw and on either side of the laryngeal prominence (Fig. 27). The bruises may be so numerous as to be confluent. There may be fingernail scratches due either to the assailant or to attempts of the victim to tear the hands away. The skin of the neck may also show the imprint of objects such as a string of beads or the woven pattern of fabric, such as a knitted polo-knecked sweater if these are compressed beneath the strangling fingers. If the death is asphyxial, the face may be cyanosed, there may be numerous tiny red spots in the skin of the cheeks, chin and neck above the strangulation line and the outer surface of

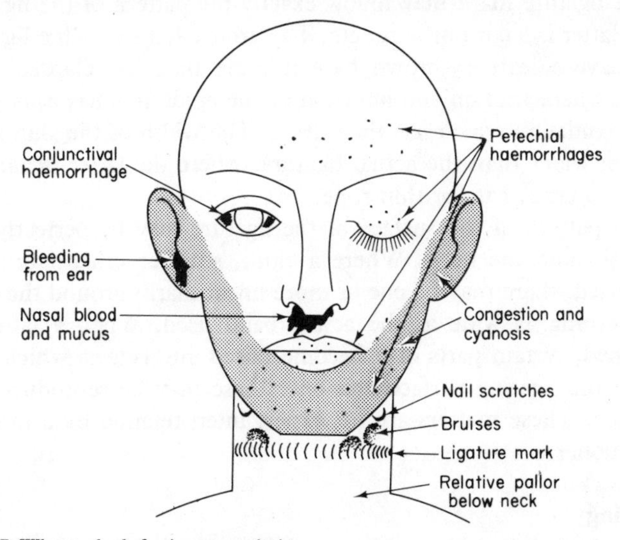

Fig. 27 What to look for in strangulation

the eyelids. The conjunctivae may show showers of fine petechial haemorrhages. There may be haemorrhages in the sclera, though these are much less common. There is commonly some bleeding from the nose or exudation of pink-tinged mucus or serous fluid. Rarely, bleeding from the ear occurs. In general, bruises and abrasions on the neck, intense congestion and cyanosis above the neck and the presence of small haemorrhages constitute the florid picture of asphyxial neck pressure. All these may be absent if death is due to rapid cardiac arrest or there may only be one or two marks upon the neck. Voiding of urine and faeces may occur, but this is such a common non-specific finding as to be of little significance.

Strangulation by a ligature

This may be suicidal or homicidal, though the former is rare and the circumstances will be obvious if some form of 'Spanish windlass' is present to maintain the pressure. Occasionally, suicides have killed themselves by knotting ligatures around their neck, sometimes managing to make several loops and knots before unconsciousness supervenes. In the more usual murder, the ligature may still be in place or may have been removed, when a linear mark or marks will be seen encircling the neck. There may be manual strangulation in addition, but in either event the general signs of congestion and haemorrhages will be present unless the rapid 'carotid reflex' type death has occurred.

The ligature mark may follow exactly the pattern of the ligature if the latter is a cord or wire, etc. The groove left by such a ligature may have a leathery-brown base if some time has elapsed since death, where friction and abrasion of the epidermis has caused serious exudation which has then dried. The width of the skin mark is often wider than the actual ligature, where the latter is narrow, as with a cord, wire or thin rope.

The pattern of the surface of the ligature may be perfectly imprinted upon the neck. Where a cloth, scarf or other fabric has been used, there may be one or more linear marks around the neck but nothing as wide as the actual band used. When a fabric is stretched, certain parts of it become raised into ridges, which constitute the ligating surface and only these may be reproduced on the skin. These matters are for expert interpretation by a forensic practitioner.

Hanging

Hanging is almost invariably suicidal, except in those masochistic accidents which are described elsewhere. Once more, death may be either asphyxial, from cerebral ischaemia or from cardiac arrest or a combination of these. As with the ligature, there may be a well defined groove around the neck with the pattern imprinted upon it. There may be a fixed or running noose, and unless the noose has tightened completely around the neck, there will be a gap in the ligature mark indicating the suspension point, where the two ends of the loop leave the skin to travel up to the knot. All sorts of suspension methods may be used and death is quite possible from such low elevations as door-knobs, bed-heads, clothes hooks etc. At autopsy, damage to the intima of the carotid arteries may be found on one or both sides. The upward direction of the ligature may block the pharynx by displacement of the tongue and also tends to occlude the carotids more than manual strangulation.

If a doctor is called to the scene of a hanging, the presence of disordered furniture in the neighbourhood of the body need not be an indication of foul play, but to the convulsive kicking which can occur during the terminal stages of asphyxia. One of the most important roles of the doctor when examining the scene of a hanging, is to immediately differentiate those accidental masochistic procedures from the true suicide. Very occasionally, hanging may be accidental and then is usually confined to toddlers who become entangled with a perambulator harness or some attachment to their cot.

Suicidal hanging is very uncommon amongst women, though not the extreme rarity of self-destruction by shooting.

Traumatic asphyxia

In this form of true asphyxia, the external signs are more gross than in any other cause. Traumatic asphyxia (a bad name, as almost all forms of asphyxia are traumatic!) consists of respiratory arrest due to mechanical fixation of the chest, so that the normal excursion of the chest wall is prevented. The notorious 'body snatchers', Burke and Hare, were alleged to have killed their victims by means of traumatic asphyxia effected by sitting upon the chest of their victims.

Virtually all cases are accidental and occur in one of the following situations:

1. Pinning beneath rubble and masonry in demolition work or building, and in mobile solids such as sand, iron-ore, coal, grain etc. Most of these tragedies are industrial in nature. Another common type of traumatic asphyxia is the collapse of a trench whilst workmen are within it; even if their heads

remain free, the pressure of soil will prevent movement of the chest.

2. Pinning beneath vehicles, especially tractors. The latter is relatively common in fatal farm accidents, especially when tractors are used laterally on hilly country and fall sideways, so trapping the driver.
3. Crushing in uncontrolled crowds. In these frightening circumstances, deaths from traumatic asphyxia might be multiple, as in the Bolton and Ibrox Park football tragedies or as in a stampede in an underground air-raid shelter during the last war, when 173 people died. One recent case involved a charity walk when a false start caused those at the front to be knocked down and crushed by pressure of bodies in the rear.

The general signs of traumatic asphyxia are similar to those of strangulation, suffocation etc., but are extremely severe, the eyes especially suffering, being suffused and haemorrhagic, the sclera sometimes being completely bloodshot. Intense cyanosis and congestion of the head, neck and shoulders is seen with numrous showers of petechial haemorrhages in the skin and mucus membranes. There is frequently a sharp line of demarcation between normal and congested skin, usually at the level of the clavicles and thoracic inlet.

The sexual asphyxias

As these are purely accidental, it is more appropriate to mention them here than under 'sexual crimes'. Not infrequently, males are found asphyxiated with surrounding circumstances which are characteristic, if the observer is aware of this frequent abberration. In the past, most cases were mis-named 'suicides', this being far from the truth, as the object of the exercise was to produce pleasure rather than death. The fatal cases obviously form only the tip of a much larger iceberg, and those who come to such an unfortunate end presumably have practised the same technique on many previous occasions, without a lethal result. Young men are more usually involved, though older men are occasionally seen as victims of this form of perversion; only one or two cases involving women have ever been described.

Partial asphyxia apparently causes cerebral disturbances with feelings of sexual gratification. Presumably, the state of impaired consciousness produced either by carotid pressure or partial obstruction of the air-way, leads to hallucinatory experiences of an erotic nature. The subject endeavours, usually successfully, to control the degree of asphyxia by mechanical means, in such a way that when consciousness recedes too far, the pressure on the neck is released and recovery occurs. Fatalities are seen when this mechanism becomes faulty. The usual arrangement is characteristic, there being a ligature around the neck (usually a running noose), the free end of which is attached either to a limb, or to a fixed object. The weight of the body is used to control the pressure. The free end of the noose may be taken down to the wrists or ankles which are commonly tied together as part of the ritual. By extending the legs or arms, the noose can be tightened, and on consciousness being lost, relaxation of the limbs releases the pressure. Alternatively, a running noose may be passed upwards to some fixed point as in suicidal hanging, or may rub over a support with the free end attached to a weight. These latter cases could be confused with true suicide, but for the other phenomena associated with these masochistic exercises. These attendant factors at once reveal the nature of the ritual to informed observers. The victim may be naked, partly clothed or clothed in female apparel, as a manifestation of transvestism. There may be padding of the brassiere to simulate breasts, and even wigs and make-up may be worn. Rubber and shiny plastic garments may be a noticeable feature, and frequently rubber masks and grotesque accessories may be present. Rubber and plastic feature largely in some cases, women's rubber boots, bath mats etc., being used.

Another frequent feature is the 'bondage' of arms, feet and sometimes waists. String, rope, electic wire, chains etc., may be used, and even elaborate measures such as padlocks and other apparatus reminiscent of Houdini are seen. There is frequently erotic or pornographic literature spread within view, and there may be evidence of a recent emission of semen. The whole picture is quite characteristic, though reluctance is sometimes found on the part of the relatives and coroner to accept the fact that this is not a deliberate suicide. Especially where the syndrome is seen in youths, the coroner or police may suggest that this was an imitative act stimulated by cowboy scenes on television: though very occasionally this may be the case with children, almost every case has a sexual motivation.

Variations of this theme are the production of asphyxia by enveloping the head in a plastic bag or even crawling into some large impervious bag made of rubber or balloon fabric etc. Several cases have been reported where fatal electrocution has resulted as an outward result of electrical stimulation for sexual gratification. Electrodes may be applied to the genitals and/or abdominal wall, usually with a low voltage supply from a battery or transformer. One case has been seen by the author where a metal comb was strapped over the umbilicus and the other conductor placed in the mouth, obviously for erotic purposes.

Similar sexual gratification may be obtained by the inhaling of stupefying substances, such as cleaning fluid (carbon tetrachloride or trichlorethylene) or general anaesthetics of the same nature. 'Glue-sniffing' where the solvent for adhesives contained these organic fluids, is also a well-known form of gratification, which may progress to frank addiction. Petrol, paraffin and many other substances have been described as the instrument of this not uncommon form of perversion.

18

Drowning

Death following immersion in water is not necessarily synonymous with drowning. Numerous cases are on record where victims have been recovered almost immediately after falling into the water, but were found to be already dead. In an appreciable proportion of autopsies on 'drowned' persons, little pathological evidence of drowning can be obtained, though the remainder exhibit the classical signs which leave no room for doubt.

MECHANISMS OF DEATH AFTER IMMERSION IN WATER

1. Instantaneous or very rapid death

A person falling into very cold water may die instantly and the mechanism is in dispute. The mode of death appears to be a reflex cardiac arrest, due either to instantaneous chilling of the skin or impact of cold water into the pharynx. A definite predisposing factor is the recent taking of alcohol, not necessarily sufficient to cause classical drunkenness. The typical story is of a sailor returning to his ship on a winter's night, after a sociable evening. He misses the gang-plank and falls into the icy water of the dock. Though recovery of the body may occur within a very few minutes, no confirmatory sign of drowning is found. The effect of the alcohol, apart from the ataxia which may lead to the fall, may well be flushing of the skin surface, which accentuates the effect of sudden chilling.

Many similar cases occur in which alcohol played no part, and the confirmation of this *rapid* mode of death depends mainly on circumstances and witnesses, as the absence of water in the lungs and air passages can occur after undoubted drowning, as well as with this sudden cardiac arrest.

2. Fresh water drowning

Submersion in fresh water is more dangerous than salt. The old idea that drowning was merely a form of asphyxia, due to exclusion

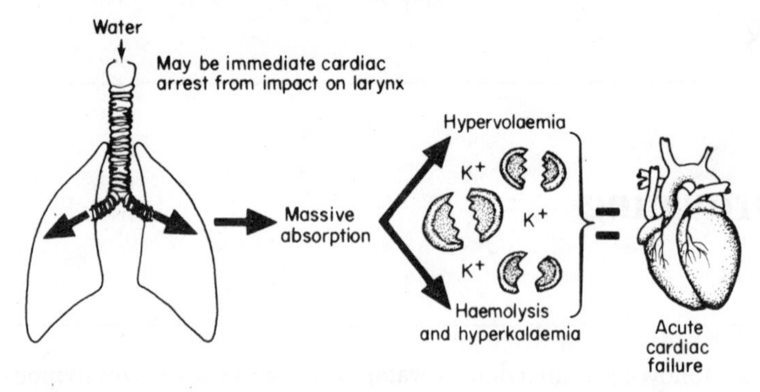

Fig. 28 Mechanism of fresh water drowning

of air from the lungs, has been shown to be quite incorrect. The true mechanism is a combination of massive absorption of water via the alveolar membranes (with a consequent acute increase in blood volume) and electrolyte and osmotic imbalance (Fig. 28). The blood volume after a few moments' submersion in fresh water may rise by over 50 per cent and the immediate cause of death may be cardiac failure from inadequacy of the heart to deal with the increased volume. Added to this is the dilution of electrolytes in the plasma with the exception of potassium, which is released from lysed red cells due to the sudden hypotonicity of the plasma. The combination of hydraemia and potassium increase may cause rapid myocardial failure. These changes can occur before pure anoxia becomes a lethal factor.

3. Sea water drowning

As sea water is hypertonic compared with plasma, no massive absorption of water into the circulation occurs. In fact, there may be a reverse transfer of lesser volume, leading to pulmonary oedema and the greater probability of frothy fluid in the air passages. No cardiac embarrassment from hypervolaemia takes place and there is no potassium toxicity. These theoretical differences are born out in practice by a much lower recovery rate of bodies recovered from fresh water as opposed to sea water. Naturally, if immersion is continued for more than a few minutes, anoxic changes then supervene, though prolonged artificial respiration and cardiac massage may occasionally achieve recovery after startlingly long periods. Probably the longest definitely authenticated case is one of 30 minutes' submersion with complete recovery; this occurred in almost icy water, where the hypothermic effects undoubtedly aided the sucessful resuscitation.

External signs of drowning

These depend largely on the length of immersion and the water temperature. After a short time in the water, the body may appear normal, though the classical sign of profuse frothing from the mouth and nostrils may be present. This is seen in a minority of cases, and is due to oedema fluid from the lungs, following damage to the alveolar walls. It is not merely inspired water blown into bubbles, as such a persistent froth is impossible to obtain from a non-proteinaceous fluid.

Bodies recovered from cold water may be a striking pink colour, almost suggestive of carbon monoxide poisoning, though it is a bright scarlet, rather than a purplish hue. The same colour may be seen in cases of hypothermia and even in bodies after refrigeration. It appears to be due to stasis of unreduced blood in the superficial skin plexuses.

The skin surface may become sodden and wrinkled after a few hours' immersion. The foot and hand pads may show this change even after an hour or so in the water. Like the skin colour, they are not indications of drowning, but merely of immersion.

Definitive evidence of drowning

This is far less easy to obtain than was formerly thought, even after a complete autopsy. The classical post-mortem appearances of waterlogged lungs and air passages filled with froth, are seen in less than half the cases of bodies recovered from the water. The so-called 'dry-lung' drowning is frequent, and the actual fact of drowning, as opposed to sudden death from cardiac arrest, is often impossible to prove. Attempts at analysing the chloride content on the left and right sides of the heart are usually futile, except in bodies examined very soon after death. The presence of foreign matter in the respiratory passages, such as weed, silt, sand etc., is useful evidence if the matter has penetrated deeply into the lung, but its presence in the trachea may be due to passive percolation after death has occurred.

The use of the diatom test has helped in some cases (Fig. 29), though is of less practical use than is suggested by some authorities. The rationale of the test is that diatoms in the water are inspired into the lungs in cases of true drowning, pass through the alveolar membrane and are pumped by the circulation to distant organs such as bone marrow, kidney and liver. When demonstrated at these peripheral sites, after acid digestion of organs recovered at post-mortem, they then proved that immersion occured whilst the heart was still beating. Conversely, if a body has not drowned, but

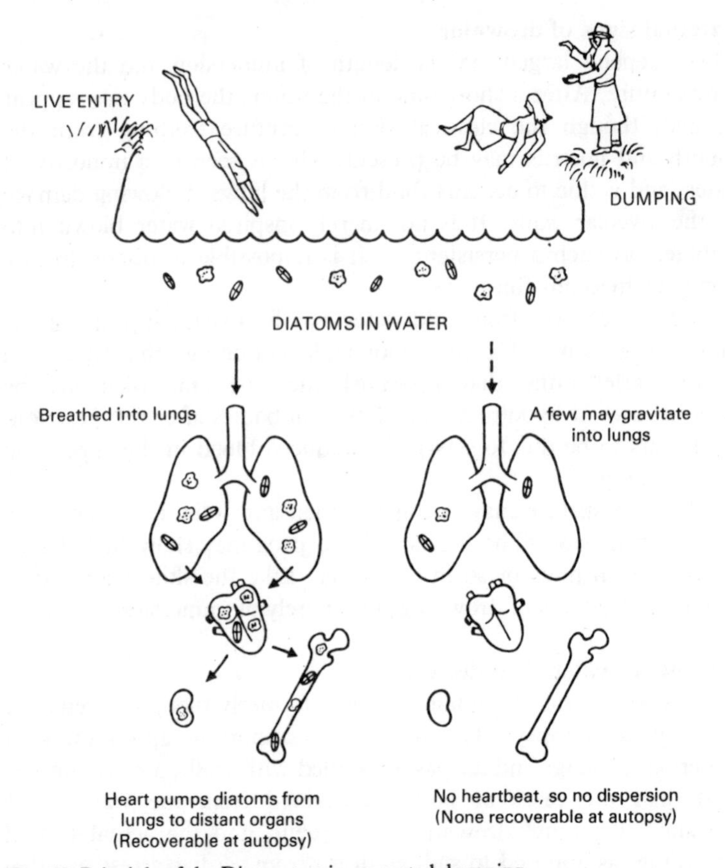

Fig. 29 Principle of the Diatom test in suspected drowning

has either died suddenly in the water or been deposited there after death from some other (possibly criminal) cause, then though there may be diatoms in the *lung* from post-mortem percolation, there cannot be any in distant organs, as the circulation had ceased. The defects of this attractive scheme are:

1. Water frequently contains no diatoms. Polluted water, which constitutes a substantial portion of inland waters in Britain, contains no diatoms. In other waters, diatoms may be both very scanty (especially in quickly-running streams) and they are seasonal in abundance, being very sparse or absent in cold weather. Sea water is more constant in its diatom content, but even here the numbers may be very small.
2. There is a small, but appreciable diatom contamination of the atmosphere and everything in contact with it. Diatoms have

been obtained from many sources around a dry body, though admittedly in small numbers. Tap water frequently contains diatoms.

3. Contamination at autopsy is extremely difficult to avoid. A body which has been recovered from diatom-containing water has to be treated extremely carefully in order to obtain tissue from the deeper parts of organs which have not been exposed to fluids or instruments in contact with the body surface. Aspiration of bone marrow is probably the safest method.

In spite of these disadvantages, where diatoms are recovered, they can be extremely useful: in the case of marine diatoms, an expert biologist can sometimes even indicate the locality where the preponderant varieties are likely to be found. This was so in a well-publicised case with criminal complications which occurred in the English Channel (R. *v.* Verrier, 1964).

19

Sexual offences

These were formerly offences under the Common Law and the Offences Against the Person Act, 1861, but recently have been codified in a series of Statutes:

1. Sexual Offences Act, 1956 – covers most offences.
2. Sexual Offences Act, 1967 – concerns homosexual practices between consenting adults.
3. Indecency with Children Act, 1960.
4. Sexual Offences (Amendment) Act, 1976.

RAPE AND UNLAWFUL SEXUAL INTERCOURSE

The law

Under the old law, rape was defined as 'unlawful carnal knowledge of a woman by force and against her will'. It was rephrased under the Sexual Offences Act, 1956 as 'unlawful sexual intercourse without her consent by force, fear or fraud'.

Following the Report of the Advisory Group on the Law of Rape (1975), usually known as the Heilbron Committee, rape was further re-defined by the Sexual Offences (Amendment) Act 1976 as *unlawful sexual intercourse by a man with a woman who at the time of intercourse does not consent to it and at the time, he knows that she does not consent or is reckless as to whether she consents.*

Rape is such a serious offence, punishable by anything up to life imprisonment, that both the legal and medical aspects must be understood in detail. The definition of rape itself needs precise clarification.

'Unlawful'

Sexual intercourse may be unlawful by virtue of the female's age or by lack of consent. Intercourse with a girl less than 16 years of age is always unlawful, consent being immaterial. Above this age, consent precludes rape, except in the case of mental defectives as will be mentioned later. It is upon the doubt surrounding the presence or absence of consent that many prosecutions for rape founder.

A man cannot be charged with raping his wife, unless a legal separation is in force between them. He can, however, be accused of assault, of causing grievous bodily harm etc., in a criminal court, and the act of forceful intercourse may constitute cruelty in civil divorce proceedings. If a man 'marries' a girl below the age of 16, it is a good defence to prove that he had reasonable cause to assume that she was over 16.

'Sexual intercourse'

For a charge of rape to lie, there must be a degree of penetration of the female by the male organ. The degree is immaterial, so long as the tip of the penis passes between the labia. Full introduction or the emission of semen is irrelevant, so long as at least partial penetration has occurred. Thus, non-rupture of an intact hymen does not preclude rape, and conversely, resulting pregnancy does not confirm rape, as conception is well known to occur from deposition of semen upon the vulva.

'Woman'

Rape is sexual intercourse without consent with or without force, but in certain circumstances, intercourse may be 'unlawful' even if apparent consent is given. In these circumstances, the distinction between a woman and a girl is important.

Consent is invalid if given by girls under the age of 16 years, so all such intercourse is unlawful. However, a man may have a defence against such a charge if he can show that:

1. he is under the age of 24 years
2. he has not been charged previously with a similar offence
3. the girl is between 13 and 16 years of age
4. he had reason to believe from the appearance of the girl (e.g. demeanour, development, dress, make-up etc.) that she was above the age of 16.

If the girl is under 13, then intercourse is unlawful in any circumstances, but it is not rape unless there was no consent. Naturally, in very immature girls or children, such consent is lacking almost by definition.

It is presumed in English law that a boy under the age of 14 years is incapable of rape. Even though this is medically unfounded, the presumption cannot be rebutted in law.

Mental subnormality

Sexual intercourse with a mentally defective woman is unlawful, irrespective of apparent consent, for as with children, the law assumes that a mentally deficient woman is not capable of forming valid consent. The degree of defect required is defined by the Mental Health Act 1959, being equivalent to severe subnormality – 'a woman he knows to be a mental defective or a woman who is under the care or treatment of an institution, certified house or approved home within the meaning of the Act or placed out on licence therefrom'. It is also a specific offence for any person on the staff of a mental institution to take sexual advantage of any female patient.

As with girls between 13 and 16, it is a defence for a man to show that he did not know, or could not reasonably suspect, that the woman was subnormal.

'Force'

The use of the phrase 'by force and against her will' covers not only physical overpowering, but other means to attain intercourse without unqualified consent.

(a) Drink or drugs

The use of stupefying drugs (such as chloroform or barbiturate) or alcohol, with the intent to reduce a woman's understanding or capabilities to the point where she would not resist intercourse, is sufficient to constitute rape. In the case of alcohol, it is frequently impossible to distinguish consent arising out of heavy social drinking, from destruction to willpower by alcohol. The surrounding circumstances, which may be no concern of the doctors, usually determine whether or not a prosecution takes place.

(b) Threat of violence

Even if no physical force is used, the use of terror or threats sufficient to allow intercourse to take place, constitutes duress and a charge of rape may still stand, even if the threats are delivered against some other person, such as children.

(c) Fraud

This has occurred either by impersonation of the husband, in a darkened bedroom etc., or by convincing gullible women that intercourse is a necessary part of some quack medical treatment (or even, in one instance, said to improve a singing voice!).

(d) Sleep
It is a debatable point whether intercourse can be achieved whilst a women is asleep, but it has certainly been alleged on several occasions.

Indecent assault
Any unlawful sexual advance which falls short of rape, i.e. absence of penile penetration, is indecent assault. In most cases this consists of manual fondling of vulva or breasts, disarrangement of clothing and so on. In theory, this may be committed by a male or a female, but the majority of cases involve older men assaulting young girls. As with rape, lack of consent must be shown, unless the girl is less than 16 years of age or a mental defective. No distinction between girls of 13–16 years is made as with rape.

There is a particular risk in medicine and dentistry of unfounded allegations of indecent assault, either through malice or through confusion following anaesthetics for dental or minor operations. Though often impracticable in general practice, it is a counsel of perfection always to have a female chaperone present when examining a female patient, and it is an unjustifiable risk to omit a chaperone when administering anaesthetics. The allegations of a woman when recovering from the affects of gas and oxygen or intravenous barbiturates are not always malicious, the effects of the narcosis sometimes leaving the genuine belief in a woman's mind that she has suffered sexual interference.

Indecent exposure
This is more a psychiatric disorder than a criminal offence, but is extremely common. Apart from the frights inflicted upon young girls and old ladies, it does little harm, and attention should be directed more to mental support of the exhibitionist than to the criminal aspects.

Indecency with children
A loop-hole existed in the law where the offence consisted of a man inciting children to handle his own genitalia, or masturbating himself in the presence of children. There was thus no assault upon the children, and to make provision for the punishment of this undesirable behaviour, the Indecency with Children Act, 1960 was brought into force. This makes it an offence for a person to commit an 'act of gross indecency' with or towards a child under the age of 14. The medical aspects are virtually nil, apart from the activities of the psychiatrist.

Incest

Though of biblical vintage, the crime of incest has been codified under the Sexual Offences Act, 1956. The list of prohibited degrees of consanguinity is shorter than the one given in the prayer books, it being an offence under English law for a man to have intercourse with his mother, sister, daughter, grand-daughter or half-sister. The same degrees of relationship are prohibited between a woman and her male relatives of equal rank. Incest most commonly occurs between a father and a young daughter, and apart from incest, there may also be an offence by virtue of the girl being under the age of 16.

Homosexual offences

Under the Common Law and older Statutes, the offence of 'buggery' was an extremely serious one. Following changes in public attitude, the Sexual Offences Act, 1967 was passed, which removes homosexual acts between consenting adults in private from the ambit of the criminal law.

It should be noted that:

1. 'Adult' means any person more than 21 years of age. This has not been affected by the recent change in the age of majority from 21 down to 18 years.
2. 'Private place' specifically excludes public lavatories, which provide a frequent locale for homosexual activities.
3. A boy of less than 14 years cannot be accused of buggery (or indeed of rape, as he is held to be sexually immature). He can, however, be charged with indecent assault.
4. This Act does not apply to Scotland or Ireland.
5. Merchant seamen and members of the Armed forces cannot take advantage of this 1967 Act, buggery remaining an offence for them under Section 12 of the Sexual Offences Act of 1956.
6. Apart from consenting adults in private, all male homosexual acts are illegal. As in rape, proof of penetration of the anus is required, but not seminal emission. Female homosexuality ('lesbianism') is no offence, but as with many male cases in which penetration cannot be proved, a charge of gross indecency could be brought.

Bestiality

Intercourse with an animal, whether vaginal or anal, is an unusual charge to be made before a criminal court, though probably the practice is by no means rare. The bulk of the evidence in these singular cases is usually scientific rather than medical, in the shape of identification of animal hairs and body exudates.

SCHEME OF MEDICAL EXAMINATION IN SEXUAL OFFENCES

Though probably at least half of the allegations of sexual interference are unfounded, especially where young teenage girls are concerned, every case must be approached by the practitioner with meticulous care, both for his own protection and in the cause of justice. In many large conurbations, a female doctor, either a general practitioner or gynaecologist, may specialise in such examinations or the regular police surgeon may deal with the matter. In one or two university cities, the forensic pathology department assumes responsibility for this work. However, in times of emergency or where no regular doctor is available, the police may request any practitioner to assist them in this serious matter. The Sexual Offences Act, 1956 states that 'a person shall not be convicted of an offence on the evidence of one witness only, unless the witness is corroborated in some material particular by evidence implicating the accused'. This corroborative evidence is frequently medical or scientific in nature, and hence considerable responsibility rests upon the doctor.

1. It is essential for the doctor to obtain consent from the woman concerned, if over 16, or from the parents or guardians of a girl below this age. Police forces usually have special printed forms of consent, but in any case the doctor should refuse a police request to examine where no consent is forthcoming.

2. Justice cannot be done to either the parties involved or to the doctor, if adequate conditions are not available for examination. The doctor should refuse a police request to examine in some ill-lit office of a police station and unless a special clinical examination room is available, the alleged victim should be taken to a surgery or hospital premises where adequate lighting, couch and instruments are available.

3. Before any examination, the doctor should become acquainted with all the background details. Though in many types of crime, the circumstantial evidence and the medical evidence remain independent, alleged sexual assaults are one case in which these are indivisible.

4. The doctor should first speak to the alleged victim and her female companion. This usually involves a girl and her mother. If the girl is of particularly tender years, she should not be distressed

by long questioning about the circumstances, but these obtained from the adult present. With a more mature woman, careful questioning should be made to ascertain her version of the events, as well as general details of her health, menstrual history etc. Part of the purpose of this is to arrive at an opinion about her character, probable truthfulness, mental state, and general awareness of sexual matters. This is not 'playing detective', as would be the case in dealing with a homicide, but a legitimate part of the examination.

5. A full record must be kept, this being equally as important as in other medico-legal matters. Apart from the usual details, the exact time of examination and the person requesting examination should be carefully and legibly recorded.

6. The general demeanour of the alleged victim, her appearance (dishevelled clothing, hair, state of agitation or emotion) should be noted. Her apparent age should be compared with her stated age, as well as an opinion as to her maturity, her mode of dress and make-up compared with her real age. The latter points are of particular relevance if the girl is between 13 and 16 years.

7. Though the minute scientific details of examination of the clothing are the concern of the Home Office forensic science laboratory, the doctor is the only person with the opportunity to observe more gross disorders of clothing. However, there is frequently a natural reluctance on the part of the woman to undress in front of a male doctor and the chaperone (usually a police-woman) should take over the actual observation of the clothing during undressing and report any relevant findings to the doctor. The undressing should be carried out with the woman standing on a large sheet of new brown paper, which must afterwards be folded carefully and sent to the Forensic Laboratory, to be searched for contact traces. If the girl has alleged that she was partly stripped, the clothes may have been replaced in the wrong order or inside out or backwards and this should be recorded. Tears, mud, blood and seminal stains should be carefully noted. Grass or other vegetable matter adherent should be carefully removed and preserved with a note of the position on the clothing. The woman accompanying the alleged victim should have been asked to bring another set of clothing, as that worn by the victim will be required for further examination. The original clothing (it is well to confirm that this was in fact the clothing worn at the time of the alleged incident) should be carefully packed in either polythene bags or clean brown paper for transmission to the laboratory. If there is to be any delay in delivery, brown paper is preferable to

polythene, as the latter tends to encourage the growth of moulds.

8. A general physical examination should be conducted first, partly for its own value and partly to reassure the alleged victim. An abrupt and immediate genital examination does nothing to allay fears and generate confidence, especially in an overwrought and possibly hysterical girl.

The whole body should be examined for injuries, mud, blood or seminal stains, particular attention being paid to the back of the upper arms, the shoulder blades and buttocks as well as the more obvious places such as thighs, neck, face and breasts. Where the offence had allegedly taken place outdoors, corroboration can sometimes be obtained by finding grass, leaves or mud-smears on the buttocks or back. Teeth marks or suction petechiae, from the assailant's mouth, may be found on the neck or breasts or abdomen, and there may be laceration of the nipples from teeth. Bruising of the lips and even tearing of the inner aspect may be found, due to blows or rough kissing. Any suspicious seminal stains on the thighs or other part of the body should be cut away from hairs if dried, or captured by a moistened swab if on the skin surface. Police forces frequently supply boxed kits for the medical and scientific investigation of alleged sexual offences. These are made up either by or on the advice of the Home Office Forensic Science laboratories and contain swabs, blood and saliva tubes, syringes, combs etc.

9. *Examination of genitalia*. A good light is essential, and the lithotomy position is preferable. Bruises, scratches, and stains on the thighs and buttocks should be looked for. The pubic hair should be examined and any matted stains or foreign material cut away and preserved. The pubic hair should be combed out, as non-matching male pubic hair may be present. All samples should be carefully retained, packed and labelled. A sample of pubic hair should be plucked out at the end of the examination.

The vulva should be inspected and palpated for scratches, swelling, bruises or other traumatic or natural lesions. Vaginal swabs and aspiration of fluid with a pipette should be made before digital examination. Smears on microscope slides should not be made unless there is to be an untoward delay (a day or more) in forwarding swabs to the laboratory.

The state of the hymen and the vaginal orifice should be examined. Considerable experience is required to differentiate between the many types of hymen, but any practitioner should be able to recognise a recent tear, with the signs of acute injury such as tenderness, swelling and bleeding. The degree of dilation of the introitus and vaginal passage can also be estimated, and it should be obvious if the woman or girl has been used to sexual intercourse. Rough assaults on young girls may cause more severe injury, such as rupture of fourchette and perineum. Fingernail scratches may be present on the labia or vaginal orifice. The anus must also be examined, swelling, reddening, tenderness and dilation being important. A swab should be taken from the anus in any case where there is any possibility of anal intercourse.

The hymen may be conveniently examined by inserting a glass globe on a stem which is then partially withdrawn so that the hymen is spread around its circumference. However, in most instances, a conventional examination using a speculum is carried out. It is said that tears of the hymen due to rupture with the fingers are usually lateral, whilst rupture with the penis are usually posterior. The truth of this is generally open to doubt, but there is another useful indicator or whether a deep indentation in the hymena border is an old healed tear or merely an anatomical variant. The latter does not extend right to the vaginal wall, whereas an old tear from previous penetration does reach the wall. The most important point is to detect a recent tear, however caused, and to ascertain whether or not hymenal tears are of long duration with healing or atrophy. This may not necessarily be due to habitual intercourse, as digital masturbation and the use of vaginal tampons may also cause dilatation of the introitus. The examination should end with deep vaginal examination, as occasionally high vaginal tears occur, especially in violent assaults on children. The swabs should be sent to the laboratory both for microscopic examination and bacteriological culture. The presence of gonococcal infection may be a relevant fact if the alleged assailant suffers from the disease.

Other precautions in serious cases include the taking of fingernail scrapings in case the victim has managed to scratch her assailant and thus have fragments of skin beneath her nails which may be blood grouped: also a venous blood sample and saliva is required from the victim for comparison studies with any alleged culprit. It is vital that medical examination should take place as soon as possible after the alleged incident. For centuries, it has been recognised that the validity of an allegation of rape often turns upon the interval between the alleged assault and the time of reporting to the authorities. It must again be emphasised that the majority of allegations are false, usually because consent was given at the time, and later regretted. There may be an interval of one or more days between a girl complaining to her mother or directly to the police. In genuine cases, the complaint will usually be made at the earliest possible opportunity. The time interval has considerable medical importance. Minor degrees of injury may fade rapidly, and vulval swelling and tenderness may vanish with a few hours. Though spermatozoa may thrive in the genital tract for a long time, the hope of recovering them also diminishes with the passage of time.

The report is of vital importance. It should be made immediately after examination and be comprehensive, containing negative as well as positive findings. Unless obvious severe genital injuries with visible seminal fluid can be seen (a relatively rare occurrence), the doctor is not in a position to say that rape has occurred, but only that recent intercourse has or has not taken place, and that various injuries are or are not present on the genitalia or general body surface. His job is to record such findings and injuries, and interpret them to the court at the time of trial, not to pre-judge the issue on medical grounds alone.

Examination of the alleged assailant in sexual assaults

This exercise is far less common than the examination of the female, but may be requested by the police. Again consent must be obtained without fail, after telling the accused person the object of the examination, thus not laying one's self open to a defence charge of obtaining evidence under pretext of some general medical examination. The clothing is equally important, and it should be confirmed that it was the actual outfit worn at the time of the alleged offence. Obvious blood or seminal stains should be noted.

A general examination should be made, looking especially for fingernail scratches on the face or arms, groins, buttocks and loins.

The genitals should be examined, with a note of the penile size, which may be relevant where serious injury has been inflicted on the woman. Again swelling, tenderness and damage, especially to the rim of the glans and the frenulum are important. Foreign material such as blood, vegetable matter or mud stains on the knees, buttocks and pubic hair should be looked for. Samples of the pubic hair should be taken, and as in the case of the female combed out for the presence of foreign hairs.

The presence of active venereal disease should be sought.

A test favoured on the Continent is that of painting the glans penis with dilute iodine solution, the rationale being that the glycogen-rich vaginal epithelium, if present, will stain dark brown. This test is rarely used in Britain.

Blood and saliva samples should be taken for group comparisons.

The detailed examination of the clothing for seminal stains is primarily the job of the forensic science laboratory.

Homosexual offences

Though the various forms of homosexuality, including anal intercourse, are now lawful in England and Wales between consenting adults in private (Sexual Offences Act, 1967), medical examination in cases of alleged buggery may still be required in cases of assault without consent, offences with persons less than 21 years of age, in Servicemen and merchant seamen and exceptionally in anal intercourse with females. Examination of the passive partner may reveal seminal stains on the surrounding skin and hair, and evidence of recent penetration of the anus. Swelling, tenderness, bleeding fissures and tears, acute dilatation and possibly faecal soiling may all provide corroborative evidence of recent forceful penetration. Rectal swabs may reveal evidence of seminal emission.

In the case of chronic passive homosexuals, the sphincter may be partly destroyed, with permanent dilation of the anus. There may be a funnel-shaped approach to the anus and thickened, possibly fissured, keratinised skin around the margin, with loss of the normal mucocutaneous junction. The normal corrugations at the anal margin may be lost as the muscle atrophies.

In either the acute or chronic case, lubricants such as Vaseline or hair cream may be present, and should be sampled by means of a swab.

The active partner

No characteristic signs are to be found, apart from perhaps the presence of lubricant and faecal soiling. Where the act is associated with violence, injuries to the penis may be found as in cases of rape.

SEXUAL OFFENCES IN SCOTLAND

The most serious sexual offences are dealt with under the common law. Previous Criminal Law Amendment Acts between 1885 and 1928 contained sections concerning such offences, but these have been consolidated into the Sexual Offences (Scotland) Act 1976.

Rape, which is prosecuted under the common law, is defined as 'the carnal knowledge of a female by a male person obtained by overcoming her will'. As in England and Wales, intercourse without consent is bound to be rape, but where apparent consent is given by a young person, similar provisions apply as in the English Act. Thus if a girl between 13 and 16 gives consent, then it is a defence for a first offender male to show that he is himself under 24 and had reasonable cause to assume that the girl was over 16.

In England, it is always unlawful for a man to have intercourse with a girl under 13. In Scotland the similar offence is 'having or attempting to have intercourse with a girl under 13', but under the common law, it is 'constructive rape' for a man to have intercourse with a girl under 12.

Whereas in England, it is an irrebuttable assumption in law that a boy under 14 cannot commit rape, no such presumption exists in Scotland.

The provisions concerning intercourse with mental defectives are substantially the same in Scotland as across the border. The law in question is the Mental Health (Scotland) Act 1960.

The Indecency with Children Act of 1960 has no parallel in Scotland, but such offences as are provided for in the English Act are referred to in Scotland as 'loose and libidinous practices'. They are dealt with under the common law when children under the age of puberty are involved, which is held to be 12 years in the case of girls. Between the ages of 12 and 16, the offence is defined in Section 5 of the Sexual Offences (Scotland) Act 1976. The child's consent nor misapprehension as to true age is available as a defence.

Where homosexual offences are concerned, the Westminster Sexual Offences Act 1967 does not have a counterpart in Scotland. There is therefore no provision for making lawful, homosexual activities between consenting adults in private, but the Lord Advocate has directed that no prosecutions are to be brought under these circumstances. Excluding these consenting adults acting in private, the law in Scotland is more severe in respect of buggery than in England. Such offences are dealt with at common law. Gross indecency between males (where there is evidence short of actual penetration) the Sexual Offences (Scotland) Act 1976 is invoked. A consenting child cannot be charged with such an offence.

Incest has interesting legal connotations in Scotland, as the law remains based on a statute of 1567 – the Incest Act which was not repealed by the 1976 Act. This ancient Act is in turn founded on Biblical pronouncements (Leviticus, Chapter 18), but is even more restrictive in the degrees of relationship than are the Old Testament provisions.

Bestiality in Scotland is again a common law offence, termed 'unnatural carnal connection with an animal' and appears to be a crime applicable only to males.

SEXUAL OFFENCES IN THE IRISH REPUBLIC

The law in the Republic of Ireland relating to sexual offences differs from that in other parts of the British Isles as follows: where English law decrees that where sexual intercourse, even with the consent of the female partner, under the age of thirteen, constitutes rape, in Ireland the age is fifteen; and where sexual intercourse with females under the age of sixteen in English law constitutes a lesser offence, the age in Ireland is seventeen. This was the result of the Criminal Law Amendment Act of the Irish Free State of 1935. Homosexual behaviour between consenting males of any age is still a criminal offence. The definition of rape in Irish law is still that of The Offences Against the Person Act 1861. It is noteworthy also that Irish law does not recognise a defence for a male committing rape for the first time under the age of 24.

20

Pregnancy

Proof of pregnancy has several medico-legal applications, whether the pregnancy be past, present or even a potential future event.

Such evidence of pregnancy may be important in the following situations:

1. In the case of alleged abortion, it may be necessary to show that the woman has recently been pregnant.
2. A similar situation may arise in connection with a charge of infanticide, child destruction or concealment of birth.
3. Pregnancy may increase the damages in an action for breach of promise of marriage or seduction.
4. In an action for defamation, where it has been said of an unmarried woman, widow or separated wife that she is pregnant, proof of the presence or absence of pregnancy is obviously vital.
5. A woman advanced in pregnancy may be excused attendance at court as a witness: the mere fact of pregnancy is not sufficient as the medical attendant must certify that her health or the imminence of delivery makes attendance medically undesirable.
6. Occasionally, the disposition of the estate of a dead husband may be affected by the expectation of a posthumous heir from a pregnant wife. Closely related to this, the potential ability of a woman to produce further children may be relevant in the disposition of property, evidence being required that a women has not reached the menopause.
7. Rarely, imposture of pregnancy may require medical evidence.

A former need for evidence of pregnancy no longer exists, this being the bar to execution of a pregnant woman convicted of murder.

PROOF OF PREGNANCY

Proof of present, recent or past pregnancy may be required in either the living or the dead woman.

Signs of existing pregnancy

Suggestive signs of early pregnancy:

Amenorrhoea.
Breast symptoms.
Frequency of micturition.
Nausea or vomiting (morning or otherwise).
Leucorrhoea.
Objective signs – discoloration of vaginal walls, softening of the cervix, Hegar's sign (ballotment of the uterus) and breast and nipple changes.

Absolute signs:

Fetal movements.
Palpitation of fetal parts.
Fetal heart sounds.
Radiological evidence of fetal parts.
Biological urine tests.

The contents of a gravid uterus may be palpated at about 16 weeks, but actual fetal parts usually cannot be distinguished until 24 weeks, when fetal hearts sounds may be heard. Radiology may reveal parts of the fetal skeleton as early as 14 weeks, but radiology should be used with reluctance, especially in early pregnancy, due to its possible effects on the fetus.

Proof of recent delivery

Uterus palpable above the pubis until about the 10th-14th day.
Dilatation and laxity of the vaginal orifice, possibly with perineal tear.
Discharge of lochia, often blood-stained until the seventh day and then brownish for a further one or two weeks.
Swelling and tension of the breasts with milk expressible after the third day. Pigmentation of areola, congested veins under the skin following recent delivery.
Striae gravidarum on the abdomen, of a pinkish colour.
Softening and wide patency of the cervix, possibly with a recent tear.

Signs of past pregnancy

White striae on the abdomen (lineae albicantes).
Frequent persistent dilatation of the vervix beyond the nulliparous state.
Old cervical scars.
Persistent darkening of the areolae of the breasts.
Signs of old tearing of the perineum.
Loss of virginal rugosity of vaginal walls (inconclusive).
Pigmented streak in mid-line of power abdominal skin from umbilicus to pubis.

All the above signs apply to the living woman: at post-mortem, direct evidence of pregnancy or recent delivery can be observed with the additional assistance of the condition of the ovaries, especially that of a corpus luteum.

Duration of pregnancy

This is likely to be a question for the expert testimony of specialist obstretrician and gynaecologist, the issue arising occasionally in divorce suits where adultery has been alleged on the grounds that pregnancy has occurred in the absence of the husband. The periods which have been accepted by courts as consistent with a legitimate pregnancy are hardly compatible with accepted medical opinion. The normal perod is 40 weeks or 280 days, though this average period may be shortened or lengthened by several weeks.

So far as extended pregnancy is concerned, a period of 349 days has been accepted by an English court, but in another case which went on appeal to the House of Lords, a period of 360 days was rejected.

At the other extreme, the birth of a 2½-lb infant was accepted as being the result of 174 days' gestation. With the advent of more sophisticated paternity testing by means of blood groups, the importance of such theorising has declined.

21

Abortion

Abortion is a spontaneous or induced evacuation of the pregnant uterus, almost always before the 28th week of pregnancy, after which it may be considered a premature labour. The term 'miscarriage' is an older synonym for abortion. About one in five of all pregnancies abort.

TYPES OF ABORTION

1. Natural spontaneous abortion

This is an extremely common condition thought to account for about 60 per cent of all abortions, though estimates vary widely. In 1950, Davis investigated almost 3000 abortions and came to the conclusion that 90 per cent had been induced, the majority by the woman herself at about the 12th week. The causes are largely unknown, but chronic disease in the mother – such as nephritis, hypertension, pelvic disease, syphilis – or an abnormality of the ovum itself, are frequently held responsible. The only medico-legal interest in natural abortions is the difficulty in distinguishing them from deliberately induced abortion.

2. Criminal abortion

(a) Induced by the woman herself

After natural abortion, this is the second most common situation, very large numbers of self-induced miscarriages occurring annually. Estimates of the number of abortions are impossible to obtain, but as long ago as 1939 it was estimated that about 150 000 abortions occurred annually in England and Wales of which 40 per cent were criminal. It was also estimated that only about 5 per cent were performed by persons other than the woman herself.

(b) Criminal abortions performed by other persons

As already mentioned, the minority of abortions are caused in this way, but these are the ones which are of most medico-legal interest, as the woman who aborts herself is almost never prosecuted. The remaining group, where the abortion is induced by others, may be the result of a professional abortionist, commonly a doctor or nurse, or may be the well-meaning amateur efforts of friends or relatives.

The law concerning abortion

The definitive statute law is more than a century old, the Offences Against the Person Act, 1861. This states that any person is guilty of an offence (formerly of the now defunct 'felony'), if he or she attempts to unlawfully procure a woman's abortion by administering any poison or other noxious thing or shall unlawfully use any instrument or any other means whatsoever. It should be noted that there is a difference in the law for the woman herself and any other party, for in the first case the woman has to be *pregnant* before any crime is committed. In the case of other persons, the *intent* to procure abortion even in the absence of the pregnancy, is sufficient to constitute the offence. As in practice, the woman herself is almost never prosecuted, this difference is academic.

A slightly less serious offence is for another party, not to procure the abortion but to supply any 'noxious thing or instrument'.

It will be noted that this old Act allowed no provision whatsoever for therapeutic termination of pregnancy and for many years until the 1967 Abortion Act, the law was in a confused state. The only concession to therapeutic abortion was in the Infant Life Preservation Act of 1929, which recognised the right of a child to a separate existence after the 28th week. As an off-shoot of this Act, an exception to criminal liability was granted if the act was performed 'in good faith and for the purpose only of preserving the life of the mother'. Though until the 1967 Act, no further legislation was enacted, the famous case of R. *v.* Bourne in 1939 gave a powerful precedent for therapeutic abortion, though this only concerned the mental and physical health of the mother, and not the other factors mentioned under the recent Act.

The penalties for criminal abortion are extremely heavy, and in addition, any doctor convicted of such an offence would be inevitably erased from the Medical Register. Though unfortunately numerous instances of deliberate and repeated exploits in criminal abortion have been proved against medical practitioners, some doctors have been unwittingly tricked into improperly terminating pregnancy by their lack of suspicion when confronted by a female patient, often one who has not previously appeared before them. The patient's gambit is either to request version of a retroverted uterus or treatment for retained products of a previous recent miscarriage. If such a case comes to light, the doctor may be hard put to prove his innocence.

Death from criminal abortion

The death rate from abortion has thankfully dropped precipitately during the last few decades, mainly due to the use of antibiotics in septic cases. In 35 years, the annual death rate has fallen from over 500 to less than 20 per cent. The actual figures are 1960 – 62 deaths, 1972 – 26 deaths and 1973 – 12 deaths. This includes spontaneous abortions, but it is an acknowledged fact that the majority of septic abortions have some basis of deliberate interference. Though mortality is low, morbidity may be high, with chronic sepsis in the pelvic organs, retained products, venous thromboses and future complications in subsequent pregnancies.

The doctor's duty in criminal abortion

The duty of the doctor, as always, is to treat the patient and observe the ethical rules of professional conduct. As long as the patient is alive, he has no cause to play detective unless it is apparent that a professional abortionist with a defective technique is liable to cause a fatal result in the future. The police do not want to hear about self-induced abortions unless a fatal outcome arises. If an aborted women should die, then the situation at once becomes completely different. The case is naturally reportable to the coroner, and all evidence must then be placed before the authorities.

The maintenance of professional confidence in abortion cases has been under fire on several occasions from learned judges. After a particularly virulent attack, the Royal College of Physicians took legal advice on the matter, and came firmly to the conclusion that the doctor has no legal duty whatsoever to report cases of criminal abortion to the authorities, unless the woman requests or agrees to this.

In actual practice, the attitude of the doctor to disclosure depends on the nature of the abortionist. A kindly neighbour attempting to relieve an acute social embarassment poses a different problem from the organised mercenary activities of a professional abortionist who fails to use aseptic methods.

METHODS EMPLOYED TO PROCURE ABORTION

Drugs etc.

These are almost invariably unsuccessful, but still enjoy consider-

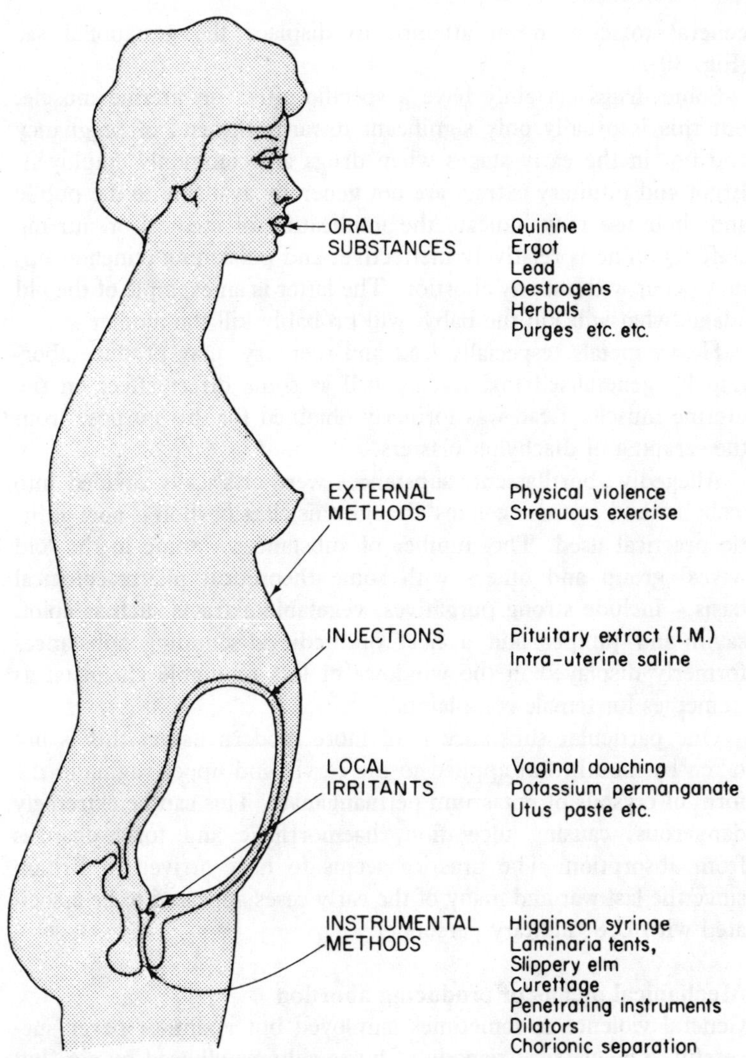

Fig. 30 Methods of attempting abortion

able popularity as an early method or attempted abortion. One exception is the recently-introduced 'prostaglandin' which is now employed as a legitimate method under the 1967 Abortion Act. Its use is so far almost totally confined to medical hands. Drugs are usually employed before proceeding to mechanical means when the problem becomes more urgent, usually after the second missed period. The number of substances which have been used is almost infinite, but all hopefully depend for their action on a direct contraction effect on the uterus or by the production of pelvic congestion and general toxicity in an attempt to displace the gestational sac (Fig. 30).

Some drugs certainly have a specific effect on uterine muscle, but this is usually only significant towards the end of pregnancy and not in the early stages when drugs are commonly employed. Ergot and pituitary extract are not generally available to the public and their use may indicate the implication of medical or nursing staff. Quinine is relatively ineffective, and poisioning (cinchonism) may occur without any abortion. The latter is an example of the old adage 'what will kill the baby, will probably kill the mother'.

Heavy metals, especially lead and mercury, may produce abortion by generalised toxicity, as well as some direct effect on the uterine muscle. Lead was formerly obtained for this purpose from the scraping of diachylon plasters.

Allegedly abortifacient, substances were classically divided into 'ecbolics and emmenogogues' though this classification is now of little practical used. The number of substances – some in the 'old wives' group and others with some theoretical pharmacological basis – include strong purgatives, vegetable extracts such as apiol, savin and juniper and a host of medieval-sounding substances formerly displayed in the windows of less reputable chemists, as 'remedies for female complaints'.

One particular substance is of more modern usage; this is not taken by mouth, but applied to the cervix and upper vagina in the form of crystals of potassium permanganate. This can be extremely dangerous, causing ulceration, haemorrhage and toxic changes from absorption. The practice seems to have arrived in Britain since the last war and many of the early cases appeared to be associated with U.S. military personnel.

Mechanical means of producing abortion

General violence is sometimes employed but is almost never successful. The classical remedy of horse-riding, followed by gin, hot bath and enema may be apocryphal, but certainly extreme violence to the abdominal wall is not unknown and has in some cases led to death from rupture of underlying organs. Displacement of the pregnancy is very rare even in these extreme cases. The co-operation of a husband or consort may be involved, heavy blows with the fist or even foot having resulted in these gross intra-abdominal injuries.

By far the most common – and virtually the only effective method – is local violence to the contents of the uterus by means of instruments or local irritants. This is always the method employed by professional abortionists.

EFFECTIVE METHODS OF PROCURING ABORTION

Vacuum aspiration of uterus

This method is becoming increasingly popular as a routine legitimate technique for emptying the pregnant uterus; it is now the most common single method used in British hospitals. As the procedure is very free from risk compared with other methods, it is also becoming the method of choice amongst illegal abortionists, especially the pregnant woman herself. In its 'do-it-youself' version, a 10 or 20 ml syringe is fitted with a length of plastic tubing, slipped directly over the nozzle. The tube is inserted into the uterus and forcible suction applied. This either aspirates part of the products of conception or so damages the uterine contents that expulsion of the remainder soon occurs. The plastic tube can easily be sterilized and there is no risk of air embolism, so the major dangers can be prevented. The worst harm that can happen, given sensible precautions, is failure to abort, but repetition is simple. Some authorities believe that this method will become almost universal medical practice and it may even become such a common-place self administered operation as to fall almost into the category of 'birth control'.

Introduction of irritant paste into the cervix

Several compounds have been used, some being proprietary substances manufactured expressly for this purpose, such as Utus paste. They are introduced into the cervical canal by means of a special applicator and are usually self-sterilising. Either by local toxic action on the foetus or by local necrosis and separation of the chorio-endometrial junction, the products of the gestation are expelled.

Direct mechanical penetration of the uterine cavity

This may be done with a variety of instruments, from the most crude implements of the pregnant women herself or her lay assistants, to the full surgical apparatus of the medical abortionist, who may virtually perform a dilatation and curettage.

The chorionic sac may either be perforated with loss of the amniotic fluid or the membranes may be partially stripped from the inside of the uterine wall, either method leading to eventual evacuation of the uterus. Catheters, bougies, uterine sounds, knitting needles, crochet hooks, nails, bicycle spokes and a wide range of other instruments have been employed. Often, mere dilatation of the cervix is sufficient to dislodge the pregnancy, and this is the rationale of the method employing slippery elm bark, which is inserted into the cervical canal, absorbs water and swells to a considerable degree.

Insufflation of the uterus

The use of the Higginson syringe to pump fluid under pressure into the cervical canal is probably the commonest method of effective abortion. Frequency employed by the woman herself, this method again depends on the stripping of the chorionic sac from the uterine wall, either with pure water, but more commonly with the addition of irritant substances such as soap or dilute disinfectant. Though effective, this method also carries the highest risk of a fatal outcome.

Prostaglandins

These recently discovered substances have been found to exert a powerful contractile effect upon uterine muscle and are used to induce therapeutic abortions. Their illegal use would appear to be only a matter of time.

DANGERS OF THE VARIOUS METHODS

Drugs

Drugs may cause generalised toxic effects or specific damage, such as peripheral gangrene in ergotism or the effects of cinchonism. General external violence may cause rupture of abdominal organs, especially liver, spleen and intestine.

In recent years, abortions have been performed both for genuine therapeutic reasons and criminally by the supra-pubic injection of hypertonic saline or glucose into the uterine cavity. Specific lesions in the central nervous system (butterfly haemorrhages in the brain stem) have been reported in fatal cases where strong saline was used.

Air embolism

Syringing of the uterus carries the special risk of air embolism. A high pressure (up to 100 mmHg) can be obtained with vigorous squeezing of the bulb of the Higginson syringe and fluid, sometimes containing toxic antiseptics, may be forced into the highly vascular cleavage plane between chorion and endometrium. The intake end of the syringe may become displaced from the fluid and instead of liquid, the operator pumps air or frothy bubbles into the uterus. This can easily happen when the level of the fluid drops, sometimes masked by a layer of froth on the surface. This air, under considerable pressure, may remain in the uterus for some time, even up to one hour, though usually the effect of embolism occur within seconds or a few minutes. Pathological diagnosis of air

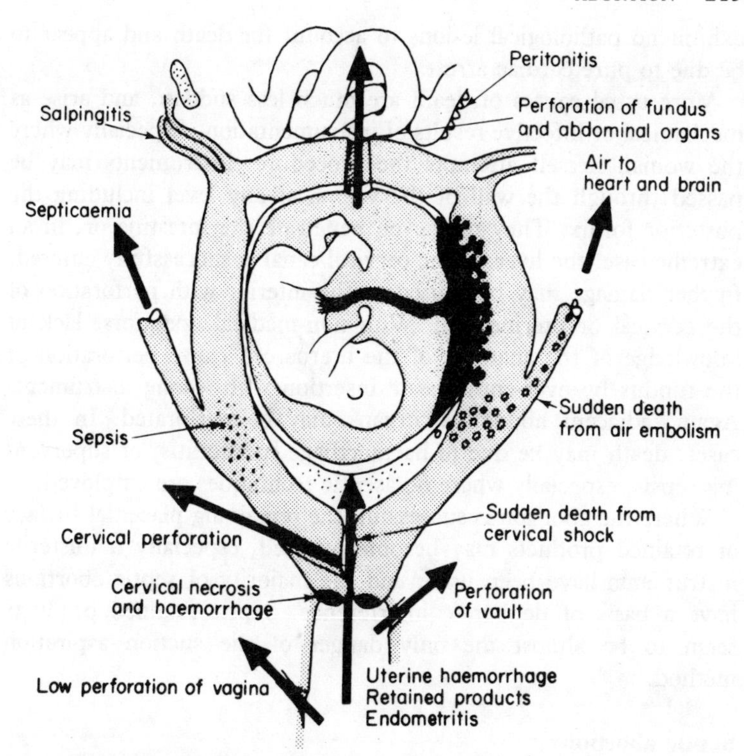

Fig. 31 Dangers of criminal abortion

embolism is of no concern to anyone but a coroner's pathologist, but death occurs as a result of cerebral embolism and failure of cardiac output due to air in the left side of the heart (Fig. 31). The amount needed to cause fatal embolism is in dispute, estimates varying from 10–20 ml, to over 100 ml. It would appear that the site of embolism determines the amount required, small quantities being able to produce actue brain stem anoxia.

The delay in some cases allows a patient to leave the premises of a criminal abortionist and die in the street or even at home, though it is quite impracticable to attempt to estimate the distance between the premises and the place of death from guesses at the length of delay between introduction of air into the uterus and a fatal embolism.

Local instrumentation

Death can occur from a variety of causes. Sudden death has been reported from mere dilatation of the cervix, especially in highly nervous, agitated victims. Loosely termed 'vagal shock', these cases exhibit no pathological lesions to account for death and appear to be due to pure cardiac arrest.

More usual causes of death are much less sudden, and arise as mechanical or infective results of instrumentation. Especially where the woman herself attempts the procedure, instruments may be passed through the wall of the vagina at any level including the posterior fornix. They may even penetrate the intestine or, in an extreme case, the liver. If the cervical canal is successfully entered, further damage may be caused to the interior with perforation of the cervical or uterine wall. With non-medical operators, lack of knowledge of the anatomy of the uterus can cause perforation of the fundus by over-enthusiastic insertion with a long instrument. Again, adjacent abdominal organs may be perforated. In these cases, death may be due to haemorrhage, peritonitis, or supervening sepsis, especially where no aseptic techniques are employed.

Where the abortion is successful, the remaining placental surface or retained products may become infected, especially if unsterile instruments have been used, and the majority of septic abortions have a basis of deliberate interference. Septic retained products seem to be almost the only danger of the suction aspiration method.

Septic abortion

The range of organisms which can cause uterine sepsis following evacuation is large, the most dangerous being *Clostridum welchii*. Other organisms include *E. coli, Strep. pyogenes, Staph. aureus* and anaerobic steptococci. The use of antiseptics in the injection fluid or as a preparatory vaginal douche or to sterilise instruments may be inadequate and when the antiseptic is too strong, may actually cause surface tissue necrosis which encourages, rather than prevents, bacterial growth. In fatal cases, the sepsis usually involves the endometrium, especially the placental bed and any fragments of retained products. Other foci of infection are the tubes, the myometrium and adjacent pelvic organs and peritoneum. Other complications of sepsis are septicaemia, renal failure, distant pyaemic emboli and the not infrequent complication of pelvic or leg vein thrombosis, with the grave risk of subsequent pulmonary embolism.

THE DOCTOR AT THE SCENE OF A FATAL ABORTION

Unless the doctor is a forensic pathologist, this matter is largely outside the province of the practitioner. The only time when examination of the scene takes place, is when death has occurred, and this will rarely involve any doctor other than the police surgeon or coroner's pathologist. As already emphasised, non-fatal cases are not the occasion for detective tactics, and the physician's sole concern should be the treatment of the patient.

If a death does occur, then the evidence of the attending physician may be requested by the coroner or the police. Many factors may point to the deliberate interference with a pregnancy. In cases of sudden death, either from cervical shock or air embolism, the woman will probably still be at the scene of the actual operative interference, often in a semi-undressed condition and often with evidence of the apparatus still to hand, especially if self-induced. Higginson syringes, bowls of soapy water, bottles of disinfectant, blood-stained towels or sheets, all give rise to suspicion that an 'illegal operation' has taken place. Where the procedure has been performed by another person, there is often considerable clearing up of apparatus and rearrangement of the clothing. This is sometimes badly performed in panic, and abortions have been detected where the underclothes or even a corset has been replaced in an obviously abnormal manner. Hot-water burns on the thighs are also suspicious.

Where the doctor has been in attendance before death, he may be able to give information as a result of his examination, including:

1. Relevant details obtained from the woman, even including an admission of induced abortion. The admissibility of such hearsay evidence is a matter for the court.
2. Signs of interference, such as scratches or bruises on the thighs, vaginal walls, cervix etc. There may be volsellum or forcep marks on the cervical lips. Severe local damage often tends to confirm that the abortion was self-induced.
3. The presence of foreign material, such as disinfectant, permanganate or soapy fluid exuding from the vagina or cervix.

THERAPEUTIC ABORTION

The law concerning medical termination of pregnancy has been drastically altered by the Abortion Act of 1967, which applies to England, Wales and Scotland, but not Northern Ireland.

Prior to this, the legal position was a confused mixture of case law (notably R. *v.* Bourne 1939), interpretation of the word 'unlawful' in the Offences Against the Person Act, 1861 and a single clause in the Infant Life Preservation Act of 1929.

Though termination of pregnancy done in non-clandestine circumstances, in good faith and with the concurrence of two doctors was never the subject of criminal proceedings, the whole mechanism needed regularising and the grounds for termination widened beyond the narrow confines of only protecting the physical or mental health of the mother.

The 1967 Act, though arousing much moral and religious opposition, has gone a considerable way towards achieving a more rational system of therapeutic abortion.

The Abortion Act, 1967 and the Abortion Regulations, 1968

The Act came into force on April 27th, 1968 and extends to England, Wales and Scotland, but not Northern Ireland.

Under its provisions, a person (inevitably a doctor) will not be guilty of a criminal offence in terminating a pregnancy if:

1. the termination is performed by a registered medical practitioner
2. two registered medical practitioners (neither of which need necessarily be the one performing the termination) are of the opinion, formed in good faith that:
   a. continuance of the pregnancy would endanger the life of the pregnant woman, or
   b. would injure her physical or mental health, or
   c. would involve injury to the physical or mental health of any existing children of the pregnant woman's family greater than if the pregnancy were terminated, or
   d. there is a substantial risk that if the child were born, it would suffer from such physical or mental abnormalities as to be seriously handicapped.

The Act further provides that in deciding whether the continuance of the pregnancy would involve such risk to the health of the pregnant woman or of her existing children, account may be taken of the woman's actual or reasonably foreseeable environment.

There are several other conditions attached to the above grounds:

1. The termination of pregnancy must be carried out in a hospital administered by the National Health Service or in places specifically approved by the Minister of Health or Secretary of State for Scotland.

2. Where termination is immediately necessary to save the life or to prevent grave permanent injury to the physical or mental health of the woman, it may be carried out anywhere and in such urgent

circumstances, no second medical opinion is required.

3. The working of the Act states that any 'treatment' must be carried out in N.H.S. or approved hospitals, but this does not apply to mere examination to decide on the need for termination.

4. The fact of the termination must be notified in a prescribed manner to the Chief Officer of the Minister of Health or the Chief Medical Officer of the Scottish Home and Health Department.

Interpretation of the various statutory provisions

The certifying practitioners

Though the Act does not specify them, they almost invariably consist of the pregnant woman's general practitioner and a consultant gynaecologist. Very commonly, the latter will be the actual operator who will perform the termination. The situation may arise where a third practitioner will be called upon to perform the termination, but declines because he does not consider that the case falls within the four categories above, or for medical reasons, he does not consider termination to be in the patient's best interest. In these circumstances, he should refer the matter without delay to another gynaecologist for a further opinion, with full consultation with the original certifiers.

Where a practitioner has ethical or religious objections to abortion in general or to any case in particular, he is at liberty to decline to participate in the treatment, even though he may have a contractual obligation to offer treatment of other types. The exception to this rule is where treatment is urgently needed to save the life or prevent grave permanent injury to the physical or mental health of the woman.

Where a doctor has such conscientious objections, he still has a duty to his patient. He should refer her without delay to another doctor if he thinks that either:

1. were it not for his own conscientious objection, it might be lawful to recommend or perform termination, or
2. if he feels that his conscientious objection makes it impossible for him to form an opinion on the question in good faith.

Risk to life or permanent injury to physical or mental health of the pregnant woman.

This matter has not changed because of the advent of the Act. The indications for termination on these grounds are soley to be determined on clinical grounds, either obstetrical, gynaecological, medical or psychiatric or a combination of them.

Children of the family

This must be interpreted in a broad sense, to include all those dependent upon the woman. It includes a single child, illegitimate children, adopted children, step-children and children over the age of 18 dependent because of some mental or physical defect. Even brothers and sisters of an unmarried pregnant woman living with the applicant might be brought within the definition. The test is whether in the broad sense, the children are members of the family and are dependent on the pregnant woman for their health, care and well-being.

Actual or reasonably foreseeable environment

The taking into account of environmental factors was one of the most controversial aspects of the new Act and was wrongly construed by some opponents as leading to 'abortion on demand'. This is far from true and the environment is relevant only in so far as the risk to the health of the woman and children of the family would be aggravated by unfavourable living conditions. Factors such as substandard housing, overcrowding, the husband's circumstances (i.e. whether he is chronically sick, an alcoholic or drug addict or in prison), the number of other children living in poor accommodation, must all be taken into account. Verification and clarification of these matters might require the service of health visitors, probation officers, children's officers, before a decision on termination is made.

Substantial risk of serious handicap

The other revolutionary aspect of the Act is accepting probable severe abnormality in the foetus as a ground for termination. The degree of both the risk and the extent of the handicap are not defined in the Act, but left to clinical judgement. The risk of serious foetal abnormality must be more than a mere possibility, but the common example of maternal rubella in the first trimester constitutes a degree of risk that is certainly sufficient.

The definition of 'serious handicap' is similarly undefined, but it is suggested as being established if the child would be unlikely to be able to live an independent life when of an age normally to do so.

Consent to therapeutic abortion

Though not a part of the Act, consent is naturally an important matter in termination of pregnancy, as with any other medical procedure.

Where the woman is married and living with her husband, her written consent is necessary and the matter should be discussed with the husband, though his consent is not strictly necessary, especially if the grounds present are for the preservation of the life or prevention of injury to the woman.

Where the grounds include the health of the woman or any existing children of her family, then naturally the husband's views are part of the 'environment' which must be taken into account.

Where the grounds consist of either the latter case or the risk of a seriously handicapped child being born, and the husband refuses his consent, the decision is very difficult; however, if the doctors both believe in good faith that termination is right and proper, they do not legally require the husband's consent and (though it has not been tested in the courts) it seems highly improbable that the husband would succeed in a civil action based on the loss of parenthood of his child.

No consent is required from the father or putative father of an illegitimate pregnancy, nor from a 'common law' husband; here again, if the grounds include considerations of environment and the woman and father have a family living together, the father will constitute one of the factors to be studied.

As regards minors, no consent is needed from the parents of an unmarried girl between 16 and 18, though it would be advisable to discuss the matter with them if the girl consents, especially if she is living at home with them.

The girl is entitled to full professional secrecy at this age (as with other medical matters, including contraceptive advice) and divulgence of her pregnancy against here wishes would be a serious breach of professional confidence.

Where the girl is below the age of 16, the parents should be informed, whether the girl wishes it or not; such a pregnancy has arisen as a result of unlawful sexual intercourse, and the doctor would appear to condone it by silence.

In the case of such young girls, consent for termination should be obtained from the parents, but if they refuse and the girl (being of sufficient maturity of mind to understand) herself desires to avail herself of termination, the parental refusal should not be allowed to interfere, if definite medical grounds within the Act are present. Again, though the parents may bring an action for assault, it is highly unlikely to succeed, in the opinion of the defence societies.

If the parents of a girl under 16 wish for her abortion, but she is unwilling, her wishes are to be dominant.

Abortion Regulations, 1968

These are the working rules of the Abortion Act, which mainly concern notifications and certification. They came into force on the same day as the Act itself and the main provisions are:

1. The forms to be used by the certifying practitioners are set out in Schedule One, as Certificate A and Certificate B. The latter is only to be used in an emergency, when only one doctor gives an opinion.

   Certificate A must be completed before the operation, Certificate B must be completed not later than 24 hours afterwards. These certificates must be preserved for three years.
2. Notification of all terminations must be made to the Chief Medical Officer, Ministry of Health (or his counterpart in Scotland) within seven days of the abortion. The form is set out in Schedule 2 of the Regulations.
3. The Regulations ensure strict confidentiality of such notifications, with the following exceptions, granted only at the discretion of the Chief Medical Officer:
   a. to authorised officials of the Ministry or of the Registrar-General, for statistical purposes;
   b. to the Director of Public Prosecution in relation to offences against the Abortion Act;
   c. to a police officer not below the rank of superintendent, in connection with offences against the Act;
   d. for the purpose of criminal proceedings which have begun;
   e. for bona fide scientific reasons;
   f. to the practitioner who terminated the pregnancy or to any other practitioner with the patient's consent.

Almost identical Regulations apply to Scotland.

Republic of Ireland

The law in the Irish Republic is unchanged from the Offences Against the Person Act, 1861, mainly that termination of pregnancy with intent to kill the fetus is a criminal offence. It is probable that a doctor could terminate the pregnancy to save a woman's life. He would however, be advised to get a supporting opinion from a colleague, preferably in writing and in the case of a married woman, both her and her husband's written or attested consent would be necessary.

At the time of writing, legal opinion has it that it is not a criminal offence for a doctor in the Irish Republic to refer a pregnant woman for a termination of pregnancy prior to viability (28 weeks) to Great Britain. The grounds given are that although the termination is considered criminal within the Republic, the offence is being committed outside the Republic and so a doctor cannot be an accessory. This legal opinion has been necessitated by the fact that the Minister for Health under the Family Planning Act, 1980, has threatened to close down those voluntary family planning clinics acting as abortion referral centres.

22

Divorce and nullity

Though these are virtually pure legal matters, the practitioner should be aware of the general outlines of divorce law, not only because medical evidence is sometimes vital, but because patients not infrequently turn to their medical attendant rather than a solicitor for their first enquiries about possible grounds for divorce.

Summary of grounds for divorce

Until recent legislation, the grounds for divorce fell into separate classes, namely adultery, desertion or cruelty. Following the enactment of the Divorce Reform Act, 1969, from January 1st, 1971, the only ground upon which a petition for divorce may be presented is 'irretrievable breakdown of a marriage'. However, the latter is held to consist of one or more of the following circumstances, the first three of which are very similar to the matrimonial causes under the old Acts:

1. that since the celebration of the marriage the respondent has committed adultery and the petitioner finds it intolerable to live with the respondent;
2. that since the celebration of the marriage the respondent has behaved in such a way that the petitioner cannot reasonably be expected to live with the respondent;
3. that the respondent has deserted the petitioner without cause for a continuous period of at least two years immediately preceding the presentation of the petition;
4. that the parties to the marriage have lived apart for a continuous period of at least two years immediately preceding the presentation of the petition and the respondent does not object to a decree being granted;
5. that the parties to the marriage have lived apart for a continuous period of at least five years immediately preceding the presentation of the petition.

The new Act does not extend to Scotland or Northern Ireland and is to be construed as one with the Matrimonial Causes Act of 1965.

As far as medical men are professionally concerned, their role as witnesses in divorce proceedings is confined to proof or rebuttal of evidence of (i) adultery, and (ii) cruelty. In addition, the fact that one party to a marriage is incurably of unsound mind and has been continuously under care and treatment for a period of at least five years immediately preceding the presentation of the petition, forms grounds for divorce. Also, a wife has grounds for divorce if her husband has been found guilty of rape, sodomy or bestiality. A husband cannot divorce his wife on the grounds that she had committed unnatural practices, though they might be held to constitute cruelty. These are included under the older Matrimonial Causes Acts, which are not completely replaced by the Divorce Reform Act. No petition can be brought within three years of marriage, except in exceptional circumstances.

In adultery, medical evidence may be called to show that pregnancy occurred during a period when the husband could not possibly have had access to the wife. The length of pregnancy may be an important factor here. Similarly, evidence may be called to show that a child could not be the offspring of the father; this may be proved to the satisfaction of the court by blood-grouping or rarely, by anthropometric methods. Evidence of adultery may also be offered by confirmation of seminal stains on clothing etc. Venereal disease may also be important, either as proof of adultery or as a direct ground for annulment or separation order. Cruelty may be shown both by evidence of physical assaults and of mental trauma. In these cases, evidence from both general or hospital practitioners, as well as psychiatrists, may be required.

Separation and maintenance orders

Under the Matrimonial Proceedings (Magistrates Courts) Act, 1960, a wife may obtain a separation order, entitling her to receive support without the necessity for cohabitation with her husband if:

- he has been guilty of persistent cruelty to her or her children;
- he has been guilty of adultery;
- has deserted her without sufficient cause;
- has contracted venereal disease and with the knowledge of this, has insisted on sexual intercourse with her;
- he had compelled her to become a prostitute;
- has been convicted in a Magistrates's Court of an aggravated

assault upon her or convicted in a higher court of an assault upon her;
- he has become an habitual drunkard or drug addict;
- he has been guilty of wilful neglect towards her or her children.

Judicial separation is now very rare, the above summary procedure having largely replaced it.

Nullity

Divorce involves the dissolution of a previously valid marriage, but in certain circumstances, a 'marriage' may be annulled, i.e. declared never to have existed in law.

These circumstances include:

- An invalid ceremony of marriage where both partners were aware of the defect in the ceremony.
- Where either party was under the age of 16 years.
- Where the partners were within the limits of consanguinity.
- Where one party was already validly married.
- Where one party was of unsound mind or a mental defective at the time of marriage, within the definition laid down by the Mental Health Act, 1959.
- Where the marriage has not been consummated due either to impotence (physical or mental incapacity) or wilful refusal.
- Where one party was subject to epilepsy.
- Where one party was suffering from venereal disease in a communicable form at the time of the marriage.
- Where the woman was pregnant by another man at the time of marriage.

If one of the last three grounds are alleged, then the petitioner must show that he or she was:

1. ignorant of the true facts at the time of the marriage;
2. sexual intercourse had not been permitted since the facts were discovered;
3. that proceedings for annulment were begun within 12 months of discovery.

In medical examination of woman for evidence of non-consummation, expert gynaecological testimony will almost invariably be called. Apart from physical defects barring intercourse, frigidity and hysteria are very relevant conditions and may require psychiatric as well as gynaecological opinion. Examination of the male partner is usually more straightforward. Impotency only has to be proved with the partner in question and the fact that either partner is fully potent with a third partner is no *prima facie* bar to an annulment. The use of contraceptives or coitus interruptus has been held not to invalidate an act of intercourse in so far as if affects nullity considerations.

It is important to appreciate that *impotency* is the only relevant factor in this contect, not *sterility*, which has no bearing on nullity suits.

The laws of the Irish Republic, being much influenced by the Roman Catholic Church, do not recognise divorce in any form. Nullities are occasionally granted by the Courts, as also are legal separations *a mensa et thoro*'. Curiously, of recent years the Roman Catholic church has been more lenient in granting decrees of nullity than the State. Therefore some persons remarrying under church law have found themselves in a bigamous situation relative to the State.

BLOOD GROUP EVIDENCE IN DISPUTED PATERNITY

The acceptance of serological evidence in cases of disputed paternity is rapidly becoming routine in British courts of law, though we have not yet adopted the practice of many Continental countries (especially Scandinavia) who compel the parties in a dispute to undergo blood testing. However, in recent years, failure of any party to conform with the direction of the court to undergo blood testing may be taken into account by the court when deciding the case. In other words, though no actual compulsion can be applied (and obviously, no doctor could be found who would be willing to take blood samples without such consent), the court may draw inferences that a refusal may mean that the party may have something to hide. This was formerly not the case and the court was specifically directed to disregard the fact of refusal.

The legal position is now codified under the Family Law Reform Act of 1969, Part 3, an extract of the relevant sections being given at the end of this chapter.

Such disputes arise in the following circumstances:

a. In divorce proceedings, a husband may sue on the grounds of adultery, basing his case on the denial of responsibility for his wife's pregnancy.
b. A man who resists an affiliation order for the maintenance of

a child of an unmarried mother, may request blood grouping to exclude himself from paternity of the child.

In addition to considering 'opportunity and conduct', e.g. inconsistencies or otherwise between the time of pregnancy and access of the man to the woman etc., the court may order medical evidence of the serological pattern of parties. As already stated, in Britain the courts have no power of compulsion, but refusal to submit to testing can be taken into account by the court.

Principles of paternity serology

The complex biological permutations of blood groups are a matter for an expert serologist, especially as newly-discovered biological systems constantly add to the complexity. However, the general principles should be grasped by any practitioner involved in such cases, so that he may explain the basic significance to the parties involved. The actual testing and interpretation is now universally performed by persons skilled in serology, but any doctor may be requested to obtain the samples and forward them for examination. Even this minor role is a responsible one, and certain precaution must be observed.

1. Blood is to be taken from the mother, the child and the putative father (or fathers).
2. These parties must be identified to the doctor taking the samples, either by them all attending together, or if this is impossible or embarrassing, each party should be identified by the solicitor who is acting in the case.
3. In the case of adults, 5 ml of venous blood is taken in the usual way and placed in a plain tube. The label should be fully completed in the view of the donor, and a declaration signed by the donor indicating that they agree that the sample so labelled was indeed their blood. In the case of the child, this declaration is made by the mother.
4. The declaration should also certify that neither party has had a blood transfusion within three months, previous to taking the sample. The wording of the form should be such that it also gives express consent for the taking of the sample, even though implied consent is obvious from the fact of the person attending the doctor's premises.
5. In the case of infants, the child should be preferably at least six months of age, and certainly more than two months of age

before testing is performed. At least 1 ml of blood should be obtained by a heel or ear prick, again into a plain bottle.

These are then despatched together with the declaration forms, to the laboratory: if this is distant, express post or some similar means must be employed to ensure that transit time is not more than one day.

Rationale of exclusion serology

Blood tests are purely an exclusory procedure and can never indicate that a given man is the father of a given child. Thus any putative father has nothing to lose (and something to gain) by submitting to such testing. The tests depend on the basic premise that certain blood group elements, being inherited on Mendelian principles, cannot appear in the blood of a child, unless contributed by the parents. As the maternity is never in doubt, any genetic element in the blood group of the child which does not appear in either the mother or the putative father, automatically excludes the latter from paternity.

The following group systems have been used for this purpose: ABO, MNS, Rh, Kell, P, Lutheran, Duffy and Kidd.

In addition, certain haemoglobin-binding proteins in human serum, called haptoglobins, can be detected by electrophoresis: three types occur and their inheritance is also determined on fixed genetic principles, thus making them of use in paternity testing. Other blood components, such as enzymes are also being used as genetic markers in the serological typing of blood.

Though all the above systems are potentially usable, the ones commonly employed are ABO, MNS, P, Rh and haptoglobins.

The child inherits one gene of each blood group from each parent. These arrive in the fertilized ovum as a result of the combination of half the normal cell chromosome-content from the father and the same from the mother. During this halving process (meiosis), the parental blood group, carried on two genes, will be split, so that it is a matter of chance as to which gene contributes to the new child. For example, a man may be Group B, this being his *phenotype*, but there are two types of Group B, that is B/B and B/O. Thus this man may pass on either B or O to the child. The fuller description of this genetic make-up, e.g. B/B or B/O, is called the *genotype*. As the same situation applies to the mother, the following table can be drawn up for transfer of the various ABO components to the children:

Blood group of			
Parent 1	Parent 2	Blood groups possible in children	Blood groups excluded in children
O	O	O	A, B, AB
O	A	O, A	B, AB
O	B	O, B	A, AB
A	A	O, A	B, AB
A	B	O, A, B, AB	None impossible
B	B	O, B.	A, AB
O	AB	A, B	O, AB
A	AB	A, B, AB	O
B	AB	A, B, AB	O
AB	AB	A, B, AB	O

From these conclusions, two 'laws' can be derived:

1. A and B agglutinogens cannot appear in the offspring unless present in the blood of one or both parents.
2. Any parent belonging to Group O cannot have a child whose blood contains AB agglutinogens and a parent whose blood is Group AB cannot have a Group O child.

Similar conclusions can be arrived at in respect of the other systems.

Chances of excluding paternity

The chances of excluding a falsely accused putative father of paternity naturally rise as the number of systems employed are increased. The following figures apply only to the British situation, as there are profound variations in blood group frequency in differing ethnic groups.

Using the ABO system alone, there is about one chance in six of establishing innocence (17 per cent). When the ABO, MNS and Rh systems are employed, a 53 per cent chance of exclusion is reached. Using the maximum practical number of erythrocyte test systems, a 60 per cent exclusion rate can be expected in Britain: with the addition of haptoglobins, etc., this rises to about 75 per cent.

As far as the relation between the doctor and the parties is concerned, it must again be emphasised that the practitioner should impress upon the parties that this is an *exclusory* test only, and does not confirm paternity.

There is no legislation in the Irish Republic concerning laboratory investigations for paternity by means of blood group tests. Thus there are no official laboratories for the carrying out of paternity tests. These needs are not required obviously for divorce purposes but occasionally for affiliation orders or problems of inheritance.

APPENDIX

Extracts from family law reform act, 1969

Part III

Section 20(1) In any civil proceedings in which the paternity of any person fails to be determined, the court may, on an application by any party to the proceedings, give a direction for the use of blood tests to ascertain whether such tests show that a party to the proceedings is or is not thereby excluded from being the father of that person.

Section 21(1) Subject to the provisions of subsections (3) and (4) of this section, a blood sample which is required to be taken from any person for the purpose of giving effect to adirection under section 20 of this Act shall not be taken from that person except with his consent.

Section 21(2) The consent of a minor who has attained the age of sixteen years to the taking from himself of a blood sample shall be as effective as it would be if he were of full age; and where a minor has by virtue of this subsection given an effective consent to the taking of a blood sample, it shall not be necessary to obtain any consent for it from any other person.

Section 21(3) A blood sample may be taken from a person under the age of sixteen years, not being such a person as is referred to in subsection (4) of this section, if the person who has the care and control of him consents. (Subsection (4) concerns the taking of blood from a person suffering from a mental disorder.)

Section 23(1) Where a court gives a direction under section 20 of this Act and any person fails to take any step required of him for the purpose of giving effect to the direction, the court may draw such inferences, if any, from that fact as appear proper in the circumstances.

23

Sterilisation and artificial insemination

The legal, if not the ethical position concerning sterilisation has changed rapidly over the course of a few decades. As recently as 1948, a professional organisation took legal advice and concluded that sterilisation was only ethically and legally justified if performed for some medical reason and not on either eugenic grounds or as a birth control method. Even more recently (1954) Lord Justice Denning stated that he would regard sterilisation of the male performed for the sole purpose of avoiding parenthood as being illegal, and that in the absence of 'a just cause' would be unlawful whether or not consent was given.

Since that date, sterilisation of both the male and female has become a routine matter and though tubal ligation in the female is frequently based upon medical considerations, which make further pregnancy undesirable, the great increase in elective vasectomy in the male cannot be considered to be for any therapeutic purpose, in the accepted sense. Sterilisation under the old concepts of law was a maiming operation, incapable of being made legal by consent, and might even constitute a criminal offence as far as the operator was concerned.

No Act of Parliament or judicial dictum has altered this situation, but the attitude of the professional medical bodies has changed radically. The representative body of the British Medical Association in 1967 stated that 'if the doctor is satisfied that an operation for sterilisation is in the interests of the health of the patient and that the patient has given valid consent and understands the consequences of this operation, there is no ethical reason why the operation should not be performed'. The defence organisations agreed that, though as late as 1961 it was doubtful whether a court might uphold sterilisation solely as a method of birth control, it appreciated that the climate of public opinion has changed and that 'a more liberal attitude to sterilisation would be taken by the courts'.

In the case of a married patient, the written consent of both the husband and wife should be obtained before the sterilisation of either party is undertaken. If sterilisation, especially in the female, is necessary on definite medical grounds, rather than as a method of birth control, the refusal of the other party to give consent need not form an absolute barrier to the procedure, if the medical opinion of the doctor, preferably backed up by a second opinion, is made in good faith.

The provision of contraceptive devices by a doctor to a girl under the age of 16, has been considered by the Medical Defence Union not to be illegal, even though she is under the age for legal sexual intercourse. The consent of the parents would appear to be a prerequisite.

These procedures are not regarded as criminal in the Irish Republic, but it is likely that doctors attempting to sterilize patients, may find themselves without nursing assistance, due to the conservative Catholic attitudes of the majority of that profession. No test cases at law are known concerning artificial insemination and there is no legislation on this subject, although the legitimacy of offspring from A.I.D. would, of course, be open to challenge in the Courts.

ARTIFICIAL INSEMINATION

This is a procedure for bringing about conception in the female where there are medical reasons why natural insemination is consistently unsuccessful. Semen is introduced into the cervical canal directly by instrumental means. There are two types of artificial insemination, which have profound legal differences.

1. Artificial insemination by husband (A.I.H.)

Here the only problems are medical, there being some mechanical defect which prevents normal post-coital penetration of the cervical canal by spermatozoa from a normally fertile husband. No legal problems whatsoever are concerned, though the Roman Catholic Church only approves the use of semen obtained from the post-coital vaginal pool, rather than the usual procedure of utilizing a masturbation sample.

2. Artificial insemination by donor (A.I.D.)

This procedure is employed where the husband is irreversibly sterile, yet a pregnancy is desired. Before A.I.D. is performed, full medical investigation should be carried out upon both partners, to exclude even a small chance of natural or A.I.H. pregnancy. When this has been done, the legal position should be carefully put to the couple, the present difficulties being explained. Full written consent must be obtained from both partners before proceeding. No legal guide lines for doctors exist, it being left to the individual practitioner's conscience. There are strong religious objections from some quarters, notably the Roman Catholic Church, as with sterilisation and other forms of conception control.

Compared with A.I.H. there are several insoluble legal problems, which include:

a. The legitimacy of the resulting child is in doubt. Though it is a presumption of English law that a child born in marriage is legitimate, this presumption is rebuttable by evidence of impotence, but it is possible to legally adopt the child to overcome this drawback.
b. When registering the birth, it was formerly necessary to give details of the father. In A.I.D., if the husband's name was entered, this might be held to be perjury, the certificate being a Statutory form. This objection is now overcome by the new form of certificate.
c. There is doubt as to whether adultery has occurred, the woman becoming pregnant by a man not the father. As adultery is not strictly defined in English law, this might prove grounds for divorce, though as the husband consented to the act, this might well prove a barrier. In Scots law, a judicial decision has been made that A.I.D. does not constitute sexual intercourse and thus could not be adultery.
d. As the previous provision of semen from a regular donor may be sufficient for many hundred A.I.D. procedures, a possibility of inadvertent incest between the offspring is possible.

In 1960, a Department Committee studied the problem and advised that:

1. The practice of A.I.D. is strongly to be discouraged, but should not be regulated by law, or held to be a criminal offence.
2. The birth of a child as a result of A.I.D., to which the parties of the marriage consented, should be a bar to proceedings for nullity of marriage on the grounds of impotence.
3. There should be no alteration in the procedure for registration of birth or of the laws relating to legitimacy.
4. Insemination of a wife with donor semen without the consent of the husband, should be made a new ground for divorce or judicial separation.

Though the problem has not been aired to any extent in the British courts, a mother of a child conceived by A.I.D. was granted a decree of nullity on the grounds of her husband's incapacity to consummate the marriage.

Strict precautions must be taken if A.I.D. is performed. The donor must not be a relative of either partner, he should be between 18 and 40 years of age and should have had children of his own. The medical attendant supervising the procedure should ensure that the donor's race and other characteristics should resemble as closely as possible those of the husband of the woman to be inseminated. His physical health and family history must be satisfactory, and the Wasserman and Rhesus testing should be checked. He must be willing to donate semen for the purpose, and his wife's permission must be obtained. The donor must be unaware of the destination of the donated fluid, and of the results of the insemination. Similarly, the recipient and her husband must give written permission for the procedure. The practitioner in charge of the procedure must keep all relevant documents in his possession, and never disclose them to the parties concerned. He must instruct that in the event of his death, the records be destroyed.

24

Infant deaths

Deaths in infancy, except where due to firmly-diagnosed natural disease, have to be treated with special care. The circumstances are often obscure, partly due to the fact that the infant patient or victim is unable to complain or give a proper history. There is also the added complication that infants and children are in the care of parents or guardians, whose treatment of their charge is not always as exemplary as could be wished.

STILL-BIRTHS

Until the Births and Deaths Registration Act of 1953, no separate certification of still-births was made in England though this was done much earlier in Scotland, by virtue of the Registration of Still-births (Scotland) Act, 1938. The present state of the law requires that instead of ordinary death certification, a special certificate must be completed by the medical or nursing attendant, if they are in a position so to do, this then being taken by the informant to the Registrar in the usual way.

The certificate has a counterfoil but no separate 'notice to informant'. The whole certificate is handed to the informant, who may be the mother, a father of a legitimate child, a person present at the birth or an occupier of premises in which the birth occurred.

The object of the separate certification of still-birth was mainly to acquire fresh knowledge to assist in determining the causes of still-births, which amount to one in fifty of all births. Unfortunately, even after autopsy, the cause of still-birth is frequently obscure. A still-birth is officially described as 'any child which has issued forth from the mother after the 28th week of pregnancy and which did not in the meantime, after being completely expelled from the mother, breathe or show any other sign of life'. When a still-birth occurs, either a doctor or a certified midwife who was either:

1. present at the birth, or

SB 000000

COUNTERFOIL

For use of Medical Attendant or Midwife, who should in all cases fill it up.

Surname of Father (or Mother) ....

Date of Still-birth ....

Place of Still-birth ....

....

Cause of death

I (*a*) ....

(*b*) ....

(*c*) ....

II ....

Date of certification ....

Post-mortem† 1 2 3

Certificate issued to

(name) ....

of (address) ....

....

† Ring appropriate digit.

CERTIFICATE OF STILL-BIRTH

SB 000000

(Births and Deaths Registration Act, 1953, Section 11, as amended by Section 2 of the Population (Statistics) Act, 1960)

To be given only in respect of a child which has issued forth from its mother after the 28th week of pregnancy and which did not at any time after being completely expelled from its mother breathe or show any other signs of life.

Registered at
Entry No.

SPECIMEN

*I was present at the still-birth of a *male/*female child born

*I have examined the body of a *male/*female child which I am in[illegible]eve was born

on the .... day of .... 19...... to ....
(NAME OF MOTHER)

at ....
(PLACE OF BIRTH)

I hereby certify that (i) the child was [illegible] alive, [illegible]
(ii) to the best [illegible] belief the cause of death and the estimated duration of preg[illegible] were as stated below.

[illegible] DEATH		Estimated duration of pregnancy
I	I	
DIRECT CAUSE State fœtal or maternal co[illegible] causing death.	(*a*)	.... weeks
ANTECEDENT CAUSES State fœtal and/or maternal conditions, if any, giving rise to the above cause, stating the underlying cause last.	due to (*b*) .... due to (*c*)	Weight of fœtus (if known)
II	II	.... lbs.
OTHER SIGNIFICANT CONDITIONS of fœtus or mother which may have contributed to but, in so far as is known, were not related to direct cause of death.	....	.... oz.

† 1 The certified cause of death has been confirmed by post-mortem.
2 Post-mortem information may be available later.
3 Post-mortem not being held.

Signature .... Date ....

Qualification as registered by General Medical Council, or Registered No. as Certified Midwife. ....

Residence ....

* Strike out the words which do not apply.
† Ring appropriate digit.

THIS IS NOT AN AUTHORITY FOR BURIAL OR CREMATION

[SEE OVER

Fig. 32 Still-birth certificate (front only)

2. who had examined the body of the still-birth is entitled to sign the certificate (Fig. 32).

If both doctor and midwife were present at the birth, then the doctor should provide the certificate. Though the legislation provides that a doctor or midwife who were either present at the birth or who had examined the body after death, may certify, in practice it is unwise for the second procedure to be followed. As it is extremely difficult (often impossible) for a skilled pathologist at autopsy to determine whether a child was born still-born or not, it is even more unlikely that mere external examination by a physician or midwife will confirm the fact of still-birth if neither were present at the time of delivery. Except where a doctor or midwife was present at the birth, it is wiser to report reputed still-births to the coroner, so that the benefit of an autopsy, however uncertain, may be added to the available evidence.

International classification of causes of still-birth

Main descriptive titles

Chronic disease in mother

- Syphilis
- Tuberculosis
- Diabetes Mellitus
- Chronic disease of circulatory system
- Chronic disease of genito-urinary system
- Other chronic disease

Acute disease in mother

- Typhoid fever
- Influenza
- Pneumonia
- Other acute respiratory disease
- Other acute disease or condition

Diseases and conditions of pregnancy and childbirth

- Ectopic gestation
- Eclampsia
- Other toxaemias of pregnancy
- Infection
- Haemorrhage

Absorption of toxic substances from mother

Difficulties in labour

- Abnormality of bones of pelvis
- Disproportion
- Malposition of fetus
- Abnormality of forces of labour
- Operative delivery
- Abnormality of tissues or organs of pelvis

Placental and cord conditions

- Prolapse or compression of cord
- Placenta praevia
- Premature separation of placenta
- Placental infarction

Birth injury (including cerebral haemorrhage), classified by cause

Congenital malformations

- Anencephalus
- Hydrocephalus
- Spina bifida
- Malformation of the cardiovascular system
- Other malformations specified by type

Diseases of fetus, and ill-defined causes

- Erythroblastosis
- Prematurity (cause not known)

The certificate also requires an estimate of the duration of pregnancy and an opinion as to direct and antecedent causes and other significant conditions which were thought to have caused or contributed to the still-birth. Once the certificate has been given to the informant, registration must take place within 42 days of the birth.

Under the 1953 Act, signs of life are defined as including 'breathing, beating of the heart, pulsation of the umbilical cord or definite movement of voluntary muscles'. Common causes of still-birth are prematurity, anoxia of various types, either due to local obstetric conditions such as prolapsed cord, or from some maternal emergency; birth trauma especially intracranial haemorrhage due to excessive moulding, placental abnormalities, toxaemias of pregnancy, Rhesus incompatibility (erythroblastosis foetalis) and congenital defects of many types.

List of indefinite or undesirable terms

Indefinite or undesirable terms (i.e. when used without further particulars such as those indicated opposite)	
Asphyxia, anoxia, etc.	Cause of condition, e.g. pressure on cord, breech delivery, etc.
Intra-uterine death	Cause whenever possible.
Maceration	Cause of condition whenever possible.
Malformation	Nature or malformation (fetal or maternal).
Birth injury	State if fetal or maternal abnormality determined the injury or if due to operation, etc.
Maternal haemorrhage	Cause or nature of haemorrhage. Placenta praevia, accidental haemorrhage, etc.
Hypertension (maternal)	State if condition arose during pregnancy or existed previously.
Nephritis (maternal)	State if condition was acute or chronic.
Toxaemia	Cause of condition, e.g. Eclampsia, Pre-eclampsia, Nephritis (acute or chronic), etc.
Prolonged labour	Cause of condition. Fetal or maternal abnormality, etc.
Prematurity	Cause of condition. Fetal or maternal abnormality, etc.

Certification of still-birth in Scotland

The procedure is almost exactly similar to the English method, a doctor or certified midwife being able to certify if present at the birth or after examining the body of the child. The informants are the same as in England and Wales, as well as the nurse who was present at the birth. As in England, the rare procedure of a declaration of still-birth by a person where no medical certificate has been issued is permissible, though very seldom employed. When the Registrar receives the certificate, he must register it in the presence of the informant, who has to verify the particulars and witness any necessary corrections. A certificate of registration is issued to the informant by the Registrar and when burial occurs, the Registrar must be notified by the person in charge of the cemetery.

Certification of still-birth in Northern Ireland

Again this is similar to the English and Scottish procedure, being governed by the Registration of Still Births Act (Northern Ireland) 1960. The certificate is either signed by a doctor or midwife present at the birth or who has examined the body. Like the English certificate, the weight of the still-birth and the estimated duration of the pregnancy are recorded.

The definition makes provision for Caesarean delivery by using the phrase 'complete expulsion or extraction from the mother'. A still-birth cannot be registered on the declaration of an informant; a doctor's or midwife's certificate is required or else the death must be reported to the coroner.

INFANTICIDE

Death at birth or very soon afterwards, is a relatively common occurrence, and undoubtedly the majority are due to natural causes. It is however significant that the 'still-birth' rate amongst illegitimate infants is twice that amongst legitimate infants. Though deliberate killing of a newborn infant, either by an act of commission or omission, is as much a homicide as the murder of an adult, the law has recognised the special circumstances surrounding a recently delivered woman and has modified the law accordingly.

In England, until 1922, the killing of a new-born infant by the mother or anyone else, was murder. However, for many years before this, juries had been unwilling to convict recently-delivered mothers and the Infanticide Acts of 1922 and 1938 regularised the position by providing the new offence of 'infanticide'.

For a mother to be able to take advantage of the leniency afforded by the Infanticide Act, the death must be shown to fall within the following description:

> 'Where a woman by any wilful act or omission, causes the death of her child, being a child under the age of 12 months, but at the time the balance of her mind was disturbed by reason of her not having fully

recovered from the affects of giving birth to the child, or by reason of the affect of lactation consequent upon the birth of the child'.

It will be seen that the child must be under one year of age – in practice these deaths almost invariably occur within minutes or hours of birth. A medical attendant or prison medical officer will invariably provide evidence as to the disturbed balance of the mind, and with these criteria satisfied, the potential charge of murder will be reduced to infanticide, which means that the woman will almost certainly be put on probation and suffer no further penalty. Rarely do matters go even this far; the pathological criteria of proving a separate existence are so hard to fulfil, that usually the charge of infanticide is dropped, often to the gratification of the police, who derive no satisfaction from investigating this type of case. Rarely, an alternative charge of 'concealment of birth' is brought, where the only evidence points to the deliberate hiding of an infant body, there being nothing to say whether it was born dead or alive.

Before a charge of infanticide can lie, it must be shown that:

a. the child had a separate existence, and
b. death was caused by a wilful act of commission or omission.

The first of these criteria poses the most difficult problem for a medical witness. In the context of infanticide, the child must be more than the legal threshold of 28 weeks' gestation (this is not necessarily synonymous with viability; seven months is taken as the point in time which the infant attains certain rights under the Infant Life (Preservation) Act, 1929). It must also be shown to have breathed or shown other definite signs of life after being completely separated from the body of the mother. This separation applies to the limbs, etc. of the infant and not the placenta and cord. Thus a child which breathes and cries whilst its lower half is still in the vagina, has no legal separate existence. Once its feet are clear of the mother (in a normal delivery) and it moves, cries, breathes or is shown to have a heart or cord pulse, then it has attained a separate existence even if the third stage of labour is not complete. Obviously these criteria, which may be separated by very short intervals of time, are virtually impossible to determine in retrospect, either by external examination or even full autopsy.

The only positive proof of separate existence are signs of continued survival for a considerable period after birth. The two most reliable are the presence of food in the stomach (or bacteria-laden meconium in the intestine) and signs of separation of the stump of the umbilical cord. This becomes dry and shrivelled after the first day, a red line of separation appears around the proximal end on the second day and complete separation of the cord occurs between four to six days, with epithelialisation of the stump at about 9–12 days.

Much effort in the past has been devoted to trying to establish definite signs of breathing after birth from the post-mortem appearances of the lungs. Many thousands of words have been written on the histological appearances of the lungs, the flotation test etc., but all these are extremely unreliable. The flotation test especially, must have led to numerous injustices in the past, and only the most obvious signs of prolonged respiration must be accepted as proof of live birth. According to the strict legal definition these need not necessarily be equated with 'separate existence', but it is hard to conceive of continued respiration in an infant who remains partially within the maternal passages.

For a charge of infanticide to succeed it must be shown that the infant lived, and this is where most charges fail – indeed are never brought. Unless the pathologist can provide adequate proof that separate existence occurred, there is no case. Occasionally, he may provide evidence to the contrary; if a macerated fetus is found or if there are gross congenital defects, then obviously no separate existence could have occurred. In all intermediate cases, the woman is given the benefit of the doubt and the birth recorded as a still-birth. The examination is often complicated by the presence of putrefaction or even mummification, as many infants have been concealed after birth and are not discovered until autolysis or other advanced post-mortem changes render examination virtually valueless. Again, a large proportion of dead new-born infants are never traceable to the mother, and are disposed of as unidentified still-births.

The second criterion of infanticide concerns the cause of death in those cases where separate existence can be demonstrated. The tenuous grip which a new-born infant has on life, can easily be broken. Even acts of omission, which are extremely hard to prove, can lead to death in the immediate post-natal period. Smothering with a pillow or obstructing the air passages by pinching the nostrils or placing a hand across the face, may well leave no marks to be seen after death. The classical congested, haemorrhagic picture of florid asphyxia is often absent in infancy. Failure to suck out the air passages may be a deliberate act, but is far more commonly seen in clandestine births where the mother, often young, unmarried and terrified, has no idea how to proceed, and indeed may not even know that she is giving birth. In such conditions, numerous injuries may be found on the baby, especially around the face, head and neck, due to frantic attempts at self-delivery. These can be multiple circumferential abrasions from the fingernails around the whole surface of the neck, and are characteristic and quite different from those of calculated violence.

Exposure of the infant to cold after birth may again be deliberate or accidental and drowning due to delivery into lavatory pans is a well-known and well-illustrated phenomenon in textbooks of forensic medicine. Again, asphyxia due to wrapping of the umbilical cord around the neck may be natural or deliberate, and no means exist to differentiate the two, apart from a voluntary statement by the mother.

Deliberate acts may include all types of injury, from severe head injuries to stabbing or laceration by knives or scissors. It is often said that precipitate delivery may cause the infant to strike its skull upon the ground and so simulate a deliberate blow upon the head. In the majority of cases, this theory has more claim to ingenuity than credibility. Strangulation by ligature is also seen as a deliberate act of commission, but all infants found with cords or tapes around their necks need not necessarily have been strangled. In the absence of signs of a separate existence, such factors become irrelevant.

Until 1929, a loop-hole existed in the law relating to deliberate disposal of infants. An abortion is a deliberate interference with the pregnancy almost always at an early stage, so that premature expulsion of the fetus is provoked. Infanticide is the killing of a child which has attained a separate existence. This left a gap between the two, whereby deliberate killing of a mature fetus *in utero* by instrument or other means, was neither an abortion nor infanticide and therefore fell outside the law and subsequent punishment. To close this gap, the Infant Life Preservation Act of 1929 was passed, which made it a grave offence to cause the death of a viable (i.e. at least 28 weeks, gestation) unborn child *in utero*. A clause in this act specifically exempted reputable medical procedures, such as the use of a craniotome, to preserve the life of the mother.

The doctor's duty in suspected infanticide

The task facing the forensic pathologist is often complex as far as the autopsy is concerned, but the duty of the general practitioner or casualty officer etc., is quite clear, when faced with a dead infant where the history and appearances are anything but straightforward. The case must be reported to the coroner. If the doctor (or a midwife) was not present at the birth, he would do well always to report to the coroner rather than issue a still-birth certificate. The interpretation of the injuries, the dubious history, is then at once removed from the responsibility of the clinician into that of the medico-legal authorities.

LAW IN SCOTLAND

The English Infanticide Acts of 1922 and 1938 and the Infant Life (Preservation) Act of 1929, do not apply in Scotland. Legislation was passed as long ago as 1690 to establish the crime of 'child murder', but this was repealed in 1809 and replaced by the less harsh Concealment of Pregnancy Act.

This provides that if a woman conceals her pregnancy for her full term, does not call for assistance in labour and subsequently the child is found 'dead or amissing', she may be convicted.

LAW IN THE IRISH REPUBLIC

The law concerning child killing in the Irish Republic is similar to that in England and Wales though it was not legislated by act of the Dail until the Infanticide Act 1949. There is no Irish equivalent to the Infant Life (Preservation) Act 1929 with its crime of child destruction.

25

Sudden infant death

One of the most neglected areas in medical research and education has been the 'sudden infant death syndrome' more commonly known as 'cot death' or 'crib death'. Little is mentioned in standard textbooks of either pathology or paediatrics, as this is a condition mainly met with by coroner's pathologists and not clinicians, except when general practitioners are called at the unexpected death of a small infant.

The incidence of cot death is hard to estimate, but a Department of Health survey published in 1965 admitted to 1500 cases in England and Wales annually. From extrapolation of figures from smaller surveys, it would appear that two or even three thousand was nearer the truth. In the United States, estimates vary between 10 000 and 20 000 cases per year; in both countries, it would appear that the incidence has decreased since 1972, the reason being unknown.

The sudden infant death syndrome is therefore a major cause of infant mortality: once passed the age of perinatal period, it is the biggest single killer of young infants, the death rate exceeding those for congenital defects, malignant disease and accidents. At three months, cot deaths exceed all other combined causes of infant deaths. About one in every 500–700 live births ends in a cot death. During the last few decades, the rapid decline in total infant mortality in advanced countries, due to control of infection and general increase in preventive medicine, has caused cot deaths to form a proportionately much larger fraction of the total deaths, so that they are now much more prominent than hitherto.

Features of the sudden death in infancy syndrome

The characteristics of the cot death are so uniform as to present a strikingly similar clinical picture.

1. Age incidence. Though the age range has been agreed upon as being from 2 weeks to 2 years, the majority of cases occur between 2 and 7 months, with a marked peak at 3 to 4 months.

2. *Sex*. There is very little significant sex variation in cot death, though most surveys show a slight preponderance of males, a fact which is seen in almost all disease processes throughout life.

3. *Twins*. There is a definitely increased risk amongst members of a twin pair, as opposed to singletons. The mean incidence in single children is of the order of 1.5 per 1000 births, whereas the incidence in twins seems to be about twice this. No less than eight cases of simultaneous death in both members of a twin pair are reported in the world literature. It was formerly held that there was no familial increased incidence in cot death and that a child born into a family which had suffered a previous cot death was no more at risk than the general infant population: there is some evidence recently to suggest that this is not so, but the increased risk is still very slight.

4. *Season*. This is probably the most striking feature apart from age. Cot deaths are almost confined to the cold months of the year, very few cases occurring between May and October in the Northern Hemisphere. The peak is usually in January with sometimes a second smaller peak about March. In the Southern Hemisphere, these months are reversed to coincide with the winter season. Even so, no evidence has been satisfactorily adduced to suggest that hypothermia is a factor.

5. *Geographical distribution*. Cot deaths appear to occur all over the world, even in tropical countries, though due to better certification and registration in advanced countries, most is known about the incidence in Europe, North American and Australasia. Also, in many tropical and sub-tropical countries, the total infant mortality is often much greater, thus by comparison making sudden infant death a relatively unimportant proportion of the total.

6. *Time of death*. Another remarkable feature of this tragic syndrome is the time of day at which death occurs. Death almost always occurs during sleep and almost always occurs in the early hours of the day. 80 per cent of all typical cot deaths occur before 10 a.m. and most of them are found dead very early in the morning. Any sudden infant death occurring in the afternoon or evening, must be examined with even greater care than usual, as these cases are frequently atypical and sometimes show a definite pathological lesion at autopsy.

7. *Prematurity and illegitimacy*. It seems fairly clear that prematurity now carries an increased risk of a subsequent cot death; illegitimacy is somewhat disputed, but is greater amongst Social Class V, in which more cot deaths occur than in other classes.

8. *Social incidence*. Cot deaths can occur in any type of family,

and numerous instances are recorded amongst professional families. However, statistically the bulk of cot deaths occur amongst the 'lower income' groups as characterized by the Registrar General's Group V. This is partly explained by the fact that this is the largest group and thus has more children at risk, the families are larger with more children per parent and also there is greater domestic overcrowding with more opportunity for respiratory cross-infections.

9. *Predisposing conditions.* The victims of cot death die not only suddenly but *unexpectedly*. The child is either quite well beforehand or may have only a minor upper respiratory infection or slight gastrointestinal upset. These conditions are so common in small children in winter time as to be of less significance as might be thought, especially as a retrospective history taken from the anguished parents often over-emphasizes minor symptoms, in a conscious or sub-conscious effort to rationalize the tragedy.

Thus the typical history of a 'cot death' is of an infant, either in good health or with a 'cold', being put to bed quite well in the evening, and being either found dead early next morning or being well at the time of the early feed, but dead when the mother returns to it at breakfast time. The common factors are those of age, season and time of death.

Autopsy appearances

The classical autopsy findings are essentially negative. If any overt pathological condition is found, then the case is not a typical 'cot death'. Occasionally a bronchopneumonia is discovered and sometimes children with congenital heart disease or other inborn defects may die suddenly and unexpectedly. In these cases, it is often found that the history is atypical, and that death may have occurred later in the day. It must be borne in mind that children with congenital or other diseases may also suffer cot death; but in the absence of a satisfactory explanation for the cot death syndrome, it is justifiable to indict the other disease as the cause of death.

At autopsy, the only frequent findings are those of petechial haemorrhages on the surface of the lungs, pericardium and thymus. For many years, these findings were ascribed to mechanical asphyxia. Much personal and social harm has occurred in the past from the assumption that suffocation has occurred either by 'overlaying' by an adult in the same bed, by the baby burying its head in a soft pillow, being covered by bedclothes, or even the cat sleeping upon the face! Another unprovable and usually erroneous assumption is the blaming of 'inhalation of stomach contents' for the death.

This aspiration of gastric material is a very common and agonal phenomenon in both adult and infant deaths from all causes. It is seen in up to 25 per cent of autopsies and in the absence of clinical corroboration, must not be invoked as the *cause* of death.

All these explanations are erroneous and have caused great suffering amongst parents, who develop feelings of deep self-reproach at having contributed, either by omission or commission, to their child's death. These feelings have frequently been reinforced by uninformed medical opinion and especially by coroner's remarks at inquests. Though fortunately less common now, it still happens that inquests are held upon these cases and death may still be ascribed to suffocation by mechanical asphyxia in the cot. As innumerable cases have been reported where this can definitely be excluded (and the whole range of features such as age, sex, season etc., rule out any such simple explanation) it is regrettable that such misapprehensions about suffocation still persist.

Until recently, no category was provided by the Registrar General for this syndrome and in order to avoid a coroner's inquest, many pathologists certify the deaths as 'acute bronchiolitis' or some such respiratory cause, which is not really borne out by the post-mortem appearances. This manoeuvre is justifiable if it avoids the coroner's enquiry which would be occasioned by calling them 'unascertainable' or 'suffocation', but it has unfortunate side-effects in that it obscures the true incidence of the syndrome, artificially inflates the statistics of true respiratory disease and also has other undesirable consequences. Amongst the latter, is the frequent belief of parents that 'acute bronchiolitis' is a treatable respiratory disease, similar to pneumonia or bronchitis. They may then reproach themselves further for having neglected a potentially curable condition, or more important from the doctor's point of view, accuse their general practitioner openly or subconsciously for failing to adequately diagnose and treat a simple disease.

Theories as to causation

Though cot death was first described in the Old Testament (Chapter 3, Kings I), the cause is still uncertain. As with all diseases of undetermined aetiology, speculation has been rife. Many theories have been put forward, including allergy to cow's milk, parathyroid deficiency, hypothermia, vitamin E and selenium deficiency, carbon dioxide toxicity, blocked air passages, spinal haemorrhages and a host of other hypotheses. Only in the last couple of years has any positive progress been made in the understanding of the condition. It is now clear that there is no one 'cause' of cot death, the fatal outcome being a final common pathway of apnoea due to a multi-factorial situation. Some of the factors are known, such as sleep, age incidence, a frequent upper respiratory infection and some inborn tendency, but the whole syndrome has yet to be fully understood. Probably the greatest advance in understanding has been provided by respiratory physiologists, who have shown that many infants suffer from prolonged sleep apnoea, having periods of up to 15–20 seconds during sleep during which no respiratory movements occur. These children appear to have an abnormal insensitivity to respiratory stimulation by hypoxia and increased carbon dioxide tension in the blood. When the respiratory pattern is depressed by sleep, possibly a mild viremia from a respiratory infection and possibly by some degree of hypoxia due to oedema and mucus secretion in the nasal passages (most children being obligatory nose breathers during sleep) a vicious spiral of apnoea – hypoxia – apnoea occurs, which if uninterrupted leads to death from respiratory failure. It has been recognised that a number of 'near cot deaths' occur, in which a child is noticed by the parents to apnoeic, pale or cyanosed and almost dead. When the child is picked up and rushed to a doctor, the stimulus causes the respiratory centres to function again and the baby returns to normal. Sometimes these children die a typical cot death within the next few days. It has been tentatively suggested that infants shown to have an abnormally long sleep apnoea pattern might be fitted with respiratory alarms, but the economic and ethical complications are yet to be solved.

Until medical research provides the cause of death, there is little that can be done in preventive medicine, though work at Sheffield in the last couple of years has indicated that non-specific intense supervision of high-risk children (determined from various maternal factors) can markedly reduce the incidence of cot death. However, this is impracticable upon a national scale and until such time that scientific advances are consolidated, attention should be turned to relieving the emotional distress of parents, especially that caused or exacerbated by suggestions of an accidental cause such as suffocation.

Several charitable organisations have been founded in both the United States and Britain to disseminate information and to give support to bereaved parents. In Britain these include:

British Guild for Sudden Infant Death Study, Pathology Department, Royal Infirmary, Cardiff CF2 1SZ, Wales.

Foundation for the Study of Infant Deaths, 5th Floor, 4 Grosvenor Place, London SW1X 7HD.

26

The battered child

Definition
The 'Battered Child Syndrome' (or 'non-accidental injury in childhood syndrome') refers to a condition in young children, usually under the age of three years, who present with injuries received as a result of non-accidental violence inflicted by a parent or guardian.

Features of the syndrome
The child is almost always under the age of three years, usually less than two years.

There is frequently an obvious discrepancy between the nature of the injuries and the explanation offered by the parent.

There is frequently an inexplicable delay between the injury and medical attention. In a recent series over 40 per cent of cases received no medical attention for over six hours, and delays of up to 24 hours are not uncommon.

The child is often, though not invariably, the only one in the family to receive repeated assaults. The child is frequently the youngest, and is often unwanted or rejected.

Though it may not be known at the time (and certainly not volunteered by the parents), the child may often have been seen by other doctors or other hospitals for previous injuries.

There is slightly more risk to male children than female, though this is common to the majority of both disease and traumatic conditions throughout life. All social classes may batter their children, even professional parents, but most cases come from the lower end of the social spectrum.

Ethnic variations differ greatly according to geographical situation, but battering tends to be predominantly an Anglo-American-Nordic phenomenon, compared with the Latin-Slav nations and may be related to the less binding family relationships. Within England, an increase in incidence has been reported in Irish and negroid immigrants, though this may be linked to the social class variation, rather than to ethnic factors.

Clinical picture

The most common injuries are:

1. Skin bruising and abrasions.
2. Head injuries, especially fractured skull and subdural haemorrhage.
3. Multiple fractures, especially of long bones, ribs and skull.
4. Visceral damage, especially rupture of the liver, intestine and mesentery.
5. Injuries to lips and mouth.
6. Injuries to the eyes, internal and external.

The constant feature is repetition of injuries at different dates, often progressing from trivial to more severe. It has been estimated that of a child presenting for the first time with injuries inflicted by a parent, there is a 60 per cent chance of recurrence of injuries at a later date, and a 10 per cent chance of eventual fatal injury.

The parents

The battering of children can occur in any type of home, but from surveys carried out at The London Hospital and by the NSPCC Battered Baby Unit, a definite pattern appears to emerge:

1. The parents tend to be young, often in their early twenties or less. The 'father' is frequently not the biological father, but a later (maybe temporary) consort of the mother.
2. Several children may have been born in rapid succession. When the mother is the 'batterer', she has often been recently delivered or is again pregnant.
3. The social class tends to be towards the lower end of the spectrum, but is not a condition associated with extreme squalor or poverty. The standard of home furnishing, clothing and nutrition is good.
4. A frequent finding is that the family is isolated, often living away from the proximity of relatives, especially grandparents. The rootless factory worker (often a caravan-dweller) is a typical example.
5. The father may be the dominant partner, sometimes aggressive though this may be masked. The mother infrequently is of a lower IQ.
6. Many of the fathers have criminal records or are unemployed or otherwise socially unstable.
7. Unhappy childhood experiences in both parents seem to be the rule rather than the exception, and many battering

parents were 'battered children' themselves. Their background cannot be better described than in this account by Miss Joan Court, formerly of the NSPCC Battered Child Research Department:

Battering parents are often victims of a very deprived, harsh background. They grew up to believe that they are worthless and inadequate. They feel that they cannot please anyone. They are bedevilled by feelings of anger and resentment towards everyone and everything. They have difficulty in dealing with agressive feelings, and cope with tension either by striking out or running away. Because they have not experienced a tender relationship with a mother person, they are crippled in their own capacity to mother, that is, in the ability to protect and feel for those weaker than themselves.

These parents are not usually mentally ill, but they are in some respects emotionally immature, and they tend to marry someone with a similar background and handicap. Such a marriage may be reasonably satisfactory until the children arrive. Then several things may go wrong. The father, for instance, may often be jealous of the new baby because he needs the mother's love for himself. Likewise the mother, if she is not getting enough support from the husband, may look to the baby to fill this need. If the baby is responsive, healthy and easy to please, all may go well. If he is whining or collicky, the mother may think the infant does not love her, or is criticising her. She may then feel rejected and batter him.

These parents have difficulty in seeing the baby as a baby. They often expect him to eat without making a mess by six months and be toilet-trained by a year. So injuries to these babies tend to occur around these issues of feeding and cleanliness. Most battering parents do not put their feelings in words too clearly. They are conscious of only unbearable tensions. This is often worse when the baby cries and when they are alone with him. It is as if the crying awakens in them their own sad feelings of being a crying and unhappy child, and in hitting the child they are punishing themselves.'

Recognition of the battered child

Certain clinical and pathological features may assist in clarifying doubts which may exist in the doctor's mind when presented with an injured child.

Certain surface injuries are highly suspicious. Bruises are frequent, especially around the distal part of the arms where the child has been gripped and shaken. Bruising of the scalp, though often not apparent due to the hair, may be detected by palpation and tenderness. Bruising of the face is extremely common, especially around the mouth. A most characteristic lesion, reported in almost 50 per cent of cases, is laceration of the mucosa inside the upper lip, often near the centre line where the frenulum may be torn. This may extend laterally, and actually separate the inner surface of the lip from the base of the gums. These injuries represent striking on the mouth, usually as an attempt of stop the continuous crying of a child. Bite marks are quite common, especially on the face and upper limbs of the child. More recently, injuries to the eyes have been described in a high proportion of cases. Vitreous haemorrhages, lens dislocations and retinal damage may be detected and an examination by an ophthalmologist is recommended in all suspected cases.

Bruises, often circular due to fingertip pressure, are common around the joints of the upper limbs, and on the neck, chest and abdomen, due to poking or prodding. Bruises may often be seen on either side of the chest, behind the axillae, and down the anterior chest wall, where the child has been gripped roughly between two adult hands and shaken. Internally, this form of trauma is responsible for the very frequent multiple rib fractures, which usually occur along the posterior angle of the ribs a short distance from the spinal column.

Fractures of the long bones may occur anywhere, but are extremely common at epiphyses, which are only loosely attached in young children. This epiphyseal separation, and calcification beneath sheath of long bones, due to avulsion of the loose periosteum of infants, presents a characteristic radiological picture. Where suspicion of battering is raised, it is essential for any child to have a full body X-ray, even bearing in mind the general undesirability of needless exposure to radiation. The same applies to post-mortem examination, when radiological examination of the cadaver is vital before autopsy begins.

Characteristic radiological features include the fractured ribs, calcified periostial lesions and the epiphyseal shearing. An important point is the estimation of age of the various injuries. In children who have been subjected to repeated trauma over a period of time, radiology may reveal fractures in various stages of healing. The presence of these is strong confirmatory evidence of 'battering'.

Ruptured viscera are frequently seen, the explanation offered being utterly inadequate to account for the gross trauma. Such injuries may consist of lacerated liver, torn bowel and multiple fenestration of the mesentery. Explanations will always be readily forthcoming from the parents, and include such facile offerings as 'he fell from my lap' . . . 'he slipped from my arms and hit the pram handle' . . . 'he slipped from the bed into the fire-place' . . . Though these explanations might be valid for one single injury, they cannot possibly explain multiple bruising, fractures of different ages and gross abdominal injuries.

Apart from these classical lesions, other more bizarre injuries are often seen. Scalding with hot fluids, burns from electric fires, cigarette burns, and other hallmarks of sadistic activities occur from time to time.

The doctor's duty in suspected battering

The battering of babies, though showing a genuine increase in recent years, is by no means a new phenomenon. It remained unrecognised mainly due to the reluctance of the medical profession to accept that gross injuries – and even death – could deliberately be inflicted by a child's own parents. The syndrome first began to come to light in 1946, when an American radiologist, Caffey, described inexplicable head injuries and limb fractures in young children. Some years later, he published a further article and his name was attached to the syndrome for some time. Soon afterwards, numerous other reports began to emerge, notably those of Silverman and Kempe, and due to almost explosive publicity over the last decade, doctors are now more ready to attribute child injuries to parental abuse. However, there is a natural reluctance to stigmatise parents, especially where the diagnosis is not absolutely clear-cut. The pendulum must not be allowed to swing too far the other way, and it must be clearly recognised that genuine accidents occur to young children as well as to other age groups. Yet where evidence of repetitive injury and discrepancy between the extent of the lesions and the offered explanation exist, then some action should be taken. However reluctant a practitioner is to initiate further investigation, he has an ethical duty to his infant patient, in a condition which carries a 60 per cent recurrence rate and a 10 per cent mortality rate.

It is not enough merely to treat the acute injuries and then return the child to a dangerous domestic situation. Once the child's lesions have been treated, then the parents should be treated. Due to strenuous efforts, especially on the part of the NSPCC, a mechanism now exists for making discreet enquiries, and for the offer of help to the parents. This is a situation where team-work is essential, and many large conurbations now have an arrangement where all the agencies concerned co-operate to supervise and treat known cases. General practitioners, health visitors, the NSPCC, the Local Authority, paediatricians and other medical specialists have a part to play, and it is no longer justifiable merely to treat a child's acute injuries and await the next episode.

In a number of cases where a child has been admitted to hospital with suspected non-accidental injuries, it appears unsafe to return the child home, either because the circumstances have not yet been fully explored or because there is indisputable evidence of battering. As a temporary measure, where the parents are unwilling to voluntarily leave the child in care, a breathing space can be gained under Section 28 (1) of the Children and Young Persons Act, 1969. The authority of a magistrate is obtained 'to detain the child in a place of safety if there is reasonable cause to believe that his/her proper development is being avoidably prevented or neglected or his/her health is being avoidably impaired or neglected or he/she is being ill treated'. This authority runs for a maximum time of 28 days, but allows the local Child Abuse Committee, where such organisation has been instituted, to further investigate and discuss the child and decide upon the best course of action.

Criminal proceedings against the parents are becoming increasingly rare, as they are now recognised as being either useless or even actively harmful. Except where death has been caused, or deliberate and sadistic brutality is evident, further splitting of the family by imprisonment causes nothing but harm. Though admittance of the child into care of the local authority might be necessary in severe cases where family circumstances are overtly dangerous, treatment is best performed under supervision at home. The Children and Young Persons Acts give local authorities power to provide advice, guidance and assistance (including material aid) to promote the welfare of children and diminish the need to receive them into care. Current research indicates that only prophylactic psychiatric attention to the parents, can alleviate the increasing prevalence of the battered child syndrome. This increases the doctor's responsibility to recognise cases at an early stage, so that parental guidance may be instituted before further serious harm or even death, overtakes the child.

Although child battering is thought to be more prevalent in Anglo-Saxon than in Latin countries, the Celts do not appear immune from this aberration of parenthood. Fatalities in the Republic of Ireland are not numerous and in a population of about 3 million the average on the State Pathologist's files is approximately one per annum with two in an occasional year. The Social workers of the Health Authorities are aware of the problem and the Irish equivalent of the NSPCC, namely the ISPCC, are active in educating the public in this area. Custodial orders either to other relatives or the a Health Board may be taken out under the 1908 Children's Act, as ammended by subsequent children's acts of the Irish Republic up to 1957.

27

Neglect, chronic alcoholism and drunkenness

In spite of the improvements brought about by the Welfare State, neglect is still present in the community, either as self-neglect or parental neglect of children. The latter are thankfully fewer than in former years, though occasional severe and even fatal cases are seen. The majority of cases of self-neglect are now seen in old persons, often living alone either from choice or necessity. The victims are frequently of a hermit-like disposition due either to senile mental changes or to some paranoid state. The condition need not be associated with poverty, and in many cases, previous offers of assistance have been rejected.

Not uncommonly, the death of such a recluse is not discovered for some time and bodies may be discovered days or even weeks later, when police break into the premises after suspicion has been aroused. The living conditions are often indescribably bad, and many of the deaths occur during the cold winter months when hypothermia or chest infections are precipitated by lack of domestic heating. In particularly cold periods, such deaths may even be seen amongst young adults, often schizophrenic males living alone in peculiar circumstances, with no heating and little food available.

Apart from the pathological signs of hypothermia in such cases, there is little medical evidence that is required, the circumstances being self-evident. Often there may have been suspicion of foul play, due to the extreme disorder of the premises and the possibility of an intruder breaking in to look for the real or alleged hoard of money. This in fact, is not infrequently found, sometimes many hundreds of pounds being discovered in bank-notes, hidden amongst the chaos.

The appearances of hypothermia are mentioned elsewhere and there may be obvious emaciation of the body, with bodily neglect in the form of dirt, extraordinary long toenails, body lice and fleas, and a profusion of ragged dirty clothing. Post-mortem examination may confirm the general appearances, the signs of under-nutrition being the body weight, empty gas-filled alimentary tract, and dilated gall bladder. There may be signs of congestive cardiac failure and oedema, partly due to the heart failure or even due to hypoproteinaemia. There may be signs of anaemia and vitamin deficiency, with skin changes.

In contrast to this self-neglect, occasional cases of deliberate fatal neglect of infants are seen, which may amount to murder or manslaughter. Though the former ruling under the Coroner's Act that the deaths of any foster-child must be reported to the coroner no longer applies, such notification must naturally be made on any of the other grounds of notification to the coroner.

The welfare of children is protected by many statutes, notably the Children and Young Persons Acts, which are particularly concerned with foster children and exposure to physical or moral danger of children in all circumstances. Under this Act, if a person undertakes for reward the nursing and maintenance of a child under nine years (not being the parents), he must give notice in writing to the local authority and should the child die or be removed from his care, he must within 24 hours give notice in writing to the local authority and to the person from whom the child was received.

The Acts also make it an offence 'for any person who has attained the age of 16 and has custody of any child under that age to wilfully assault, ill treat, neglect, abandon or expose him, or causes or procures him to be assaulted, ill-treated, neglected or abandoned, or exposed in a manner likely to cause him unnecessary suffering or injury to health'. A further section of the Acts made it an offence for any adult person to have gone to bed under the influence of drink, if any child under three years of age in the same bed died of suffocation. This rather curious ruling was a response to the assumption that children dying from what is now called a 'cot death' were in fact 'overlain', though this is now considered to be a spurious explanation. It is also an offence for a person over 16, having the custody of any child under the age of seven, to allow the child to be exposed to the risk of burning or scalding whereby he is killed or seriously injured.

The same Act of 1933, amended by the 1963 Act of the same name, also provides for children and young persons who are in need of care and protection. They are deemed to be such if they lack such care, protection and guidance as a good parent may reasonably be expected to give, to such extent that this is likely to cause him unnecessary suffering or seriously to affect his health or proper development. In such cases, a juvenile court may commit him to the care of a 'fit person' willing to undertake the care of him (usually the local authority) or to order his parents or guardian to enter into a recognisance to exercise proper care and guardianship.

From the practical point of view, the doctor will recognise such children by virtue of his experience, powers of observation and common sense. The 'battered baby' described elsewhere, is a particular type of child neglect, where the acts are of *commission* rather than *omission*. Fortunately, the incidence of dirty, unkempt, underfed and ill-housed children is less now than in the latter part of the last century, when organisations such as the NSPCC were founded primarily to relieve their suffering. However, the Welfare State has by no means eliminated this picture and both in rural and urban surroundings, child neglect to the point of death may occasionally be encountered. As the general appearance of the child presents such as obvious picture, the doctor will not be in such a difficult position as with the battered baby syndrome, where nutrition, clothing and housing often leave little to be desired. In cases of emaciation, natural disease must be eliminated, including congenital metabolic diseases, and in fatal cases this duty to eliminate natural causes is a duty for the pathologist. In young infants, extensive urine dermatitis, sometimes sufficient to have caused ulceration of the sacral region may be seen. In very cold weather, neglected infants have been found dead with actual freezing of urine-soaked clothing and florid ulceration of the extremities from exposure to low temperature.

In fatal cases, the duty of the practitioner is, of course, confined to notifying the coroner and complying with his subsequent requests for a statement and evidence at an inquest. Where the child is alive, the matter is best handled by the NSPCC and Children's Officer of the local authority. Where doubt exists as to the true nature of emaciation etc., the opinion of a consultant paediatrician is often very helpful.

Chronic alcoholism

One form of self-abuse is of particular interest in relation to notification to the coroner. This is chronic alcoholism, for which there was a separate verdict available at a coroner's inquest. Though now more widely recognised to be either a form of drug dependence or a frank psychiatric condition, from the coroner's point of view, it is akin to 'self-neglect', for which there is also a separate inquest verdict available. Any death certification mentioning alcoholism, whether acute or chronic, must be rejected by the Registrar of Births and Deaths and reported to the coroner. Often, even the bare diagnosis of 'cirrhosis of the liver' will also cause the Registrar either to query or reject the certificate, unless the condition is stated to be 'not due to alcohol'.

From the medical point of view, chronic alcoholism is far better identified from the general circumstances and clinical history than from post-mortem examination. Though chronic gastritis, fatty change in the liver and portal cirrhosis may be seen (as well as the frequently associated signs of personal neglect and malnutrition), all these conditions can occur in the absence of chronic alcoholism, and vice versa.

Other hazards of either chronic alcoholism or frequent bouts of acute alcoholism are:

1. *Death from burning* – a not uncommon terminal event being the ignition of bedclothes by a lighted cigarette whilst in alcoholic stupor. Other deaths from burns have occurred from knocking over paraffin stoves or falling into open fires whilst incapacitated by drink.
2. *Falls*, either in the roadway or at home may lead to death from head injuries or other fractures.
3. *Terminal infections*, especially bronchopneumonia, are particularly common in chronic alcoholics.

Drunkenness

Acute alcoholic intoxication, as opposed to chronic alcoholism is an extremely common condition and one which often involves the doctor. To be drunk is no crime in itself, but numerous situations come within the criminal law where drunkenness may lead to some public danger. A notable example is driving a motor vehicle, a subject which is dealt with in a separate chapter. Drunkenness whilst in charge of a child, in charge of a horse-drawn vehicle, and many others are on the Statute Book, but in most of these cases the diagnosis of drunkenness is left to a police constable. The police surgeon or the doctor is primarily concerned with drunkenness, but there are some aspects which primarily affect the safety of the drunken person himself, and any doctor may be called upon to examine him.

The differentiation of the drunken state from head injuries is a perennial problem for casualty officers and where there is any substantial possibility of the two existing together, the person should be admitted for observation. The head injury may have occurred whilst the person is drunk, or a head injury may completely mimic the effects of drunkenness. Confusion may naturally arise when alcohol is smelt on the breath, though this is naturally no guide to the amount consumed. The clinical state may present the most profound clinical problem in distinguishing the two conditions, especially when both are present together. A particular danger is the confinement of a drunken person to police custody overnight, where apart from the risk of dying of pure alcoholic intoxication or aspiration of vomit, the concurrent existence of a head injury may lead to a fatal outcome whilst in a police cell.

The symptomatology of acute alcoholism varies greatly, but the following points might assist in the differentiation of drunkenness from head injury, as well as the obvious features such as external head injury and X-ray of the skull:

> In head injuries with concussion, the victim tends to be pale, with moist, cold skin and a thin pulse of normal to slow rate. The pupils may react normally to light, the breathing is shallow and slow and the demeanour generally is subdued and co-operative, though there may be well-established amnesia.
>
> In drunkenness, the typical picture is of a restless, confused and often unco-operative patient, whose condition gradually improves as time goes on. The skin is warm, dry and flushed, the pulse rapid and full. The pupils react sluggishly to light and the breathing is irregularly deep and sighing, with belching and snoring. Memory may be normal, though distored by alcoholic confusion.

Other factors are common in both conditions, such as blood pressure, inco-ordination and temperature; when both conditions are present simultaneously, it may well be impossible to separate the relative contributions of drunkenness and the head injury. Only careful observation can then be recommended, new decisions being made as further clinical signs become obvious.

28

The drinking driver

The examination of the drinking driver and the collection of blood samples is almost always the province of the official police surgeon, but occasions may arise when practitioners other than recognised police surgeons, may be requested to assist the authorities in this matter. There is no legal obligation to do so, and although motives of public duty may conflict with personal reluctance, it is entirely a matter for the individual doctor to decide for himself. The legal responsibilities and subsequent court proceedings may be both onerous and arduous, especially where the doctor is not habitually engaged in this practice.

A doctor may also become involved at the request of one of his patients who is exercising his legal right to have his own practitioner in attendance during a police surgeon's examination. Though the partisan spirit of representing the defence versus the prosecution is hard to eliminate, it must always be remembered that both medical witnesses are there to seek the true facts of the matter, and not fight tooth and nail either 'for' or 'against' the defendant.

In view of the frequency of this medico-legal exercise and the potentially serious results of a conviction, it is well for the basic facts of the law and procedure to be understood by all doctors engaged in either general practice or casualty and accident medicine.

The law and the drinking driver

The Road Traffic Act of 1972 combined in their entirety, two separate provisions for the prosecution of drinking drivers which were formerly included in two separate Acts of Parliament.

The driver of a motor vehicle may be proceeded against by the police on either of two grounds:

1. If his ability to drive properly is for the time being impaired through drink or drugs (previously included in the Road Traffic Act, 1962).

2. If he drives a motor vehicle whilst exceeding a minimum of 80 mg of alcohol per 100 ml of blood or 107 mg alcohol per 100 ml of urine (previous included in the Road Safety Act, 1967).

It is most unusual for the police to proceed under the old provisions, though they must do so if some other drug besides alcohol is involved. For virtually every case of drinking and driving, the finding of an excess of alcohol in the blood or urine above the statutory limit is automatically used for conviction, without reference to the impairment of ability of the accused person to drive a motor vehicle.

The use of a blood or urine threshold for conviction arose from the defects in the previous legislation. Great controversy and most energetic defence efforts revolved about the last word in the phrase of the 1962 Act which reads 'A person shall be taken to be unfit to drive if his ability to drive properly is for the time being *impaired*'. The degree and manifestations of 'impairment' in this context have never been satisfactorily defined, and in arriving at a decision, the court must take into account the evidence of the police officer, the medical examination and the results of blood and urine analysis where available. The scheme of examination is given in great detail in various publications, especially in those intended for the police surgeon, but basically the objects of the examination are:

1. To exclude natural disease which may mimic the effects of alcohol or drugs.
2. To exclude injuries, especially head injuries, which may mimic or aggravate the effects of alcohol or drugs.
3. To detect and evaluate impairment of reaction time, co-ordination etc., due to the effects of alcohol or drugs.
4. To decide whether the driver is fit to be released to the charge of his vehicle, whether fit to be detained in police custody or whether he should be admitted to hospital.

The following scheme of examination applied mainly to the old 1962 Act, but is still valid when examining for impairment of driving ability thought to be due to drugs other than alcohol.

When called to examine a driver suspected of having an impaired ability due to alcohol or drugs, the doctor (if he agrees to attend) should follow a meticulous routine both to protect himself and to ensure that justice is done. He should note the time of commencement and completion of the examination and endeavour to see that it is carried out in the best possible surroundings, though this is often impossible in the often forbidding environment of older police stations. The presence of a police officer cannot be forbidden, and may be a considerable comfort where an obstreperous subject is concerned.

The next vital matter is the obtaining of consent. Except where the subject is unconscious or completely uncomprehending, legally valid consent must be obtained. The purpose of the examination must be explained, it being made clear that the information gained will be used in evidence at subsequent legal proceedings. The doctor must make it clear that the driver is not obliged to submit to the examination and that he may exercise his right to have it conducted by a doctor of his own choice on with such a doctor present at an examination conducted by the present doctor.

The doctor must also indicate that if samples of blood and/or urine are taken they wil also be used for analysis and the evidence offered to the police. Consent, though ideally obtained in writing, is usually obtained verbally with a police officer as witness.

If the driver refuses consent, the doctor may only make such observations as will assist him in determining whether the patient suffers from some illness or the effects of some injury, and should not question the patient in any way that could incriminate him.

If the patient is unconscious or incapable of giving consent, the doctor should examine with the purpose of detecting disease or injury, estimate the degree of intoxication if any, and take blood samples. However, the results of all of these should be withheld form the police until the patient recovers consciousness or sobriety, and gives proper consent. The only exception is the statement to the police about the subject's fitness to be detained or the necessity for further medical treatment.

The examination should be conducted as soon as practical after the doctor is called, as naturally the effect of any alcohol progressively diminishes. If the patient insists on the presence of his own doctor, the examination must not be unduly delayed because of his non-arrival.

Form of medical examination

This varies from practitioner to practitioner, but a satisfactory scheme is similar to that given in the BMA booklet *The Recognition of Intoxication*.

It again should be remembered that the purpose of the examination is not only to detect and evaluate alcoholic or drug intoxication, but to confirm or eliminate the presence of natural disease or injuries which may mimic or exaggerate any intoxication. Particular attention should be paid to the scalp for recent bruises, abrasions or tender spots. If detention of the suspect has followed a road accident, details of the latter should be obtained from the police before examination, the severity and nature of the accident being relevant in expected nervous and possibly physical state of the driver.

A medical history should be obtained from the patient, this preliminary conversation also assisting in an assessment of the state of speech, confusion, memory and general competence. The time of the last meal, the amount and nature of any drink or drug taken should be elicited. Direct questioning should be made as to the presence of diabetes, insulin dosage, fits of any sort and the current taking of any medicines or tablets.

A general impression should be made of deportment and behaviour, state of dress, general coherence and co-ordination and specially speech. General tests of memory and awareness are recommended, which may be incorporated into general questioning such as name and address, occupation, date, time and a few simple questions of general knowledge.

The subject should then be asked to write something, both his name and address, and simple paragraph copied from a book or newspaper. In assessing both this and the previous matter of knowledge and awareness, the apparent level of intelligence and education must be taken into account. The pulse should be taken, that in alcoholic intoxication being classically full-bounding and rapid. The month temperature, state of the mouth, any smell of alcohol on the breath and the state of the skin (flushing, pallor or sweating) should be noted.

The eyes should be examined carefully, allowance being made for the wearing of glasses, contact lenses and any pre-existing disease, such as a false eye, deformed iris or evidence of previous injury or surgical treatment. A simple test of visual acuity should be applied. The full range of eye movements should be studied, and the ability to converge noted. Any strabismus must be carefully noted, as this may be either temporary, due to the subject's condition or a permanent defect. Nystagmus is important and true lateral nystagmus must be distinguished from nystagmoid jerks due to the examiner's finger moving beyond the field of vision.

Ears should be examined with an auriscope and a general assessment of hearing ability made.

The ability of the driver to walk should be studied, a note being made of his gait whilst crossing the room and back. Any pre-existing disability in this context, such as lameness, must be detected and allowed for. Irregularity, staggering, a wide-based walk and other peculiarities should be noted. The old test of walking a straight line is invalid, as many people in normal circumstances are unable to do this. The manner of turning and the reaction time to commands to stop and start should be noted. The ability to stand straight and still with the eyes shut must be tested.

Muscular co-ordination is important, especially the degree of ability with which he can perform ordinary movements rather than artificial clinical tests. Doing-up and undoing buttons, picking up coins, and lighting a cigarette are some good tests, the only purely clinical tests employed being the finger-nose and finger-to-finger tests.

General examination of the respiratory, cardio-vascular and central nervous system should be carried out, to detect and eliminate natural disease. Apart from the exclusion of injury and disease, the object of the report is to offer an opinion as to the degree of impairment (if any) of driving ability of the accused at the time of the doctor's examination. In arriving at this opinion, the doctor must take an overall view of his findings, and these should be communicated to the driver at the time. He should again be reminded of his right to obtain his own medical adviser.

The report to the police should be completed at the time, giving the name of the person, the date and time of the examination. Any disease or injury which may have contributed to the state of the accused must be described. A direct opinion as to whether alcoholic intoxication has impaired his driving ability should be offered. Finally, his fitness to be either discharged in charge of his vehicle, discharged without a vehicle, detained by the police, or admitted to hospital must be made.

Usual procedure under the 1972 Act

Recent legislation does not attempt to penalise a driver for impairment of ability to drive, but merely for having drunk sufficient alcohol to raise his blood level to more than 80 mg by weight in 100 ml. of blood by volume (or 107 mg of alcohol by weight in 100 ml. of urine by volume). As far as the Act itself is concerned, no clinical examination is necessary, though this is invariably done to safeguard the suspect's interests and indirectly to protect the police custodians. The legal function of the doctor is to take blood specimens in a proper manner, urine specimens being taken by the police. The most important legal aspect of this new Act is that refusal to provide blood or urine samples automatically leads to conviction. Incidentally, this is the first occasion in English Law that makes it an offence to withhold evidence that might be self-incriminating.

The sequences of events leading to prosecution under this Act are as follows:

1. After contravening any traffic regulation (which excludes random testing) a police officer is authorised to stop any driver and

request him to take a breath test. This first screening-test is performed at the roadside, and consists of blowing into a plastic balloon via a glass tube containing a crystalline bichromate-sulphuric acid mixture. The constitutents of this mixture are so compounded that the crystals will turn green to a pre-determined distance if the blood alcohol is 80 mg/100 ml or more. (At the time of writing, trials are being made with a new form of breath-testing device based on the fuel cell, which gives a more accurate reading of the breath alcohol level. A Bill was introduced into Parliament in December 1980 to make the results of a breath-test the definitive criterion for an offence of driving with excess alcohol, in preference to the use of a blood sample.)

If this test is positive, the police officer will request the driver to accompany him to the nearest police station, and the breath test is repeated. If it is again positive, the police officer will inform the driver that he must submit to a blood test or to give two specimens of urine within the next hour, and that failure to comply with this request constitutes an offence with automatic conviction.

The reason for the second breath test is that it is recognised that alcohol may remain in the mouth after even a small drink, and may cause a false positive first test. This residual alcohol in the mouth does not persist more than 20 minutes, and a test taken again after this interval would be negative if the initial positive breath test was due to this spurious factor.

2. If either the first or second breath is negative, the suspect will normally be dismissed from police interest, though it is still possible that if the driver appears overtly intoxicated, the police may proceed to evaluate his ability to drive, if they suspect that it is impaired by drugs.

3. When the second test is positive, the station officer will summon the police surgeon (or another doctor who expresses willingness to assist) to take the blood sample.

On his arrival, it may be found that the accused refused to have blood taken: without such consent, the doctor must not in any circumstances attempt to obtain the samples, as this constitutes an assault. Since refusal carries automatic conviction, there is little need for the doctor or police to strain their powers of persuasion. The accused may refuse permission for the doctor summoned by the police to take the samples, but agree to his own doctor doing so. As this might be a stratagem to delay matters whilst the blood alcohol falls, it must be explained to the driver that unless the other practitioner can arrive before preparations to take blood are complete, refusal beyond that point will constitute automatic conviction. Refusal of the driver's own doctor to attend does not alter the position in any way, the accused either submitting to the police doctor's ministrations or suffering automatic conviction.

4. Instead of blood, the driver may elect to give two urine samples within an hour. These are taken under police supervision, the doctor not being involved. If the second specimen cannot be produced, then a blood sample must be taken or again automatic conviction will ensue.

5. Though it is wise to make at least a superficial assessment of the driver's physical state, if the police do not intend to detain him after the blood samples have been taken, the doctor has no further responsibility. If however, the police intend taking him into custody, then they will request a report from the doctor as to his fitness for detention. Consent for this examination must be obtained separately from the driver from that for the taking of blood, whether the latter has been granted or refused. A clinical examination, directed at the medical state and not to the degree of intoxication, should then be performed, with a direct view to the safety of the driver during detention in police premises, usually for the remainder of the night.

As in the previous section, special attention should be directed to head injury, the presence of pre-existing disease such as diabetes and the taking of drugs such as insulin or barbiturates. If any condition is found which makes immediate medical treatment necessary, the patient should be advised accordingly, and either treatment arranged in the police station or transfer to hospital arranged. If permission to examine is refused and obvious clinical abnormality is apparent, due to disease or injury, the patient should be informed of this, and then reassured that any information gained from the examination of his present physical state will be withheld from the police unless and until the driver gives permission.

6. Where permission for blood taking has been granted (in the presence of a police officer), the actual technique of collection is vital. The police have ready-packed kits for this purpose prepared by the Home Office Forensic Science Laboratories. Four plastic cups with wired-on lids are provided, two of which are for analysis on behalf of the prosecution (one is a reserve in case the first is unsuitable or insufficient) and the third is offered to the driver for his own private analysis if he so wishes. A spare cup is also included. Sterile lancets and dressings are also provided. Re-packing and labelling of the tin are particularly important to ensure proper identification and continuity of evidence of the samples. As many police surgeons now prefer to take samples of venous blood in pre-

ference to capillary blood, larger bottles are also available, which after filling are placed in outer containers which have an unremovable snap-lid.

Blood-taking

When the introductory formalities mentioned previously have been performed (including the vital *consent*), the site of blood-taking must be stated to the patient. When originally planned, it was envisaged that the site of blood-taking would always be from a skin prick in either ear or finger, but experience has shown that venepuncture is often far more satisfactory. The choice is up to the doctor, not the driver, and insistence on taking blood from some unsuitable place can be construed as refusal to allow sampling, with the inevitable consequence of automatic conviction. Soon after the introduction of the new Act, several drivers attempted to evade the issue by requesting sampling from ludicrous places, such as toes or even in one instance, the penis! The defence societies have stated that the election of site is the doctor's choice, and that refusal to comply can be construed as total refusal.

If skin-pricking is chosen, the skin of the finger or ear-lobe is cleaned with soap and water (naturally not surgical spirit) and the skin punctured with the lancet provided. The caps should have been removed from the cups previously, and three drops of blood are placed into each – something often easier said than done! The cap must be replaced, usually by the police officer, who mixes the cup to dissolve the anti-coagulant. When three cups are filled (the fourth is provided in the kit as a reserve) the wired labels are attached through the lugs of the cups, which are numbered consecutively. Two cups are replaced in the tin, sealed with Sellotape and labelled. The other cup is placed in an envelope, which is sealed and signed by the police officer and the accused, when it is placed with his effects ready for collection on his release. After the procedure is finished, a triplicate Home Office (R.T.5) is completed, the top copy being kept by the doctor for his own records.

As frequently happens, the doctor may well prefer venepuncture to the difficult and uncertain business of obtaining at least nine drops of blood from the skin prick. The method is also more accurate, in that less time is taken to fill the cups and there is much less opportunity for evaporation of alcohol from the sample. With the advent of disposable syringes and needles, police forces frequently have equipment available for venepuncture, no particular technique being prescribed in the Act.

PROCEDURE IN SCOTLAND AND IRELAND

The Road Traffic Act, 1972 runs to Scotland exactly as in England, but the law in both Northern Ireland and the Republic of Ireland differs.

In the *Republic of Ireland* the Road Traffic Act of 1968 was very similar to the British legislation in that a screening test by breath analysis is employed, followed by a definitive analysis of either blood or urine. However, the level for conviction was not 80 milligrams per 100 millilitres, but 125 milligrams per 100 millilitres. This level was found to be too high and was amended by the Road Traffic (Amendment) Act 1978 which reduced the limit to 100 milligrams of alcohol per 100 millilitres of blood and the equivalent in urine, namely 135 milligrams of alcohol per 100 millilitres of urine. Another slight difference of the 1968 Act, unchanged by the 1978 Act is that if the acused person opts to provide a urine sample instead of blood, the medical practitioner is responsible for overseeing its collection, whereas this may be done by a police officer under English law. The doctor must be present when the Gardai formally cautions the arrested person and there are slight differences in the procedure for ensuring that the specimens are identified and sealed to ensure continuity of evidence.

In *Northern Ireland*, there is a double system of penalty for persons found driving with an excess of alcohol above statutory limits. The 80 mg per 100 ml of English law and the 125 mg per 100 ml of Republican law are combined so that the level of alcohol is directly related to the severity of the sentence imposed by the courts.

The 'Major Offence' may be brought if a motorist is deemed either to be under the influence of drink or drugs to such an extent as to be incapable of having proper control of a motor vehicle (as proved by the clinical examination of a police surgeon) or, more usually, by demonstration of a blood alcohol level of at least 125 mg/100 ml or a urine level of 167 mg/100 ml.

The 'Minor Offence' is an alternative which is not related to behaviour, but only to an alcohol level in excess of 80 mg/100 ml in the blood or 107 mg/100 ml in the urine.

Motorists can be stopped at random by specially-trained policemen and to be required to take breath tests. The apparatus is an 'Ethanograph' used in a specially-equipped van. If the reading is over a specified limit, the motorist can choose between having the breath test used in evidence or to having a blood or urine sample taken. Blood is always taken as a venous sample, not from fingerprick.

29

General aspects of poisoning

Toxicology has become such a vast and explosively expanding subject that both the non-specialist doctor and the forensic pathologist have little hope of keeping pace with pharmacology and toxic effects, still less with the details of analytical techniques and the interpretation of results. These have become the province of the toxicologist, but there are certain common causes of poisoning and certain general effects common to most poisons of which all doctors should be aware.

As there is no convenient classification possible, the most common poisons will be dicussed in an arbitrary order.

BARBITURATES (SCHEDULE IV, PART A OF THE POISONS RULES)

Although in 1973, 60 per cent of fatal poisonings in England and Wales were due to barbiturates, more recent years have seen a marked fall in such cases. This is due both to an active move on the part of doctors to restrict prescribing and also to the advent of non-barbiturate hypnotics and the greatly increased use of tranquillisers and other psycho-active drugs. The dangers inherent in having large quantities of these drugs circulating in the community have prompted a movement in the medical profession to progressively phase out the prescribing of barbiturates, similar to the virtual outlawing of amphetamines in recent years. The first Area Health Authority to recommend this action was that of South Glamorgan, in May 1975. However, barbiturate poisoning is still important and some knowledge of its toxic effects is essential.

The drugs act by an extension of their normal pharmacological action, that is, depression of the central nervous system. Used therapeutically for inducing sleep or a general hypnotic or sedative action on mental activity, in large doses they disable the lower brain centres and cause brain stem paralysis, especially of the respiratory centre. The normal therapeutic actions of drowsiness, loss of concentration and co-ordination are accentuated by overdose to the point of stupor, coma and death.

Various barbiturate compounds have different uses, mainly by virtue of the rapidity of their effects rather than the type of effect.

The fastest acting are those used for induction of anaesthesia such as thiopentone (Pentothal), which is normally given intravenously, as an aqueous solution. Due to their mode of administration, toxic effects are rarely seen outside hospital practice.

The short-acting barbiturates are represented by substances such as hexa-, cyclo- and quinal-barbitone, whose therapeutic effects after normal dosage persist only for up to four hours.

The medium-acting barbiturates such as amylo- and butobarbitone are probably the most commonly employed, giving up to eight hours' hypnotic affect, ideal for inducing sleep at night.

The long-acting barbiturates, the first to be employed for therapeutic purposes, consist of barbitone itself (Veronal) and phenobarbitone, widely used for long-term maintenance of epileptics and patients who require day-and night-time sedation. The duration of activity of these drugs is up to 24 hours.

The fatal does of barbiturates is impossible to tabulate, as there is great individual variation in tolerance. Patients who have been prescribed barbiturates for a long period can tolerate dosages far in excess of a person who has never before received them. In general, the maintenance of a high blood level for a relatively short time is enough to cause respiratory failure and death. This peak can be reached with a much smaller dose of the short-acting drugs than with the long-acting drugs, and a rough guide is that 1–2 grams of short-acting barbiturates, 2–3 grams of medium-acting and 3–4 grams of long-acting barbiturates are likely to cause death. These are roughly ten times the normal therapeutic dose, though, as already stated, the individual variation is great and deaths can occur at much lower or much higher levels of administration.

The speed of toxic effects also varies greatly and depends not only on the dose taken, but on other factors such as food in the stomach and personal absorption rates. However, after a massive dose of a short-acting barbiturate, death may occur in as short a time as 20–30 minutes. With large doses of medium-acting barbiturates such as amylo-barbitone (probably the most common suicidal barbiturate) death is common within a couple of hours.

Death is due to pure respiratory failure from brain stem depression, but may also be accelarated by hypotension, and cerebral anoxia from airway obstruction during profound coma, either by secretions in the air passages or pharyngeal blockage. When rendering first aid in a barbiturate poisoning, one of the most urgent necessities is to maintain a clear airway. Where coma is prolonged more than one day, chest infections prove the most usual cause of death.

Diagnosis of barbiturate or other hypnotic poisoning

Where a previously healthy person, especially one who is young or middle-aged, suddenly goes into coma, then the differential diagnosis lies between poisoning by a hypnotic, such as a barbiturate, or a cerebral vascular accident, especially subarachnoid haemorrhage. If a practitioner is called to a case of this type, apart from the urgent treatment of the patient and despatch to hospital, he should also examine (or cause to be examined) the immediate surroundings, in order to assist in the differential diagnosis by the discovery of a possible toxic cause. This is not meddling in detection, but an integral part of the clinical treatment. In fatal cases, though such investigations are the job of the coroner's officer or police, his medical knowledge of the appearance of drugs may legitimately be called into use to clarify the circumstances. Indications that coma or death may be due to an overdose of a drug include:

- Empty tablet bottles or boxes at the scene, especially on beside tables. The original contents may be rapidly identifiable by the pharmacist named on the label.
- Dropped capsules or tablets in bedclothes etc. These should be retained for identification.
- Cups or glasses near by with a white sediment or capsule remnants present, which again should be retained for analysis.
- Vomit upon clothing or pillows, which may contain coloured capsule material or white granular remnants.
- Marked cyanosis of the patient, though by no meams pathognomonic, is often present.
- Where coma has been present for many hours, there may be typical blisters especially on the hips, legs and buttocks. Again these are not pathognomonic of barbiturates, but are probably more common in this condition than any other.

If the patient is conscious and the drug has been taken a very short time before (often the young suicide-gesture girl will present herself immediately after taking capsules) then emetics and gastric lavage may be justified, otherwise rapid transportation to hospital is the only form of treatment indicated, with adequate safeguards as to airway and oxygenation during transit.

The interpretation of analytical results will be a matter for the clinician or coroner's pathologist. Such interpretation can be extremely difficult and misleading, as deaths are very frequent with low blood levels, even within the therapeutic range, whilst patients far from being in coma may have levels in the theoretically fatal range. Though a coroner may earnestly desire an answer, it is extremely difficult to relate blood levels to the number of capsules or tablets taken. Such snap calculations in the witness box of a coroner's court are fraught with errors. The absence of sufficient natural disease to cause death, the clinical picture, the detection of any apprecible amount of barbiturate or other drug and the local signs in the oesophagus and stomach at autopsy are of more value than blood levels, though analyses of organs such as liver may assist in confirming drugs as a cause of death.

TRANQUILLISERS (SCHEDULE IV, PART B)

The great proliferation in both variety and quantity prescribed has made poisoning by drugs used for their psycho-therapeutic properties much more common. These drugs comprise tranquillisers proper, together with anti-depressants and non-barbiturate hypnotics.

Though only mildly toxic, compared with powerful hypnotics like the barbiturates, transquillisers can cause death in large doses, or where some personal idiosyncrasy exists. They are being seen increasingly in both fatal cases and in admissions to hospital. Their use presents peculiar problems both to the pathologist and to the analytical toxicologist, as the autopsy signs may be minimal or absent and the methods of detection in body fluids both technically difficult and hard to interpret.

As far as the clinician and practitioner are concerned, much depends on the surrounding circumstances, such as empty bottles giving a clue to the diagnosis, as well as reference to recent prescriptions and dispensing records from chemists. The pharmacology and toxicology of these substances is complex and even obscure; from the practical point of view, one fact to be kept in mind is the dangerous potential toxicity of the mono-amine oxidase inhibitor group with tyramine-rich foods such as cheese, which may provoke a hypertensive crisis.

SALICYLATE POISONING

Though less common than barbiturate or tranquilliser poisoning, the taking of large numbers of aspirin is a fairly frequent occurrence in Britain, though strangely it is virtually unknown in many parts of the Continent. As a suicidal gesture, usually in teenage girls, it is often the method of choice, fortunately resulting usually in nothing but sickness and ringing in the ears. The individual tolerance to aspirin varies enormously, and cases have been reported where death followed even therapeutic doses. As a general guide, anything over 25–40 tablets is dangerous, though recovery has been recorded after several hundred five-grain tablets. Large doses are very often returned by vomiting, and the conditions may be almost self-curing. However, many fatalities have occurred and the constant feature of many of these is the *delayed* action. Where an appreciable number of aspirin tablets have been taken, it is most unwise to rely upon the good clinical state as a guide as to the progress during the next 24 hours. Many deaths have occurred suddenly up to a day or more following consumption of aspirin and if possible it is best to detain the patient for observation for the first 36 hours. Children are particularly sensitive to aspirin toxicity, and even in the absence of symptoms should be carefully watched. In all cases, stomach washout is worth while even hours after the drug was taken, as it tends to mass in large, relatively insoluble lumps, which may be removed even after long delay.

CARBON MONOXIDE

The poisonous affect of carbon monoxide is due to its effective replacement of oxygen in the red cells, as it has almost 300 times the affinity of oxygen for haemoglobin. It is thus really an asphyxiant, in that it causes oxygen deprivation at cellular level. Due to this efficient competitiveness with oxygen, even small concentrations of carbon monoxide can build up over a period and cause symptoms and even death. Where high concentrations, are present, death may be very rapid.

The progression of symptoms is a slow build up is usually as follows: headache, nausea, stupor, vomiting, coma, convulsions and death. Marked pulmonary oedema may occur and plumes of froth may appear at the mouth and nostrils. Vomiting is also a conspicuous features. In cases which recover, there may be permanent damage to the basal ganglia of the brain, carbon monoxide poisoning being one of the causes of a Parkinsonian syndrome. Even if actual neurological changes are escaped, there is often a lengthy, or even permanent personality change.

The origin of this type of poisoning has changed radically during the past few years. Formerly, the vast majority of deaths and nonfatal poisonings were due to the 7–15 per cent of carbon monoxide that was present in domestic coal-gas, but since the almost universal replacement of this fuel by natural 'North Sea' gas (which contains a mixture of non-poisonous hydrocarbons such as methane), the incidence of suicidal and accidental cases has been much reduced. Though natural gas is asphyxiating, in that it cannot support respiration, it requires appreciable displacement of oxygen to cause death, which in turn needs very effective blocking of ventilation in the room concerned.

Diagnosis of carbon monoxide poisoning

This is usually obvious from the circumstances, but a considerable number of fatal cases have been missed or detected at a late stage, because the body had either been removed from the scene or the surroundings had been altered before viewing by the doctor. This may occur inadvertently in accidental poisoning or sometimes deliberately in suicide, when the relatives wish to avoid the true nature being discovered.

Carbon monoxide poisoning should always be considered when a person is found dead in a tightly closed room which contains some form of flame heating, be it gas or paraffin. Numerous cases have been seen in winter-time, where undoubtedly accidental circumstances have caused death by incomplete combustion of the fuel in either gas or paraffin stoves. The colour of the post-mortem lividity or even the general skin surface may be suggestive or even immediately diagnostic in florid poisoning. A normal colour of the lividity does not exclude carbon monoxide, especially in anaemic persons, and post-mortem analysis of a blood sample is the only sure way of confirming or eliminating carbon monoxide poisoning. In non-fatal cases, no abnormal skin colour might be visible, shock and circulatory failure causing the skin to be very pale.

Occasionally, suicide from the carbon monoxide contained in exhaust gases may be used. The deceased may be seated inside his car, with a tube leading from the exhaust into the passenger compartment or the deceased may lie on the floor of the garage near the exhaust pipe, with doors and windows tightly closed. Exhaust fumes from a normally effective engine contain about 6 per cent carbon monoxide and a 1.5/2-litre vehicle within a single garage will generate enough gas in a few minutes to cause death. Occasionally, accidental deaths are seen in similar circumstances, though the presence of tools etc., will usually indicate the non-suicidal nature.

As long as domestic gas continues in some areas to contain carbon monoxide, the well-established pattern of accidental deaths will continue. These mainly effect old persons, as they tend to live alone, are forgetful and inefficient when handling gas taps. Their living premises are often small, so that percolation of gas from one part to another is easy. They tend to feel the cold and use gas fires and stoves for heating, as well as frequent tea-making. Their sense of smell is often atrophied and all these circumstances combine to put them more at risk than younger people. In addition, the resistance of old people to carbon monoxide is less; they frequently die at blood saturation levels of only 25–35 per cent as opposed to the figures of 60–70 per cent often seen in younger suicides. Children are similarly more susceptible to carbon monoxide, and unfortunate cases were seen each year where whole families are wiped out by some nocturnal gas leak. These latter accidents must be carefully differentiated from the pathetic murder/suicide tragedies where a mother will commit suicide and take her children with her, usually by coal gas.

Accidental sources of carbon monoxide poisoning (apart from senile forgetfulness with stoves and fires) include the following:

1. Faulty appliances, especially gas geysers in bathrooms. Since the widespread advent of natural gas, leakage from the supply system is now relatively innocuous, but carbon monoxide may still be generated by combustion of the hydrocarbon constituents in an oxygen-deficient atmosphere. This may be due to decline in the efficiency of the burners or to obstruction of the outlet, or to blockage of ventilation in the room. Bathrooms are particularly prone to fatal accidents, and are certainly the most dangerous part of the

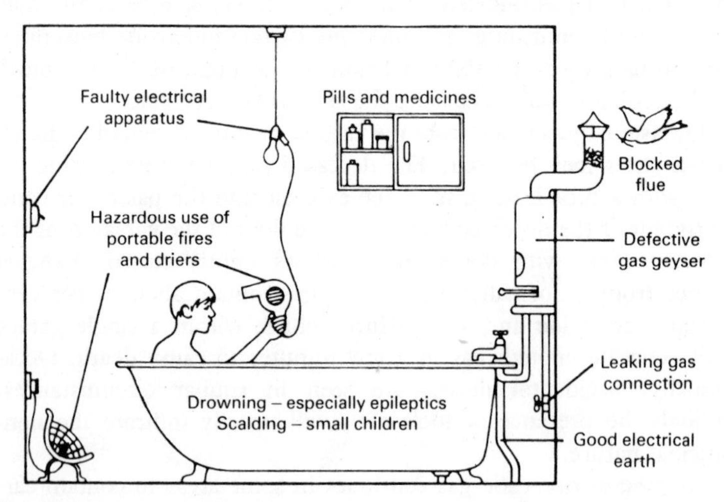

Fig. 33 Fatal hazards of the bathroom

house. Coal gas poisoning, incomplete combustion poisoning, electrocution (due to the good earthing and damp conditions), falls from slippery floors with consequent fractured femora, and poisoning from the contents of the bathroom cabinet are well-known hazards, added to which is the risk of scalding to young children in the bath, and drowning of epileptics (Fig. 33).

2. *Paraffin heaters in rooms*, where the ingress of air is obstructed by draught exclusion (frequently seen in very cold weather), may lead to a fatal production of carbon monoxide and sometimes multiple deaths of the occupants.

When an intrinsically innocuous fuel gas, such as North Sea gas or bottle propane or butane is burnt in a faulty apparatus or where the amount of oxygen is severely reduced by poor ventilation, then combustion may be incomplete. Instead of the hydrocarbon fuel being burnt to carbon dioxide, a proportion may be released as monoxide. This is a particular danger with gas geysers in bathrooms and with appliances such as gas refrigerators in confined spaces, such as caravans. In July 1975, a family of four were killed simultaneously in a motor caravan, due to carbon monoxide released from a gas refrigerator.

3. *Incomplete combustion* either from general or localised conflagrations, produces large quantities of carbon monoxide. This is often seen when furniture, bedding, carpets or curtains smoulder in a closed room and is a special risk for alcoholics who retire to bed smoking a cigarette. This may drop on to the counterpane and though local burning may be minimal, sufficient carbon monoxide is produced to cause death. Where the fire is more severe, it may be difficult or impossible to tell whether carbon monoxide or burns caused death, but it is often merciful to be able to tell relatives that there was evidence that carbon monoxide poisoning must have caused unconsciousness or even death before the flames reached the deceased.

Tragically, children are very much more at risk from house fires and many die from carbon monoxide poisoning, their burns being partly or wholly post-mortem in nature.

30

Drugs and the doctor

One of the most onerous 'privileges' which the doctor acquires on registration with the General Medical Council, is that of being able to prescribe drugs. The responsibility in this respect is profound. Prescribing irregularities are a frequent cause of both erasure from the Register and disputes with the National Health Service. With the increasing complexity of therapeutics, the proliferation of administrative and legislative rules and the upsurge in drug addiction, every prescription becomes a potential source of trouble for the practitioner.

The prescribing of substances not approved by the National Health Service, the too-liberal dispensing of potential drugs of addiction, the over-availability of drugs usable for suicide, the forgery or alteration of prescriptions by patients, theft of prescriptions and other irregularities of omission or commission, all form a thickening forest of difficulties for the prescriber. Though nothing can replace constant watchfulness and careful script-writing, at least a working knowledge of the regulations is a sound basis for safety.

At least 28 Acts of Parliament and a number of statutory rules dealing with drugs and poisons, have been enacted over the years, but the matter is now dealt with by three major Acts:

Pharmacy and Poisons Act, 1933 (together with the Poisons Rules, 1971)
Medicines Act, 1968
Misuse of Drugs Act, 1971 (together with the Misuse of Drugs Regulations, 1973).

PHARMACY AND POISONS ACT, 1933

The classification of poisons under this Act is somewhat confusing, as it is divided into *Parts* and *Schedules* which overlap. The workings of the Act are supervised by the Poisons Board, who publish the *Poisons List*, dividing substances into Part 1 or Part 2 categories. They further make the *Poisons Rules* which differentiate certain poisons into the Schedules.

Part 1 contains substances used in medicine, dentistry, verterinary and other sciences. They may only be obtained from authorised sellers, i.e. recognised pharmacists who are members of the Pharmaceutical Society who, like doctors themselves, are on a Register, from which they may also be erased.

Part 2 contains toxic substances most of which are not used for therapeutic purposes but mainly for industry, agriculture and horticulture. These can be sold by any wholesaler or retailer who is a 'listed seller'.

Under the Poisons Rules, as opposed to the Poisons List, substances are divided into 15 *Schedules*. Of these only the First, Third and Fourth have any relevance to medicine. Schedule 1 contains most of the poisons in Part 1 of the Poisons List, and a few of those in part 2. The Rules are mainly concerned with storage, labelling, and sale and records.

First Schedule drugs may not be sold to the public without certain safeguards:

1. The buyer must be known to the seller or produce a certificate signed by a householder or, if the householder is unknown to the seller, by a police officer, indicating that the buyer is a person to whom such a poison may be entrusted.
2. These poisons may only be sold on registered premises under the supervision of a registered pharmacist.
3. The buyer must sign the seller's Poisons Book or give an order in writing, with his signature, name, address, profession, name and quantity of the substance acquired and the purpose for which it is to be used.
4. In lieu of this entry in the Poisons Book, the buyer may produce a prescription signed by a doctor, which replaces the entry. In urgent circumstances, the doctor may telephone such an order, but he must supply a signed prescription within 24 hours to comply with the regulations.
5. If a doctor dispenses a Schedule I substance to a patient, he must similarly keep a record in a Poisons Book in the same way as the pharmacist. When he personally administers a drug to a patient, no such formality need take place.

The Third Schedule partly concerns many substances of a non-medical nature, such as organic chemicals, solvents, explosives and metallic poisons, but also concerns medicinal substances which contain small quantities of active ingredients. Examples are topical anti-histamines, inhalers and dilute ephedrine and formaldehyde.

The Fourth Schedule is the most important medically, being divided into two parts, A and B. The main purpose is to prevent members of the public obtaining medical substances with potentially dangerous properties in the absence of any prescription from a doctor, dentist or veterinary surgeon. Schedule 4 contains a list of substances where records must be kept exactly as for the Schedule 1 substances. Prescriptions for these drugs must therefore follow the legal requirements of the rules for Schedule 1 substances. Most of these drugs are hypnotics and sedatives, the barbiturate group being the main member. Schedule 4(A) substances must be prescribed on a form setting out the following:

Name and address of the doctor.
His signature and the date.
Name and address of the patient.
Name of the drug.
Total amount to be dispensed.
Amount to be taken at each dose.

If issued by a dentist or veterinary surgeon, the prescription must also indicate that the substance is to be used only for these purposes. Repitition of the prescription may be allowed if it states so clearly upon the document: the number and interval of 'repeats' must be stated. If this is omitted, the pharms may repeat only three times in all, and if no interval between repeats is indicated, then he may not dispense at closer intervals than three days. The pharmacist must keep the prescription for at least two years, unless it is the National Health Service FPC 10 (which cannot be repeated).

Schedule 4(B) is a very long list of synthetic pharmaceuticals including hormones, hypnotics and the ever increasing group of 'tranquillisers' and psychotherapeutic substances. Unlike Schedule 4(A) substances, they do not require that prescriptions should be in the same strict form as Schedule 1 drugs, though they naturally must carry the name, address and signature of the prescribing physician.

It is illegal for a representative of the drug house to leave a Schedule 1 sample with a medical practitioner, unless a signed order has been sent the company's headquarters and an entry made in a Poisons Register *prior* to delivery. Failure of a doctor to confirm a telephone order for a Schedule 1 drug within 24 hours carries a maximum penalty of £50 fine and the possibility of disciplinary proceedings by the General Medical Council.

Under the Act, the medical practitioner is obliged to keep poison ous substances in proper containers, impervious to the poison and sufficiently strong to prevent leakage during transport and handling. Liquids up to 120 fl. oz (other than medicines) must be bottles with fluted exerior surfaces, to distinguish them in darkness.

All Schedule 1 poisons must be recorded in a book, though not necessarily one used exclusively for that purpose. A normal day book containing other information may be used for this purpose. The entry must be made either on the same day or on the day following, giving the name of the person to whom supplied, the substance and the quantity and the date. Such records need not be kept for National Health Service prescriptions or those issued under the aegis of the local health authority. Doctors may also administer drugs personally to patients and may leave a single dose with the patient without necessity for recording the fact. The record book must be kept at the premises at which is was dispensed and retained for at least two years: if a doctor possesses more than one surgery, he must have separate records for each place.

The Medicines Act, 1968 is primarily concerned with the commercial aspects of therapeutic substances, especially as regards their manufacture, safety, clinical trials and mode of presentation. Advertising, promotion and sale are more closely regulated than formerly and much more comprehensive publication of the pharmacological action, contraindications and possible hazards are ensured. Undoubtedly some stimulus for the provisions of this Act arose from tragedies such as the thalidomide catastrophy.

MISUSE OF DRUGS ACT, 1971

The control of drugs of dependence and addiction was effected by a number of Acts between 1920 and 1967. Most of these were variations of the Dangerous Drugs Acts, an latterly the Drugs (Prevention of Misuse) Act, 1964.

All this old legislation was swept away by the Misuse of Drugs Act, 1971, together with its associated Misuse of Drugs Regulations, which came into force on July 1st 1973. This completely new legislation was designed to control the misuse of drugs of many kinds, but especially narcotics and other drugs of dependence. It also categorized drugs of dependence into various degrees of harmfulness and also graded the penalties for misuse. It controlled unlawful possession and trafficking, prescribing and supply, trading and production of such drugs and afforded means of constant surveillance of the problem of drug dependence in Britain. It also has provisions for notification of addicts and the fostering of education and research in relation to drug dependence.

The Act applies to Northern Ireland as well as to England, Wales and Scotland. It contains 40 sections and six Schedules. Some of the major provisions of the Act are given here, but these are by no means exhaustive.

Section 1 established a statutory body called the *Advisory Council on the Misuse of Drugs* which is to advise the government of all aspects of the drug problem, with particular emphasis on the social aspects. This Council has at least twenty members, drawn from the medical, dental, veterinary, pharmaceutical and chemical industries.

Section II deals with the categorization of drugs of dependence, classing them into three groups, *Class A, Class B and Class C.*

Class A list the most dangerous drugs of dependence such as heroin, morphine, cocaine, pethidine, L.S.D., methadone, cannabinol and injectable amphetamines.

Class B contains addictive drugs of intermediate potency including oral amphetamine, cannabis, codeine, dehydrocodeine, methylamphetamine and a number of other synthetic substances.

Class C drugs are rarely involved in dependence, but are included for the sake of completeness. These include substances such as chlorophentermine, methaqualone, pipradrol etc.

The classification into these three groups is mainly for the purpose of categorising the maximum penalties which may be applied for offences, on the basis of the drug's potential harmfulness when misused. A totally different classification is used for the purposes of the controls to be applied to their use for legitimate purposes: this is the classification which mainly concerns the pharmacist and is set out not in the actual Act, but under the Regulations. This second classification is broken down into four Schedules.

Further legislation under the Act, is the reconfirmation in 1973 of the Notification of and Supply to Addicts Regulations. A person is regarded as being addicted to a drug if, and only if, he has as a result of repeated administration become so dependent on a drug that he has an overpowering desire for the administration of it to be continued. Under the regulations, any doctor who attends a person whom he considers is addicted to any drug in the following list, must within seven days furnish certain particulars to the Chief Medical Officer of the Home Office. The drugs concerned are *cocaine, dextromoramide, diamorphine, dipipanone, hydrocodone, hydromorphone, levorphanol, methadone, morphine, opium, oxycodone, pethidine, phenazocine and peritramide*. No doctor may administer or authorize the supply of cocaine or diamorphine or their salts to an addicted person, except for the purpose of treating organic disease or injury, unless he is licensed to do so by the Secretary of State.

Sections 3, 4, and 5 concern the import or export of controlled drugs, the production, supply or an offer to supply such drugs and the possession of drugs of dependence. Apart from exempted persons such as doctors, dentists, veterinary surgeons etc., it is an offence to possess or to attempt to possess a controlled drug unless to prevent an offence or to hand the drug to some suitable person.

Section 6 makes it an illegal act under any circumstances to cultivate the cannabis plant.

Section 7 contains the exemptions granted by the Home Secretary to certain drugs or to persons from the foregoing sections. This is naturally intended to allow those persons properly entitled to handle such drugs to obtain the legal possession of such substances.

A number of other sections control the use of premises for the preparation and smoking of opium, cannabis etc. and a number of other matters mainly of concern to the police.

Sections 10 and 11 control the packaging, labelling, transport and disposal of controlled drugs and the documentation of possession and transactions etc. This section particularly concerns doctors and pharmacists. It also includes the notification of addicts to the proper authority by doctors, as brought into force by the previous legislation. This notification of addicts was reconfirmed in Notification and Supply to Addicts Regulation of 1973.

Section 13 concerns prohibitions for failure to notify addicts and authorising prescribing to addicts. Though neither of these matters is an offence under the Act, they would lead to an investigation and to possible prohibition of prescribing in the case of individual practitioner who flounts the regulations.

Section 15 provides that if the Home Secretary considers that a doctor is prescribing in an irresponsible manner in respect of drugs of dependence, he can refer the matter to a professional panel for quick action and depending on their advice, the doctor may be prohibited from further prescribing of such drugs. Other sections provide for safeguards relating to withdrawal of right to prescribing and describe tribunals and advisory bodies with nominated members from such bodies as the GMC and the Royal Colleges, as well as the BMA.

Section 17 states that the Home Secretary may require any doctor or pharmacist to provide information about prescriptions if it appears that there is a social problem arising in a certain area.

The Misuse of Drugs Act, 1971 and the associated Misuse of Drugs Regulations, 1973 form a long and comprehensive document, the contents of which should be thoroughly studied by any doctor who habitually has cause to prescribe the drugs mentioned in the Schedules. The penalties are potentially quite heavy for contravening the Act and the possibility of prohibition of prescribing and even the further danger of attracting the notice of the GMC Professional Conduct Committee must always be borne in mind, as drugs are a frequent cause of serious professional misconduct.

Practical matters connected with the misuse of drugs act

The only persons authorized to possess controlled drugs apart from patients who have had them prescribed, are registered medical practitioners, dentists, sisters in charge of a ward or operating theatre, veterinary surgeons, certified midwives who have an order from a community physician of the AHA (restricted to medical opium, tincture of opium and pethidine) and authorized pharmaceutical chemists in retail trade, hospitals, health centres etc. Certain persons in charge of laboratories may be approved for the possession of such drugs, as may be public analysts, sampling officers, inspectors of drugs, ship's captains on vessels without a medical officer and farmers who may possess 32 ounces of tincture of opium on a police certificate. A dentist may only give drug by personal administration and cannot prescribe for a patient.
The actual prescription must comply with certain criteria:

1. It must be written, dated and signed by the prescriber and except under NHS conditions, must give the prescriber's address. The name and address of the recipient must be stated.
2. The total amount of the drug to be supplied must be stated and this cannot be repeated more than three times on the same prescription. If given by a dentist it must be marked 'For local dental treatment only'.
3. When the prescription is made up, it must be dated with the day of supply and must be retained by the dispenser.

Records of receipt and supply must be kept in a prescribed form and completed on the day of supply or receipt. Each of the three classes of drug must have a separate register or part of register for their recording. Any corrections or cancellations must be made by marginal notes and dated, not by alteration of the original entry. All Scheduled drugs must be kept in locked receptacles and the courts have held in the past that a doctor's car is not a receptacle, unless the drugs ar further locked in a doctor's bag or locked in the boot of the vehicle.

Republic of Ireland

Addictive and other potent drugs are controlled by the Misuse of Drugs Act, 1977, which in many ways mirrors the equivalent English Act of 1971, though it lacks any form of central notification of addicts. The Act empowers the Minister for Health to direct the Medical Council to set up a Committee of Enquiry into doctors who are prescribing irresponsibly. The controlled drugs are listed in a schedule in the Act, but are further classified under the Misuse of Drugs Regulations 1979. These regulations also give instructions for the prescribing and storage of drugs by medical and dental practitioners and others legally entitled to possess them. A further regulation, the Misuse of Drugs (Designation) Order 1979, withdrew permission for possession of substances such as Cannibis and its derivatives, L.S.D., mescaline, raw opium and related drugs from any practitioners; they may only be in the possession of *bona fide* research workers or forensic scientists. The 1979 regulations also specify the details which must be entered on prescriptions, including the number of instalments and the intervals between dispensing them. These are essentially the same as the British regulations. A large number of therapeutic substances, including antibiotics, hormones, tranquillizers, anti-inflammatory agents etc. are controlled by the Medical Preparations (Control of Sales) Regulations 1966. The regulations limit repeats of prescriptions to a period of six months from the day of writing.

31

Legal aspects of mental disorders

Previous legislations such as the Lunacy Act, 1890 and the Mental Treatment Act of 1930, has been replaced by a complete codification of the law relating to mental disease, the Mental Health Act, 1959.

This consists of nine parts, covering a wide range of circumstances relating to mental disease, but a basic classification of the types of disorder is common to all parts.

The legal sub-divisions of 'mental disorder' are:

1. *Mental disorder* covering all types of acquired and congential disease, including the psychoses, arrested developments, psychopathic disorder etc.

2. *Severe subnormality* – a state of arrested or incomplete development of mind of such a nature or degree to render the patient incapable of living an independent life or guarding himself against serious exploitation.

3. *Subnormality* – a state of arrested or incomplete development of mind (not amounting to severe subnormality) which requires medical treatment or special care of the patient.

4. *Psychopathic disorder* – a persistent disorder or disability of mind (whether or not including subnormality of intelligence) which results in abnormally aggressive or seriously irresponsible conduct on the part of the patient and requires or is susceptible to medical treatment.

The older classification is replaced by the above, so that 'idiocy' or 'imbecility' described before 1959, would fall under the category of severe subnormality and 'backwardness' or 'feeble-mindedness' under subnormality. The Act further provides that the old description of 'moral defective', which could lead to detention, no longer applies, and that no person shall be dealt with under the Act as suffering from mental disorder by reason only of promiscuity or other immoral conduct.

This part of the Act also emphasises voluntary admission to mental institutions to be preferred above all other methods, and that the age of 16 is the age of consent to such treatment if the patient is capable of expression.

METHODS OF ADMISSION TO MENTAL HOSPITALS

1. Voluntary admission

As stated, this is the method to be used whenever possible, available to all over the age of 16 in exactly the same way as with physical disorders. Discharge from hospital is equally informal, and must be granted without notice at the patient's request, unless the mental state has deteriorated so markedly that the safety of the patient or the public requires certification.

2. Compulsory admission

When the safety of the patient or the public demands it, compulsory admission may be enforced under the Sections 25–29 of the Act.

(a) Admission for observation

Where the patient suffers from mental disorder of a nature or degree which warrants admission for observation, this may be done for a preliminary maximum period of 28 days. Application must be made by either a relative or the Mental Officer of the local authority (the official called the 'Duly Authorised Officer' before the 1959 Act).

The Mental Welfare Officer must have seen the patient within 14 days before application. The application must be accompanied by written recommendation from two doctors, one of whom must be a specialist in mental disease. In practice, this means that one doctor is the general practitioner and the other is a consultant psychiatrist called in for the purpose.

These medical certificates do not necessarily indicate the nature of the disorder but must state that it is necessary in the interests of the patient, his relatives or the public. The applicant must be either a relative or the Mental Welfare Officer, not one of the doctors.

This observation order runs only for 28 days, during which time the patient may be discharged, admitted for voluntary treatment or further certified.

(b) Admission for treatment

This long-term compulsory order may be obtained for a patient of any age if suffering from mental illness or *severe* subnormality, but only in the case of a patient less than 21 years if suffering from psychopathic disorder or subnormality.

Again the applicant must be the nearest relative or the Mental Welfare Officer, but in this case, this official cannot initiate certification if the next-of-kin objects.

A similar recommendation must be provided by two doctors, one of whom is a specialist in mental disease. This time, the medical reasons for detention must be stated, identical opinions being required from each doctor. They must further agree that other methods of treatment are unsuitable. The maximum duration of a Treatment Order is 12 months, when it may then be renewed for a further period of one year. Beyond this first two years, renewals may be made for further two-year periods.

(c) Urgency order

Where an urgent situation exists, either from a dangerous or intolerable domestic situation or from an acute psychiatric condition endangering the patient himself, an immediate 'breathing space' may be obtained for a period of 72 hours. Application may be made again by the nearest relative or Mental Welfare Officer, but this need be supported by the medical opinion of only one doctor, usually the general practitioner. The doctor must have seen the patient within three days before making application. Such detention may only last for three days, but during this time a further extension of either 28 days' observation or one year's treatment may be arranged.

Emergency admission can also be implemented by any police officer who considers that a person in a public place is apparently suffering from a mental disorder sufficient to place him in need of care and attention. The police officer can remove that person to ' a place of safety' for 72 hours, when he can then be seen by the Mental Welfare Officer and doctors. This place of safety can either be police custody or the observation ward of a mental hospital; in practice the latter is the almost invariable choice.

Where two doctors complete any certification, they must have seen the patient within seven days of each other, and although it usual for both doctors to examine at the same time (as the general practitioner usually asks for a specialist consultation), there is no legal necessity for this to occur.

A doctor may not make a medical recommendation for one of his own relatives, the relative of a partner or assistant or if he has a financial interest in the patient's affairs.

Section 30 of the Act applies to an informal patient already in hospital and who wished to take his discharge against medical advice. The procedure here is similar to the urgency order, one doctor being able to provide a certificate compulsorily detaining him for a further three days, during which time a second medical recommendation to detain the patient either for a further 28 days or a 12-month period is obtained.

Certification of the sub-normal and psychopaths

If seen under the age of 21 years of age, these patients can be detained in the normal way as described above, and the order may be extended by one-year periods up to the age of 25, if they are already in an institution. Beyond the age of 25 they must be discharged unless a special certificate is issued (Section 44) called a 'barring' certificate. This must be provided within two months of the expected date of discharge.

If first seen above the age of 21, or if he has been discharged after 25 and re-examined, the only method of detention is by a Court Order. Before certification in the usual way can be implemented, such a person must be shown to have a mental disorder of a degree that warrants detention for observation or his own protection or that of other people. The Court Order is only made available if the psychopath is convicted of an offence normally punishable by imprisonment.

Guardianship

Where a person suffering from a mental disorder needs care and protection, he may be placed in guardianship (of an individual or, more usually, the local authority) which is normally outside a hospital. This guardian is placed *in loco parentis* and has the same powers as if he were the father of the patient and the patient were under the age of 14. Applicaitions are similar to those for compulsory admission to hospital, being supported by two medical certificates, patients under guardianship may be discharged from it by the responsible medical officer, the local health authority or the nearest relative. In the latter case, 72 hours' notice is required in writing from the relative, and if the medical officer in charge does not agree, no further application can be made for six months. The guardianship ceases at the age of 25 years in the case of subjects suffering from subnormality or psychopathic disorders.

Mental health review tribunal

One such Tribunal is established in every Regional Hospital Board area. They are under the jurisdiction of the Lord Chancellor, and must consist of at least one member from the legal profession, the medical profession and persons with experience of social welfare. The purpose of the Tribunal is to review cases of compulsory detention or guardianship, where appeals have been made by either patients or their relatives. Except under the detention as a result of Section 65 (detention following a conviction for a criminal offence at Quarter Sessions or Assizes) the Tribunal has powers to direct the discharge of the patient whom it considers is not suffering from a sufficient degree of mental illness at the time of examination. Those detained under Section 65 have their case reviewed regularly by the Home Secretary.

Detention for medical treatment by the courts

Magistrates courts and Crown courts may order detention of a convicted offender in a mental hospital under Section 60 or 61 of the Mental Health Act, the only exception being conviction for murder where special provision applies. Section 65 allows a 'Restriction Order' to be imposed by a superior court, so that premature discharge may be prohibited below a fixed number of years.

For these sections to be applied, there must be evidence of two doctors, one of whom has special experience of mental illness, to show that the offender suffered from one of the classifications under the Act, of a nature or severity to require his detention. It must also be shown that this is the best method of dealing with the offender and must also be shown that some hospital or guardian is willing to receive the offender.

As the Mental Health Review Tribunals normally have the power to order a patient's discharge, sometimes a Restriction Order is made at the trial, restricting the date of discharge of the patient on the grounds of the nature of the offence or the antecedents of the offender, making it necessary to protect the public. A magistrate's court may not impose this order, and if it feels encumbent to restrict discharge, it must refer the case to a higher court for sentencing.

Procedure in Scotland

Scotland has broadly similar legislation on Mental Health, but there are differences of detail in the parallel Mental Health (Scotland) Act, 1960. Unlike England and Wales, this Act established a *Mental Welfare Commission*, to exercise a protective function on behalf of mentally incapacitated persons. The procedure for compulsorily detaining patients is also different, in that is a quasi-judicial element. In addition to the certificates of two doctors, the application has to be approved by a Sheriff. The patient may be detained for up to one year, with a further renewal for another year, but thereafter, a new application must be made. An urgent admission may be made on the application of only one doctor (without the ratification of the Sheriff) but this lasts for a maximum of only seven days.

Section 54 of the Scottish Act empowers a Court to remand a convicted person to a mental hospital, rather than jail; the evidence of one doctor is sufficient for this, but psychiatric reports from the hospital must be supplied to the Court in due course. Section 63 of the Scottish Act provides for accused persons to be found 'insane in bar of trial' – equivalent to 'unfit to plead' in England and Wales.

If an accused person is acquitted by reason of insanity, the Court also makes an order for detention in a State Hospital.

Republic of Ireland

In the Irish Republic at the time of writing a new Health (Mental Services) Bill 1980, is in the final stages of modification, but is being heavily criticised by the medical profession and may well be modified before it becomes law. The present arrangements for mental treatment are described in a booklet produced by the Irish Government Stationery Office, 'Mental Treatment Acts 1945–1961; Statutory Provisions, Regulations and Explanatory Notes regarding the reception, treatment, detention and discharge of mentally ill patients'. In simple terms patients in mental hospitals fall into three categories:

1. Voluntary patients. The only restriction is that hospitals require 72 hours notice of a desire on the part of such patients to discharge themselves. The purpose of this is to enable the medical authorities in the hospital, if they consider some more custodial form of treatment necessary, to invoke the emergency procedures.

2. Temporary patients. These patients are detained in hospital for a period of six months which can be extended for six months at a time up to a total period of two years.

3. Persons of unsound mind. This category is used as little as possible and is normally applied to persons of such subnormality or abnormality as are likely to require lifelong detention. Its undesirability is chiefly because of the loss of citizen's rights which it entails. The three categories above are further subdivided in each category to private and public patients, since private patients require an extra certifying doctor. The procedure for admission of patients to public mental hospitals for both temporary and unsound mind categories, is that a relative applies to a medical practitioner, or an official of the Health Board, for a recommendation for reception to a mental hospital. The family practitioner usually then examines the patient and makes the recommendation' to the local mental hospital. The Health Board, if necessary with the co-operation of the Gardai (police) then remove the patient to the hospital where he or she is examined by the Medical Officer in charge of that hospital. The hospital doctor then makes an 'eligible patient reception order' for that patients detention 'until his removal or discharge by proper authority or his death'. As previously mentioned two outside medical practitioners are necessary for a private patient reception order'. This is to safeguard the patient against a medical proprietor of a private mental hospital who might have a pecuniary interest in their continuing detention.

Criminals who are unfit to plead through mental illness or have been convicted but are found to be insane are detained during the Governments pleasure at the Central Mental Hospital, Dundrum, equivalent to Broadmoor or Rampton.

No statutory category of mental subnormality, psychopathy or diminished responsibility exits in Ireland, though Courts will take into account criminal behaviour influenced by mental illness in making a decision on disposal and sentence (State -v- Hayes and Doyle -v- Wicklow County Council). The McNaghten Rules still apply otherwise. Insanity is rarely pleaded in murder cases as the death sentence applies only to murderers of policemen, warders, foreign diplomats, categories of killing associated with political rather than insane offenders. Release from prison after a 'life' sentence with good conduct remission, can often be sooner than from the Central Mental Hospital. There is no Irish guardianship.

WILLS AND TESTAMENTARY CAPACITY

Patients not infrequently turn first to their doctors for advice which is more legal than medical; the matter of wills is an example, especially as the subject often arises when a patient is very ill or of advanced years.

Testamentary capacity refers to the mental ability of a person to make a valid will. The latter may be contested by heirs and relatives at a later date and medical evidence may be needed to determine the testator' capacity at the time of making the will.

For any will to be valid, the following conditions must be satisfied:

- The testator, though not necessarily free from all mental illness, must have a sound, disposing mind as far as making the will is concerned.
- He must know that he is actually making a will, must know the general extent of his property (not necessarily an exact inventory) and knows the person to whom he may reasonably leave his possessions.
- His mind must be free of any delusions or obsessions which might pervert his judgement in disposing of his property. He may be utterly deluded in other directions, but as long as his mind is clear in this respect, the will need not be invalidated.
- The testator must not be under the effect of any drugs, including alcohol, if it tends to distort his mental capacity as far as making the will is concerned.
- He must not be under any undue influence from another person. This particularly affects the doctor, who may be in a very close emotional relationship with a dying patient. If any large legacy is left to the doctor, relatives may suggest that this relationship constituted undue influence.
- The will must be signed (or marked) by the testator in the presence of two witnesses, neither of whom (nor their spouses) can then become legatees under the will. A doctor may well be asked to be one of the witnesses, and apart from the fact that this excludes him from any benefit, he should be reluctant to agree as he may be called at a later date to become involved in the often bitter family feuding and to have to testify as to the deceased's testamentary capacity.

SUGGESTED FURTHER READING

Adelson L 1974 Pathology of homicide: a vade mecum for pathologists, prosecutors and defense counsel. Thomas, Springfield

British Medical Association 1980 Handbook of medical ethics. BMA, London

Burges S H, Hilton, J E (eds) 1978 New police surgeon: a practical guide. Hutchinson, London

Camps F E (ed.) 1969 Recent advances in forensic pathology. Churchill, London

Camps F E 1976 Gradwohl's legal medicine, 3rd edn. (work completed by Robinson A E, Lucas B G B) Wright, Bristol

Glaister, J, Smith H 1973 Medical jurisprudence and toxicology, 13th edn. Churchill Livingstone, Edinburgh

Hadfield S J 1958 Law and ethics for doctors. Eyre & Spottiswoode, London

Mason J K (ed.) 1978 Pathology of violent injury. Arnold, London

Mason J K 1978 Forensic medicine for lawyers. Wright, Bristol

Polson C J, Gee D J 1973 Essentials of forensic medicine, 3rd edn. Pergamon Press, Oxford

Polson C J, Marshall T K 1975 Disposal of the dead, 3rd edn. English Universities Press, London

Removal of cadaveric organs for transplantation – a code of practice 1979. DHSS, London

Report of the committee on death certification and coroners 1971 Cmnd 4810. HMSO, London

Simpson C K 1963 A doctor's guide to court. Butterworths, London

Simpson C K 1965 Taylor's principles of practice of medical jurisprudence. Churchill, London

Simpson C K 1979 Forensic medicine, 8th edn. Arnold, London

Taylor J L 1980 Medical malpractice. Wright, Bristol

Thomson W A R 1977 Dictionary of medical ethics and practice. Wright, Bristol

Index